Twice Orphaned

Michi Nishiura and Walter Weglyn
Multicultural Publication Series

Arthur A. Hansen, Series Editor

Published Titles

Song of Anger: Tales of Tule Lake
Barney Shallit

Between Two Adversaries:
Korean Interpreters at Japanese Alien Enemy Detention Centers
During World War II
Hyung-Ju Ahn

Behind the Orange Curtain:
Religious Pluralism in a Southern California County
M. Margaret Tanaka and Cheryl Amarasuriya Eberly, Editors

Silent Scars of Healing Hands:
Oral Histories of Japanese American Doctors in
World War II Detention Camps
Naomi Hirahara and Gwenn M. Jensen

Forgotten Patriots:
Voices of World War II Mexican American Veterans of Southern California
Charlene Riggins and Miguel A. Garcia, Editors

A Different Shade of Orange:
Voices of Orange County, California, Black Pioneers
Robert Johnson and Charlene Riggins

Twice *Orphaned*

Voices from the Children's Village of Manzanar

Catherine Irwin

Library of Congress Cataloging-in-Publication Data

Irwin, Catherine, Ph. D.
  Twice orphaned : voices from the Children's Village of Manzanar /
Catherine Irwin.
      p. cm. -- (Michi Nishiura and Walter Weglyn multicultural publication
series)
  Includes index.
  ISBN 978-0-930046-24-8 (pbk.)
  1. Manzanar War Relocation Center. Children's Village--History. 2.
Japanese American children--California--Manzanar--History--20th century.
3. Children--California--Manzanar--History--20th century. 4. Orphans-
-California--Manzanar--History--20th century. 5. Japanese Americans--
Interviews. 6. Japanese Americans--Evacuation and relocation, 1942-1945.
I. Title. II. Series.

  D769.8.A6I67 2008
  940.53'1779487--dc22

                              2008040530

Published by Center for Oral and Public History
California State University, Fullerton

Cover design: Kathleen Frazee
Cover art work: Prior to departing Manzanar, Kango Takamura presented a painting
of Children's Village to Lillian and Harry Matsumoto, the assistant superintendent and
superintendent of Children's Village. It may be one of the few images of how Children's
Village actually looked. The original painting is on permanent loan to the Eastern
California Museum in Independence, California. Permission to use this image was
granted by Lillian Matsumoto.

To Tom

Manzanar Children's Village

There are a hundred thousand
stars out tonight,
Pulsing waves of pale light
Releasing yesterday's layered memories
Inviting echoes of the past
buried deep in pain and longing.

The earth remembers
the generous tears of children.
The gnarled trees bear witness
to their anguished state.
The blossoms that fell across
their tear-stained cheeks
will return again and again
to celebrate their passing.

I tremble, standing here
on this hallowed ground,
Feeling the aching silence
Reaching out to take your hand
Exhorting the ghosts of memory
to come gently across the silence
and fill this void with song.

—Wilbur Sato

Table of Contents

List of Illustrations

Pictures provided courtesy of the following individuals and institutions:

Foreword

One Japanese American social activist, whom Michi Nishiura Weglyn (1927-1999) as well as her husband Walter Weglyn (1926-1995) especially admired, was Sue Kunitomi Embrey (1923-2006). Sue, likewise, held Michi and Walter in great esteem for their exemplary social activism. By the time that the two Nisei (US citizen children of Japanese immigrant parents) women first met in the late 1970s or early 1980s, each had already emerged as an iconic figure within the Nikkei (Japanese American) community and beyond. Sue had achieved this status largely on the basis of her leadership of the Los Angeles-based Manzanar Committee, which since 1969 had spearheaded an annual pilgrimage (the first of its kind) to the World War II site of the Manzanar War Relocation Center in eastern California's Owens Valley. Michi, on the other hand, gained her distinction mainly for authoring in 1976 the first major book about the WWII Japanese American experience from the perspective of one of the 120,000 victims, *Years of Infamy: The Untold Story of America's Concentration Camps.* Both the Manzanar Pilgrimage and *Years of Infamy* helped mightily to lay the groundwork for the redress and reparations movement for Japanese Americans that climaxed in the passage of the Civil Rights Act of 1988.

It is my good fortune to have had these two dedicated and talented Nisei women as close friends and valued allies, from the early 1970s until their respective deaths, not only with respect to documenting for posterity the wartime exclusion and detention experience of Americans of Japanese descent, but also in attempting to transform the historical interpretation and public memory of that social disaster. However, because Michi (and Walter) lived across the continent in New York City, while Sue and I lived in the adjacent southern California counties of Los Angeles and Orange, I quite naturally enjoyed more of a face-to-face relationship with Sue. I mention this fact here because it meant that I was more inclined to call upon Sue for assorted favors, one of which figures prominently in the origins story for this particular volume in the Michi Nishiura and Walter Weglyn Multicultural Publication Series.

During the 1970s through 1990s, I intermittently taught a pro-seminar for history majors (but open to other majors as well) at California State University, Fullerton (CSUF), titled the "Japanese American Evacuation."

The culminating assignment for each student in that class was to write an original research paper on some specified topic in relation to the wartime concentration camp experience of Japanese Americans, and for which one of the documentary sources was to be an oral history interview with a knowledgeable participant or observer. The first half of the semester was devoted to reading and discussing books, articles, and films focused on this experience. Then, midway through the semester, the class took a weekend field trip to the site of the WWII War Relocation Authority (WRA)-administered camp closest to our university campus: the aforementioned Manzanar camp, which was situated some 225 miles away on State Highway 395 between the two small Inyo County towns of Lone Pine and Independence.

Every class field trip followed a familiar agenda: on Saturday morning we traveled by auto from the CSUF campus to Lone Pine, where we had reserved lodging at the Willow Motel, a modest hostelry consisting of refurbished barracks from the Manzanar camp. There we were met by our two Nisei guides for the weekend, both of whom had been detained with their respective families in Manzanar for all or part of World War II. On Saturday afternoon, the guides treated the class to a narrated tour of the campsite, which was then bereft of any staffed interpretive center or even informational signage which now await visitors to the National Park Service-administered Manzanar National Historic Site (MNHS). In preparation for this experience, I instructed the students in advance to be on the alert for anything seen on the tour and/or discussed by the Nikkei guides that might serve as a suitable research paper subject to pursue. During the evening following the tour, all of the students talked informally with their guides about research paper topics that appealed to them. Then on Sunday, the highlight was a visit to the permanent Manzanar exhibit at Independence's Eastern California Museum and a short program involving the two Nisei guides and several non-Nikkei residents of the Owens Valley who had either worked at Manzanar or lived proximate to it during the war. The students ruminated further about their tentative research paper topics. This process continued on the long ride back to the CSUF campus and up until the time, in the following week, when each student at the regularly scheduled class meeting had to submit a research paper topic for my consideration and approval.

The spring 1993 Japanese American Internment class was blessed by having Sue Embrey and Wilbur Sato as its Nisei guides for the field trip. Like Sue, Wilbur was affiliated with the Manzanar Committee, and like her, he had participated during the wake of World War II in the activities of the Nisei

Progressives, an activist group of Japanese Americans who supported Henry Wallace for the presidency of the United States and who championed civil liberties, human rights, and social justice. Armed with maps that they had prepared especially for the occasion, Sue and Wilbur toured the class around the mile-square Manzanar site, stopping periodically to provide commentary about a particular place of interest. At one point, in the northwest portion of the camp, the guides halted the group in an area that, they explained, had been the location for both the 250-bed hospital complex and the Children's Village. When questioned by one of the students as to the nature of the latter, Sue indicated that it was an orphanage, the only one among the ten WRA detention camps, and had been "home" to approximately 100 orphaned children of Japanese American or mixed heritage. She then remarked that in spite of its warm-sounding name, those who lived there "had a pretty tough time," since they were rejected by the mainstream society because of their "Japanese blood" and even looked down upon by many Japanese Americans because they were suspected of being less than "pure-blooded Japanese." Wilbur added that Sue was right in saying what she did, but observed that he had gone to school with some of the orphans, had lived in a barracks block next to the Village, and had often played with the children there.

Immediately after the tour, one of the very best students in the class, Lisa Nobe, an American Studies graduate student of Japanese ancestry specializing in Asian American history, approached me and said, "I can tell you right now that the topic I want for my research paper is the Children's Village orphanage." As it turned out, Lisa not only stayed with this topic, but three other students in the class convinced me that they were so taken by the subject as to want to make it the focus of their research as well. Two of these students, Noemi Romero and Celeste Cardenes, were Mexican Americans whose undergraduate major was history but whose minor was Japanese, while the third student, Reiko Katabami, an American Studies graduate student like Lisa, was an exchange student from Japan emphasizing comparative women's history. Because of this convergence of interest, it was agreed that the four students would work as a project team, with Lisa acting in the capacity of project director. It was further decided that they would extend their research into the summer on an independent basis so that they could conduct interviews with a substantial number of the onetime orphans at the Children's Village as well as the Village's surviving former superintendent, Lillian Matsumoto, who made her home in the San Francisco Bay Area city of Berkeley.

When the decision had been made for the Children's Village study to function as a project, I contacted Wilbur Sato to see if he would be willing to be the advisor. He was agreeable to this arrangement, but also suggested that another advisor should be Tamotsu Iozaki, who during the war had initially been one of the youthful charges at the Village but then later worked as a counselor there. In a subsequent series of meetings, Wilbur and Tamo spoke to Lisa, Noemi, Celeste, and Reiko in great depth about the Children's Village, and then drew up a list of former children and staff who had attended an earlier Village reunion to suggest some possible interview subjects. Capitalizing on these leads, the student interviewers made contact with their prospective interviewees and audio tape-recorded their wartime memories of life at the Manzanar Children's Village orphanage. Thus, an oral history project was born.

Because of the graduation of most of the students on this project, coupled with a lack of funding in the CSUF Oral History Program (OHP), these Children's Village interviews were not immediately transcribed. However, I was constantly on the lookout for funding opportunities to get the transcription done. One promising opportunity presented itself in 1996 when the CSUF University Advancement office contacted me to see if I would be willing to work with the president of the CSUF Alumni Association, who was then employed with the US office of a Japanese beer company, to secure funding support related to the OHP's oral history work with Japanese Americans. With the transcription of the Children's Village interviews uppermost in mind, I met with the Alumni Association president to discuss my intention, and he advised me to write up a proposal that would indicate the work to be done, the nature of the project to which it was connected, why that project was significant, and how much the work in question would cost. Once he had this proposal in hand, he would make a presentation to the public relations officer of his company—which he eventually did. Unfortunately, the public relations officer turned down the request because of the possibility that the Children's Village interviews might touch on topics that would be sensitive within the Japanese American community and thus potentially harm relations between that community and the beer company.

Very shortly after I received this disappointing news, though, I got a telephone call from Renee Tawa, a Japanese American reporter at the *Los Angeles Times*. She asked me if anything new and exciting was on the horizon in relation to the OHP's Japanese American projects. At this point, I told her about the Children's Village interviews and the recent proposal I had written to garner funds to have them transcribed. She then expressed an interest in seeing this proposal. Not much time elapsed after I sent the proposal to her before she contacted me again and said that she found the Children's Village story to be a fascinating and strangely neglected chapter of the World War II experience of Japanese Americans, and was eager to write a piece about it for her paper. I was naturally pleased by this turn of events.

But I was simply overwhelmed when, on the morning of March 11, 1997, I opened up my copy of the *Los Angeles Times* and there, on the first page, situated atop the feature story in column one, was the following headline: "Childhood Lost: The Orphans of Manzanar." The response to this lengthy, well written, and stirring story was tremendous. By the end of the day our OHP office was deluged with informational inquiries and invitations for promotional opportunities from a variety of local and regional media. By the end of the week, these sorts of opportunities had broadened into national and international ones. The most appealing came from the popular American television magazine *60 Minutes*, which wanted to devote a segment of a future weekly broadcast to telling the story of the Children's Village.

Project director Lisa Nobe, by then an OHP research associate, took the lead in dealing with the needs of the advance representatives from *60 Minutes* assigned to the Children's Village story, and helped to negotiate an arrangement. In return for lining up selected interviewees in the Children's Village project for the *60 Minutes* interviewer, Morley Safer, and his filming crew to re-interview on videotape, the OHP would get the original audio interviews transcribed and Lisa would be granted a modest stipend for her consulting services.

At last, on the evening of December 7, 1997, a thirteen-minute segment, "Orphans of Manzanar," was broadcast nationwide on CBS. This deftly edited piece, which specifically credited the students of Cal State Fullerton for their resourceful fieldwork, was so dramatically powerful as to set in motion a second wave of interest in the Children's Village story. This led first to a panel on this story at the Japanese American National Museum in Los Angeles, in which Lisa and I participated, that drew a large and spirited audience of wartime Village denizens, including virtually all of those interviewed by the CSUF students. At this event, too, I announced that the OHP would someday publish a book featuring the oral histories that the students had transacted a few years earlier, and that these likely would be supplemented by new interviews done with other informants.

It appeared that this promissory note would soon be redeemed when the OHP was contacted by a Los Angeles-based book manufacturer interested in having Lisa and me work with him on producing a coffee-table book of words and images about the Children's Village for mass marketing and distribution. But this prospect, following some promising and productive meetings, ended with a whimper rather than a bang when the book manufacturer moved his office first to Santa Barbara County and then, not long afterwards, moved still again, but without leaving behind a forwarding address or any other contact information.

For the time being, the Children's Village book was set aside, but it was not forgotten. In April 1999, in a special issue of the *Journal of the West* on "Japanese American Relocation in the American West," there appeared a fine article by Lisa Nobe entitled, "The Children's Village at Manzanar: The World War II Eviction and Detention of Japanese American Orphans." In Lisa's biography at the conclusion of this article, it said: "She is currently co-authoring a book on the Children's Village with Arthur A. Hansen." That this book was not published thereafter had far less to do with desire or will than with the shifting responsibilities and priorities of its well-intentioned authors.

Fortuitously, some four years ago, in anticipation of the Manzanar National Historic Site's opening of an interpretive center and a bookstore, our new Center for Oral and Public History (COPH), which had supplanted the OHP in 2002, was visited by two MNHS representatives, National Park Service Ranger Richard Potashin and bookstore manager Mary Daniel. Working through a group called the Manzanar History Associates, Mary and Richard were interested in stimulating our Center to republish some of its earlier books and to develop new books for sale in the MNHS bookstore. Highest ranked in the new books category for development was "a compilation of interviews profiling the orphanage." In a follow-up correspondence, Mary candidly remarked, "I truly do understand these projects will take hard-to-come-by funding [and] while I regret my organization is not in a position to commit dollars at this point, I will do my best to meet the terms you establish for their sale."

In response to this new opportunity and challenge, I lined up an editor for the Children's Village volume, Alan Koch, who as a seasoned American Studies graduate student had been enrolled in the same 1993 "Japanese American Evacuation" class in which the Children's Village project had emerged. I also worked with COPH's financial officer, Kathy Frazee, on arranging resourceful funding for this book so that it could be included in the Weglyn Series. When Alan's personal financial needs prevented him from continuing his editorial duties, by a stroke of blind luck I encountered a former Asian American Studies Program colleague, Dr. Catherine Irwin, who evinced an interest in picking up where Alan had left off. Cathy was then at the point of transitioning from a part-time position at CSUF as an adjunct faculty member to assuming a full-time tenure-track position as an assistant professor of English in the Modern Languages Department at the University of La Verne. She expressed an interest in transforming the plan for the Children's Village book from an edited anthology of existing interviews in the COPH archives to a volume for which she would not only generate many new interviews, but also, in the manner of an author, to produce a general introduction and to organize all of the interviews into appropriate topical chapters contextualized by analytical and explanatory text.

As a direct result of Catherine Irwin's inspired authorial role in *Twice Orphaned*, the Manzanar Children's Village project has exchanged its own longtime orphaned status in the COPH archives for a sustaining public home between two covers. Published in 2008 at the time of the twentieth anniversary of the passage of the Civil Liberties Act, *Twice Orphaned* can properly be regarded as embellishing the principle and process of redress enshrined in that measure.

* * *

The Michi Nishiura and Walter Weglyn Multicultural Publication Series aims to memorialize the humanitarian legacy of the Weglyns. Their estate has made the series financially possible, while their lives have invested it with palpable meaning and high-minded purpose.

As a twelve-year-old, Walter Weglyn secured the last space on a transport, that in 1939 brought two thousand German Jewish children to a special children's camp in Rotterdam. To stay alive, he was forced after Holland fell to the Nazis to flee from one shelter to another, eleven in all. Thereafter, a kindly Dutch diplomat's wife, who nightly buried him under a goat stable, saved his life. German aerial bombings in the Lowland killed most of the refugee children, and of those spared, only Walter and one other child survived the war. So also did his parents, who had been interned at Theresiendstat concentration camp in Czechoslovakia. Walter Weglyn, whose wartime odyssey was later featured along with Anne Frank and other Holocaust victims in Harvey Shapiro's book, *What Evils Men Do*, arrived in the United States in 1947. While living at Columbia University's International

House in New York City, he met Michi Nishiura, who had come there when personal misfortune forced her to withdraw from Mount Holyoke College in Massachusetts to become a costume designer. After Michi was diagnosed with tuberculosis and temporarily confined in an upstate New York sanitarium, Walter proposed to her. Following their 1950 marriage and the establishment of their home in Manhattan, Walter embarked upon his long and successful career as a perfume chemist, and Michi pursued her profession in broadcast television (including an eight-year stint as costume designer for the popularly acclaimed *Perry Como Show*) and also wrote poetry and painted.

After the war in Vietnam and the Watergate scandal opened the actions of the US government to increasing scrutiny and criticism, Michi began to question the decisions responsible for the detention of herself, her family, and her ethnic community during World War II. Unsalaried and without the aid of grant monies, she spent years systematically searching through the archival records in repositories like the National Archives and the Franklin Delano Roosevelt Library to find evidence proving that "military necessity" was only a pretext for the racist wartime policy of mass detention for people of Japanese ancestry. "Persuaded that the enormity of a bygone injustice has been only partially perceived," Michi explained her decision to write *Years of Infamy*: "I have taken upon myself the task of piecing together what might be called the 'forgotten' or ignored parts of those years." The release of this book in 1976, in the words of Phil Tajitsu Nash, "finally gave redress advocates the facts they needed to press their righteous claims in the courts and in Congress." Michi was greatly assisted in both the researching for and the writing of her seminal book by Walter, who was outraged by the incarceration experience of Japanese Americans (as he also was of the treatment of African Americans in the South, where he lived before settling in New York). "Walter is my most exacting critic and mentor," Michi was quoted as saying. "I was able to write *Years of Infamy* because of the critical feedback he gave me, and his determination that I *must* expose the lies used to justify that atrocity." Truly, as the writer Frank Chin and the oral historian Paul Tsuneishi pointed out in their obituary of Walter Weglyn for the *Rafu Shimpo* (Los Angeles Japanese Daily News), Walter was "passionately committed to others who were disadvantaged or suffering oppression everywhere . . . [and] shared his wife's zeal in Asian American civil rights issues."

In 1993, while both of the Weglyns were still alive, President Bob Suzuki of California State Polytechnic University, Pomona, announced the establishment of the Walter and Michi Nishiura Weglyn Endowed Chair in Multicultural Studies. As an addendum to his moving tribute to Michi written shortly after her death on April 25, 1999, Phil Tajitsu Nash remarked that because she had been a person of action as well as ideas, one very fitting memorial to her would be for admirers to think of ways to build ongoing institutions such as the endowed chair at Cal Poly Pomona and to further their own vision of a better world. It is in this spirit that the Michi Nishiura and Walter Weglyn Multicultural Publication Series is dedicated. Parallel with the purpose of the endowed chair at our sister campus in Pomona, we hope this series publishes works of fiction and non-fiction that will promote a profound understanding of racial-ethnic diversity and a concomitant practice of authentic cultural pluralism in the United States.

Arthur A. Hansen
Series Editor
Center for Oral and Public History
California State University, Fullerton

Preface

By now, the story of the Japanese American imprisonment during World War II, in outline at least, is familiar to many readers. In 1942, the United States Army removed more than 110,000 Americans of Japanese ancestry from their homes, farms, jobs, and businesses on the Pacific Coast. In one of the most infamous failures of justice in American history, anyone who bore a Japanese name, features, or family connections was deemed a security risk and jailed. The inmates were transferred from the army to the War Relocation Authority, a newly-created civilian agency, and incarcerated in concentration camps in remote, barren parts of the western states. There they sat out the war behind barbed wire. Some of them cooperated with the government, some protested their imprisonment, and some joined the US Army and fought heroically for their country.

Students learn this history in school. There are books, movies, and museums dedicated to telling the story and keeping alive the memory of the unjust suffering of an entire American ethnic group. This is only appropriate, but a generation ago, it was not so. In the 1950s and 1960s, very few Americans allowed themselves to be conscious of this episode, and fewer still contemplated the dismal implications for American liberties. Even Sansei (third-generation Japanese Americans), growing up in those decades, seldom had a clear idea of what their parents and grandparents had endured, for the older generations generally did not want to talk about an experience of pain and shame.

And then the story began to be told. In landmark volumes in 1971 and 1976, Roger Daniels and Michi Nishiura Weglyn stripped away the cloak that had shrouded the concentration camp episode from public view.[1] Japanese American groups began to rebuild the community's memory. Memorial pilgrimages were organized to Manzanar, the first of the camps, and then to others; some became annual events. As the Nisei generation aged, they began to talk more and more about their experiences, to organize reunions, to fund museum exhibits—indeed, to create whole museums and archival repositories. Twenty years ago, by the Civil Liberties Act of 1988,

---

[1]Roger Daniels, *Concentration Camps USA: Japanese Americans and World War II* (New York: Holt, Rinehart and Winston, 1971); Michi Weglyn, *Years of Infamy: The Untold Story of America's Concentration Camps* (New York: Morrow, 1976).

the US government finally apologized for the injustice it had perpetrated and made token monetary reparations. Since the 1970s, scores of books have been written on the concentration camp episode.

For all this public and scholarly attention, some aspects of the World War II concentration camp experience remain unknown to this day. The Japanese American story, including the concentration camp era, has usually been told as a family story. So we have many accounts of families sticking together in this hard time, living together in tight quarters and quiet desperation in camp, and then rebuilding their lives together outside after the war.[2]

By contrast, we have heard relatively little about individuals and outliers. We have only begun to hear the stories of people like Ralph Lazo, a Mexican American teenager who voluntarily went with his Nisei friends to Manzanar and was imprisoned for two and a half years, and Estelle Ishigo, the white wife of a Nisei artist who joined her husband Arthur at Heart Mountain.[3] We know very little about the gay population among the Japanese American inmates, and almost nothing about people like Liwa Chew, Mary Ventura, and Riyoko Patell, who were imprisoned while their non-Japanese husbands remained free.[4]

In *Twice Orphaned*, Catherine Irwin and her collaborators bring to life a little-known and long-neglected group within the inmate population: children who were interned without families.[5] In the years before the war,

---

[2]E.g., Monica Sone, *Nisei Daughter* (Boston: Little, Brown, 1953); Jeanne Wakatsuki Houston and James D. Houston, *Farewell to Manzanar* (Boston: Houghton Mifflin, 1973); Yoshiko Uchida, *Desert Exile: The Uprooting of a Japanese-American Family* (Seattle: University of Washington Press, 1982); Lauren Kessler, *Stubborn Twig: Three Generations in the Life of a Japanese American Family* (New York: Penguin, 1993); Louis Fiset, *Imprisoned Apart: The World War II Correspondence of an Issei Couple* (Seattle: University of Washington Press, 1997); Stephen S. Fugita and Marilyn Fernandez, *Altered Lives, Enduring Community: Japanese Americans Remember Their World War II Incarceration* (Seattle: University of Washington Press, 2004); Mary Matsuda Gruenewald, *Looking Like the Enemy: My Story of Imprisonment in Japanese-American Internment Camps* (Troutdale, Ore.: New Sage Press, 2005).

[3]Lazo and Ishigo have been the subjects of documentary films: *Stand Up For Justice: The Ralph Lazo Story* (Nikkei for Civil Rights and Redress and Visual Communications, dir. John Esaki, 2004); *Days of Waiting* (PBS and National Asian American Telecommunications Association, dir. Steven Okazaki, 1990).

[4]Chew, Ventura, and Patell are mentioned briefly in Paul Spickard, "Injustice Compounded: Amerasians and Non-Japanese Americans in World War II Concentration Camps," *Journal of American Ethnic History*, 5.2 (1986), 5-22.

[5]The only prior treatments of these orphans are Helen Elizabeth Whitney, "Care

three orphanages served the Japanese American populations of northern and southern California: the Salvation Army Home in San Francisco, and the Shonien and Maryknoll Catholic Home in Los Angeles. By 1942, these three institutions were home to nearly a hundred homeless or orphaned Japanese American children. Many of them were children whose parents had died; others had seen a father taken away by the FBI in the weeks after the Pearl Harbor attack, or a mother break down and become unable to care for them. A significant minority were mixed-race children whose Japanese families did not want them. All of the children at those institutions were interned at Manzanar, together with some other Japanese American orphans such as six-year-old Richard Honda, a foster child placed with a white family in Oxnard since infancy. At Manzanar, they entered a special part of the camp set aside as Children's Village.

Beginning in the 1990s, Lisa Nobe, Art Hansen, and their colleagues at the California State University, Fullerton, Oral History Program (now the Center for Oral and Public History) tracked down eighteen former orphans and staff members who had been interned at Children's Village. This book, ably compiled, edited, introduced, and set in context by Catherine Irwin, tells their story. The participants tell in their own words what their lives were like in the prewar years, what it felt like to lose their parents, and how they related to other children on the outside, both Japanese Americans and non-Japanese Americans. Then it takes them into the camp at Manzanar, describes their everyday lives and privations there, and probes the double abandonment they experienced, first by their parents and then by their country. Subsequent chapters bring their lives full circle, through the end of the war, the camp closures, re-entry into civil society, and their growth in subsequent decades.

It is a compelling story and an important one, vividly told.

Paul Spickard

---

of Homeless Children of Japanese Ancestry during Evacuation" (MA thesis, University of California, Berkeley, 1948); Ford Kuramoto, "A History of the Shonien, 1914-1972: An Account of a Program of Institutional Care of Japanese Children in Los Angeles" (PhD dissertation, University of California, Berkeley, 1972); and Lisa Nobe, "The Children's Village at Manzanar: The World War II Eviction and Detention of Japanese American Orphans," *Journal of the West*, 38 (1999): 65-71.

Acknowledgments

This book would never have come into fruition without Dr. Art Hansen. His unwavering dedication and generous support of this project was inspiration to finish this book, fifteen years after his graduate students Lisa Nobe Wong, Celeste Cardenas, Noemi Romero, and Reiko Katabami first began conducting interviews with former orphans of the Children's Village. Dr. Hansen read multiple drafts of this manuscript and provided invaluable suggestions, guidance, and encouragement. It was an honor working with him.

Special thanks also go to the staff of the Center for Oral and Public History: Kathy Frazee not only read the entire manuscript and offered her erudite advice, but worked on the layout and design of the book as well. Archivist Stephanie George provided the support and help needed to retrieve and prepare the oral history interviews and photographs for this book. Kira Gentry also provided support during the hunting and gathering stage of archival work.

I would also like to especially thank and acknowledge Lillian Matsumoto, Karyl Matsumoto, and Greg Marutani for their assistance and for providing many of the photographs in this book (including the front cover painting by Kango Takamura).

I would also like to extend my thanks to Dr. Natalie Fousekis, Director of the Center for Oral and Public History, as well as the following people at California State University, Fullerton: Dr. Bill Haddad, Chair, Department of History; Dr. Craig Ihara and Dr. Thomas Fujita-Rony of the Asian American Studies Program; and Dr. Tom Klammer, Dean, College of Humanities and Social Sciences.

Thanks also go to Susan Sang for her work as copy editor; to Debra Gold Hansen for assistance constructing the index; and to Suzanne Walters, Garnette Long, and Adriana Ruvalcaba who transcribed many of the tape-recorded oral history interviews in this book.

I would also like to acknowledge and thank the following people and organizations for their generous support and interest in this project throughout the years: Alan Koch; Risa Hirao; Dr. Paul Spickard, Professor of History and Asian American Studies at University of California, Santa Barbara; Dr. Amy Sueyoshi, Chair, Department of Ethnic Studies at San

Francisco State University; Marie Masumoto and the Japanese American National Museum; Renee Tawa and the *Los Angeles Times*; Morley Safer and *60 Minutes;* and Alisa Lynch, Chief of Interpretation, Manzanar National Historic Site, and her staff, especially Richard Potashin, Mary Daniel, and Kirk Peterson.

The completion and publication of this book was made possible through financial support from the Michi Nishiura and Walter Weglyn Multicultural Series, a research grant from the University of La Verne's College of Arts and Sciences, and the Center for Public and Oral History.

I extend my sincerest gratitude and appreciation to the men and women who were interviewed for this book and shared their memories and experiences of orphanage life. I would especially like to thank Mr. and Mrs. Takatow Matsuno, Tamo Isozaki, Annie Sakamoto, Sohei Hohri, Mary Miya, Dennis Bambauer, Robert Yamashita, and Lillian Bonner. I would also like to thank the friends and family of those interviewed, especially Wilbur Sato and Kazuye Suyematsu.

Finally, I would like to thank my own family for their constant support, especially to my husband Tom who lovingly pushed and encouraged me through every stage of this book. This one's for you, TP.

Introduction

On June 23, 1942, social worker Lillian Matsumoto boarded a military bus with thirty-one orphan children and five of her staff and traveled 235 miles from Los Angeles up through California's central valley to their new home behind barbed wire in Manzanar Relocation Center.[1] The children with Matsumoto, including Dennis Tojo, Ira Iwata, Clara Hayashi, and Tak Matsuno, were from the Shonien and Maryknoll Catholic Home, two orphanages or "children's homes" for minors of Japanese descent.

These children were relocated to Manzanar for the same reason that 120,000 other American citizens and residents who lived on the coast of California, Oregon, and Washington were: because they were of Japanese ancestry, they were considered a threat to national security, and were "instructed" by President Franklin D. Roosevelt's Executive Order 9066 to prepare for military exclusion and detention. As Lisa Nobe writes, "As was true of the West Coast Americans of Japanese descent, Japanese American orphans were subjected to United States governmental policies based primarily on race and carried out as a direct result of prejudice and discrimination. No distinctions were made between 'certain' Japanese Americans and others, and this denial of a person's rights did not exclude orphanage children."[2]

Lillian Matsumoto and her husband Harry would become the assistant superintendent and superintendent, respectively, of the orphanage at Manzanar, and would oversee the staff that cared for the orphan children. Other children from San Francisco's Salvation Army Home and those orphaned during exclusion or while living in the camps would also be placed in their care. Three one-story buildings, "wider than the usual barracks," contained a boys' dormitory, a girls' dormitory, a nursery, a small children's dormitory (one for boys, the other for girls), staff housing, a dining hall, kitchen and store room facilities, a recreation room, and bathroom facilities.[3] As the only orphanage within the ten camps, this institution within an institution would be called "Children's Village."

---

[1] Helen Elizabeth Whitney, "Care of Homeless Children of Japanese Ancestry during Evacuation" (M.A. thesis, University of California, Berkeley, 1948), 18, 28.

[2] Lisa Nobe, "The Children's Village at Manzanar: The World War II Eviction and Detention of Japanese American Orphans," *Journal of the West* 38 (April 1999): 65.

[3] Whitney, 18.

Eighteen former orphans and staff members who were incarcerated at Children's Village were interviewed for California State University at Fullerton's Center for Oral and Public History Children's Village Project, which was started by graduate student Lisa Nobe in 1993 and has been under the direction of Dr. Arthur Hansen. One of the main objectives of the Children's Village Project was to explore the impact of detention on these orphans. What was life like for orphans of Japanese ancestry before World War II? How did this specific population of children cope with incarceration at Manzanar internment camp? Where were these children sent after the war ended and the camps closed? What were the effects of institutional life on these children? These oral histories reveal the effects of war and abandonment on children as stories expose the confusion, anger, fear, and sadness that a child probably once felt as he or she was left behind in an orphanage as a result of a father's arrest by the FBI after Pearl Harbor or a mother's physical or mental breakdown due to tuberculosis, mental illness, or the stress and shame of incarceration. Harry Kitano has argued that while it is "far too complex" to measure precisely the effects of internment on Japanese Americans, "traces of the experience are probably still a part of every person who went through the trauma."[4] The personal stories and experiences presented in this book explore how children coped and survived separation from their parents and then abandonment by their country.

Before World War II: The Rise of Japanese Children's Homes in California

Many of the Nisei and Sansei children who were sent to Children's Village became orphans before the war as a result of family and economic instability. Because of anti-immigration laws, such as the Gentlemen's Agreement of 1907, the early Japanese immigrant population, which was predominantly male, was restricted to sending for their wives or arranging "picture bride" marriages. Without an extended family with multiple adult wage earners, many families in the early twentieth century struggled as farm laborers, servants, fishermen, and small business owners.[5] Usually, husbands and wives both had to work to earn enough to survive. In addition, because few of the Issei or Nisei families in the early immigrant community included

---

[4] Harry Kitano, "The Effects of the Evacuation on the Japanese Americans," in *Japanese Americans: From Relocation to Redress*, ed. Roger Daniels, Sandra C. Taylor, and Harry Kitano (Seattle: University of Washington Press, 1991), 157.

[5] Paul Spickard, *Japanese Americans: The Formation and Transformations of an Ethnic Group* (New York: Twayne Publishers, 1996), 37-46, 70.

grandparents or relatives who could act as child-care givers, families whose parents could not afford to raise their children had to break up to survive. As Ford Kuramoto argues, "The absence of strong, extended family systems in the early Japanese community in the United States precipitated the need for an out-of-home care program."[6]

In addition, Issei and Nisei families in the United States could not always rely on social organizations or other community members for economic help. Economic instability in the larger mainstream community meant unemployment and business failures in the ethnic Japanese community. In 1908, two Japanese community banks went bankrupt because of an economic depression.[7] In some cases, men who had emigrated alone to America were "adopted" by Nikkei families who helped these single men survive.[8] At the same time, as a result of both financial instability and racial discrimination, many Japanese families living in the city had no choice but to settle in ghetto neighborhoods where poor housing and low-wage jobs were the norm.[9] Many children became temporary or half-orphans because the stress of these poor living and working conditions led to the death or illness of a parent.

Before World War II and the opening of Children's Village, there were three orphanages in California specifically for children of Japanese ancestry: the Salvation Army Home in San Francisco, the Maryknoll Home in Los Angeles, and the Shonien in Los Angeles. The Shonien was the first of these homes to open its doors. In 1912, Rokuichi "Joy" Kusumoto, along with other community leaders, formed the Japanese Humane Society (*Rafu Jindokai*), to help young picture brides in "unsuccessful marriages" and the growing number of homeless children in their ethnic community.[10] This society founded the Shonien, or the Japanese Humane Society Children's Home, that was "understood to care only for Japanese dependent children."[11] When the first Shonien facility opened its doors in 1913, the staff was able to house six infants. By August of 1916, after the purchase of a larger residence, there

---

[6] Ibid, 70. See also Ford Kuramoto, *A History of the Shonien, 1914-1972: An Account of a Program of Institutional Care of Japanese Children in Los Angeles* (San Francisco: R and E Research Associates, 1976), 10.

[7] Kuramoto, 11.

[8] Spickard, 70.

[9] Kuramoto, 12.

[10] Ibid, 12.

[11] Ibid, 13. See also William H. Slingerland, *Child Welfare Work in California: A Study of Agencies and Institutions* (New York: Russell Sage Foundation, 1916), 89.

were nine children at the home. Three children had been sent to the Shonien by their father as a result of marital separation, and the other six children had lost a parent to death or illness.[12] Two years later, eight out of nine children placed at the Shonien were half-orphans.[13]

The need for orphanages in the early twentieth century was a concern not only in the Japanese immigrant community, but in the larger American culture as well. Lori Askeland has noted that orphanages existed in America even before the Revolutionary War: "They were relatively few in number until the 1830s, when several were constructed in response to the poverty and the breakup of kinship networks resulting from large-scale immigration and urbanization."[14] Most orphanages were segregated by race and run by Catholic, Protestant, and Jewish religious organizations.[15] Many of these agencies believed that they were providing "'child rescue' or salvation from an otherwise dismal life."[16] In the 1850s, Charles Loring Brace of the New York Children's Society began "placing out" or relocating homeless or orphan children from urban centers into rural areas further west, where children were sent to work and live "a new, wholesome life."[17] According to Marilyn Irvin Holt, these "rescue" operations, also known as "orphan trains," placed "at least 200,000 children and teenagers" until its gradual demise in the 1920s, when child-care and social work advocates demanded a "'more intelligent' approach to child placement and criticized states that retained indenture laws."[18]

As a result of early twentieth-century racial segregation and discrimination, many child-care resources in the larger community were closed to Japanese children. At the same time, according to Ford Kuramoto, "Foster care and adoptions of children as an alternative to institutional care were not well known or favored by the majority of Japanese people. Non-Japanese institutions were not desirable because of cultural differences and the disruption

---

[12] Kuramoto, 14.

[13] Ibid, 16.

[14] Lori Askeland, "Informal Adoption, Apprentices, and Indentured Children in the Colonial Era and the New Republic, 1605-1850," *Children and Youth in Adoption, Orphanages and Foster Care*, ed. Lori Askeland (Westport, CT: Greenwood Press, 2006), 9.

[15] Ibid, 9.

[16] Marilyn Irvin Holt, *The Orphan Trains: Placing Out in America* (Lincoln: University of Nebraska Press, 1992), 23.

[17] Marilyn Irvin Holt, "Adoption Reform, Orphan Trains, and Child-Saving, 1851-1929," *Children and Youth in Adoption, Orphanages, and Foster Care,* ed. Lori Askeland, 18.

[18] Ibid, 18, 27. See also Neva R. Deardorff, "Bound Out," *Survey* 56, no. 8 (1926): 459.

of kinship ties."[19] While this was the Nikkei perspective on childcare, on the West Coast prior to World War II, many county welfare departments and agencies had placed one or more Japanese American children with foster parents, usually of the same race.[20] Orphanages, hospitals, and other institutions were also called upon to accept an occasional child of Japanese ancestry; but with the building of the Shonien and Maryknoll Catholic Home for Japanese children both in Los Angeles, and the Salvation Army Home for Japanese children in San Francisco, the care of most homeless or orphan children of Japanese descent was provided by these three race-specific orphanages or by distant family members.[21]

In particular, the Shonien would grow into a facility that by 1942 was caring for thirty-eight children and teenagers year round; Maryknoll had thirty-three children and teenagers; and the Salvation Army had twenty-two.[22] Unlike mainstream orphanages that placed children as laborers who were to work for room and board, teenagers at these three orphanages were usually allowed to stay in their care until they were eighteen years old.[23] One former orphan, Mits Yamasaki, remembers how living at the Shonien instead of working as a houseboy allowed him to play varsity football and be on student government at Marshall High School in Los Angeles.[24] However, many Nisei teenagers living in one of the children's homes left at sixteen years of age to live with nearby families (usually Caucasian) to work as domestics or "schoolboys" or "schoolgirls" while they went to high school.[25]

1942: World War II and the Move to Children's Village

The lives of Nisei and Sansei orphans changed after the bombing of Pearl Harbor by Japan on December 7, 1941. Like other Japanese American school children, many of the orphans were unaware of the ramifications until the FBI arrested a father or community leader. Life at the Shonien changed the day after Pearl Harbor, when Joy Kusumoto, Shonien's director, was arrested by the FBI and sent to an internment center in Missoula, Montana.[26] Without the leadership of Kusumoto and other community lead-

[19] Kuramoto, 13.
[20] Whitney, 13.
[21] Ibid.
[22] Kuramoto, 32; Whitney, 15.
[23] Kuramoto, 30.
[24] Mitsuru Yamasaki, Interviewed by Cathy Irwin, 24 January 2007, CSUF-Center for Oral and Public History.
[25] Kuramoto, 30.
[26] Ibid, 42.

ers at the helm of the Shonien, two Nisei staff members—Harry and Lillian (Iida) Matsumoto—became responsible for overseeing the operation of the home and the other seven staff members.[27] During this time, as businesses run by Issei were shut down and bank accounts and other assets of Issei and Nisei were frozen, the Matsumotos had to struggle to find ways to keep the Shonien financially stable.[28] These Nisei staff members, along with Nisei staff members at the Salvation Army and Maryknoll homes who were preparing for removal, also worried about the future of the orphan children and who would care for them, as military authorities had excused "inmates in institutions" from incarceration.[29]

The decision over who would care for the children at the three orphanages was ultimately left to the federal authorities and the California State Department of Social Welfare (SDSW).[30] However, staff and community leaders at the Shonien fought to keep staff and children together. For example, in a letter to federal authorities, Shonien's board chairman, Dr. T.G. Ishimaru, made a plea on behalf of the Shonien staff for exemption from relocation:

> The present staff understands the nature and background
> of each child and has already begun the work of readjust-
> ment which of necessity must be continued if full and
> normal development is to be assured [. . .] The staff is
> "father and mother" to these children. Love, understand-
> ing, and guidance are just as essential as food and shelter.
> Any change in the present staff will unnecessarily bring
> undue hardship on these children. The staff members are
> more than just parents; their responsibility is greater in
> human relationships.[31]

Dr. Ishimaru's letter to federal authorities underscored how important staff members were to the growth and development of the children in their care. In addition, Dr. Ishimaru emphasized how important the staff was to the assimilation process. By the end of his letter, he asks federal authorities to look beyond the anti-Japanese sentiment and to look upon the Japanese American

---

[27] Whitney, 13.

[28] Kuramoto, 32.

[29] Ibid, 33

[30] Ibid, 34.

[31] Letter from Dr. T.G. Ishimaru, March 24, 1942, in Kuramoto, 33-4.

Shonien staff as Nisei who were "interested in making good American citizens of these children" and how "(a)ll members of the present staff are citizens and all are active members of their respective denominational churches. English is spoken at all times within the institutions."[32] Subsequently, the military army "allow(ed) temporary exemption for seven staff members of the Shonien Japanese Children's Home, the same number of Japanese-American staff of the Salvation Army home, and for all the children remaining in the three orphanages."[33]

This special exemption lasted long enough for military personnel, the United States Children's Bureau, and the Social Security Board to analyze the circumstance of each child and to agree on the army's position of promptly "relocating" all staff members and children over fourteen. In the first week of April 1942, the SDSW, which would act as a liaison between the federal agencies and the three orphanages, "assumed coordination" of relocation and decided that, instead of training a new non-Japanese staff for the Shonien, the Shonien staff would remain with the children and relocate with them.[34] Less than a month later, on April 28, 1942, Dr. Ishimaru and Lillian and Harry Matsumoto drove up to Manzanar camp with members from the United States Children's Bureau and the Social Security Board to inspect and approve the "three tar-paper barracks" that would be "euphemistically named Children's Village."[35]

For many of the half-orphans and their families, relocation meant not having to worry about money. As a result, most of the children at the Shonien and Maryknoll home who had at least one parent or relative alive were reunited with their families before going to camp. However, in some cases, the emotional stress and shame of being confined behind barbed wire in makeshift barracks took its toll on adult family members. Kuramoto writes that in one instance, "a mother in poor health suffered a nervous breakdown because of the internment of her husband. She was placed in the psychiatric ward of the county hospital, leaving five children without parental supervision. These children were emergently placed at the Shonien."[36]

By the end of June 1942, Children's Village had a population of sixty-one children.[37] Ninety percent of the children were from California

---

[32] Ibid.
[33] Whitney, 16.
[34] Kuramoto, 34.
[35] Ibid, 35.
[36] Ibid, 33.
[37] Whitney, 28.

8 *Children's Village*

with over one-third from Los Angeles County.[38] Approximately 50 percent of the admitted were under seven years of age and 29 percent under four years of age.[39] Children admitted after June of 1942 were mostly under fourteen years of age; by early 1943, teenagers between sixteen and eighteen years of age were usually transferred to the regular barracks, either to live with relatives or to a dormitory, such as the YWCA barrack.[40] However, teenagers with younger brothers and sisters in the Village usually stayed to maintain family unity.[41] In some cases, such as the Matsuno family, when there were younger siblings staying in the Village, an older sister or brother would transfer to the regular barracks and have a parent and younger family members join them later.[42]

While most of the children at the Village were from the Shonien, Maryknoll, or Salvation Army children's homes, seven children became orphans after relocation. In the case of the Kodama family, two daughters were placed in the Children's Village after their parents committed suicide in their barrack.[43] Between September 1942 and September 1943, seven more children were sent to the Children's Village from foster and broken homes; in addition, the Village offered temporary (a few days to eight months) care to sixteen children and long-term care to eight children sent from hospitals and maternity homes.[44] For many families, the stress and trauma of being sent to an American concentration camp tore apart the family unit, as parents were driven to extreme actions and choices. In some of these cases, the reason for placement was kept secret. Ronald Kawamoto, born at the Santa Anita Assembly Center, was separated from his Mexican American mother and Japanese American father and sent to the Children's Village. He never found out why he had been orphaned during the war.[45]

Mixed-race children like Ronald Kawamoto had a particularly hard time at the Children's Village because they faced rejection by the larger racial-ethnic community not only for being orphans, but also for not being (or

[38] Ibid, 29.

[39] Ibid.

[40] Ibid.

[41] Ibid.

[42] Mary Miya, Interviewed by Celeste Cardenas, 13 March 1993, CSUF-Center for Oral and Public History. See also Tak Matsuno, Interviewed by Noemi Romero, 13 March 1993, CSUF-Center for Oral and Public History.

[43] Sharon Kodama, Interviewed by Richard Potashin, 9 September 2005, Manzanar National Historic Site Oral History Program.

[44] Whitney, 28.

[45] Ronald Kawamoto, Interview by Cathy Irwin, 4 February 2007, CSUF-Center for Oral and Public History.

looking) "pure" Japanese.[46] Even before incarceration, approximately nineteen children who had been placed at the Shonien were orphans of mixed-race parentage.[47] One explanation for the large proportion of mixed-race children in the home was "the reluctance of Los Angeles Japanese families to take in children of mixed parentage, while they were quite willing to provide homes for most pure Japanese orphans."[48] Out of the 101 children who were cared for at the Children's Village from 1942-1945, an estimated 19 percent of the population was mixed-race. The known racial combinations of some of these children included Mexican-Japanese, Indian-Japanese, Filipino-Japanese, and Italian, Irish, and French descent.[49] Of the fourteen children who were certain to be mixed-race, eleven of them were under seven years of age and the rest were between eight and fifteen years old. Interestingly, twelve out of these fourteen children were Sansei, or third-generation Japanese American, which suggests that Nisei may have crossed racial lines socially and romantically despite the community's taboo and stigma against interracial marriages and children during that time.[50]

Internment Life for Children

In general, the life of the Nisei child or adolescent interned at Manzanar's Children's Village was in many ways different from the life of the Nisei child or adolescent who lived in the barracks with their families. Before internment, Issei parents were teaching their children the primacy of family solidarity and conformity.[51] However, among the families living in the barracks, the different ways that adults and children coped and adjusted to camp life disrupted family unity because of the breakdown in the family routine. Instead of eating together at traditional meal times, for example, parents and children ate in community mess halls where "young Nisei spent more time with their generational peers than with their elders."[52] In addition,

[46] Nobe, 68.

[47] Paul Spickard, "Injustice Compounded: Amerasians and Non-Japanese Americans in World War II Concentration Camps," *Journal of American Ethnic History* 5 (1986): 14.

[48] Ibid, 14.

[49] Nobe, 69; Whitney, 32.

[50] Whitney, 32-34.

[51] Paul Spickard, *Japanese Americans: The Formation and Transformations of an Ethnic Group* (New York: Twayne Publishers, 1996), 70, 72-3.

[52] Benson Tong, "Race, Generation, and Culture among Japanese American Children and Adolescents During the Internment Era," *Asian American Culture: A Historical Handbook and Guide, Ed. Benson Tong* (Westport, CT: Greenwood Press, 2004), 89.

overcrowded barracks sent children out of the family home to explore and seek friendships with other children, and as their children realized that they were now dependent on the government for provisions, parents began to lose authority over their children.[53]

One obvious reason why the Nisei orphans living in the Children's Village experienced camp differently is because many of the boys and girls in the Children's Village had already experienced the breakdown of the family unit before the war, primarily as a result of the illness or death of a parent, the FBI arrest of a father, and/or a financial crisis. Moreover, the majority of Nisei orphans sent to live at Children's Village had already experienced institutional life; their previous living quarters were one of the three California orphanages or children's homes specifically for children of Japanese descent. As a result, children from the Shonien and other homes were used to communal living and to the free time spent playing with other children.

At the same time, what made the experience harder for some of the younger orphans at Manzanar was the feeling of being stigmatized by the larger community for being orphans. When she was working in the community in Los Angeles, Lillian Matsumoto recalls hearing parents warn their children that if they didn't behave, they would be sent to the Shonien, and she believes this sentiment was carried over to the Children's Village.[54] Many of the children remember playing within the Children's Village grounds, but no one remembers being invited by children from the other barracks to socialize or play. Even before the war, Tamo Isozaki remembers the prejudice in the ethnic community against orphans. "Oh, yeah," says Isozaki, "I felt that. At school, they'll play with you, but that's all. They'd never say, 'Hey, Tamo, why don't you come over to my house?'"[55]

The stigma that Isozaki felt continued after he got to Manzanar; however, Isozaki believes that the close bonds formed among the orphans in the Children's Village were a result of this social rejection by the community:

> Even the Issei in the community wasn't so fond of us because they would never come to our orphanage or say, "I want to come and see Tamo. He's my friend." They might see us, but they don't come in and visit us. I think that's

---

[53] Ibid.

[54] Lillian Matsumoto, Interviewed by Lisa Nobe, 12-13 May 1993, CSUF-Center for Oral and Public History.

[55] Tamotsu Isozaki, Interviewed by Lisa Nobe, 13 March 1993, CSUF-Center for Oral and Public History.

why the orphanage kids were pretty close to each other. It was like, if you fight him, you're fighting me too because he's my brother. It was that kind of attitude.[56]

As one of the older children at Children's Village who served as a role model to many of the younger boys, Isozaki tried to cultivate a sense of unity among the children by helping to organize sports teams. And today, Isozaki believes that sports is what provided many of the boys at camp with not just an emotional outlet, but a sense of independence and achievement:

I would say that I was proud that we were able to get together and have a basketball team, have a baseball team, with the amount of people who were in our Children's Village and be able to make a team. And it was successful, without any supervision. The older boys were in charge, and they kept things straight. We were independent from everybody else, even the head people of the Children's Village. We picked our own teams to play against, and we clicked together. There was no fighting among ourselves over who's better or who's lousier, and that kind of stuff, so I liked that. Sports was the most important thing to keep us from crying about every little thing.[57]

Besides sports, other activities also brought children from the barracks and the Village together. While the larger barrack community seemed to maintain a distance from the Children's Village, the poor educational system in place during the 1942-1943 school year made camp life miserable for all children regardless of their family situation. The student-teacher ratio was forty-eight to one for elementary, and thirty-five to one for secondary instruction (compared to a national average of twenty-eight to one).[58] Lack of school equipment and course material for science laboratories, home economics, and other classes, coupled with the shortage of qualified teachers, prevented many students from getting the quality education that they needed to continue to develop at the rate of their peers outside of camp.[59] Ira Iwata

---

[56] Ibid.

[57] Ibid.

[58] Thomas James, *Exile Within: The Schooling of Japanese Americans, 1942-1945* (Cambridge: Harvard University Press, 1987), 43.

[59] Tong, 91.

remembers being over a year behind in school after leaving camp and starting school in Colorado.[60]

Most educators and especially the older students were aware of the irony of the teaching of American democratic ideals to students of a racially segregated community detained behind barbed wire.[61] In some cases, the lack of previous contact with Japanese Americans, training, and cultural sensitivity among teachers led to discrimination in the classroom. Celeste Teodor recalls that teachers never called on the orphans in class, which kept them from moving to an advanced class.[62] Consequently, the boredom, frustration, and anger felt by students manifested in more than just the inevitable acts of truancy and dropping out. Clara Hayashi recalls that her high school class demanded an early graduation and ended up planning their graduation themselves.[63] Other social problems appeared and seemed to be magnified by incarceration. A memorandum from Miya Kikuchi to Manzanar Director Ralph Merritt notes:

> Youth problems and juvenile delinquency were among the most pressing to the adults. Strict curfews for young people were suggested in order to curb vandalism, fighting, and other disorderly behavior. Much of this problem was attributed to the breakdown of the family structure due to the difficult housing situation at Manzanar.[64]

Among administrators, disorderly conduct among the youth was attributed to the disintegration of family rather than manifestations of frustration and anger over their circumstances. Unlike the Issei generation and older Nisei who had experienced and understood the laws and social norms that limited their access to housing, employment, and other resources, many youth were experiencing for the first time the culminating effects of anti-Japanese sentiment. They learned what it meant to be Japanese American in the United States.

---

[60] Ira Iwata, Interviewed by Cathy Irwin, 9 August 2007, CSUF-Center for Oral and Public History.

[61] Tong, 91.

[62] Celeste Teodor, Interviewed by Cathy Irwin, 9 August 2007, CSUF-Center for Oral and Public History.

[63] Clara Hayashi, Interviewed by Reiko Katabami, 17 July 1993, CSUF-Center for Oral and Public History.

[64] Memorandum from Miya Kikuchi, 18 May 1942, Ralph Merritt Collection, Special Collections, Research Library, University of California at Los Angeles.

While the parents and children incarcerated at Manzanar Relocation Center struggled with problems such as the breakdown of the family structure and the poor education system, ironically, the staff at Children's Village maintained a semblance of order and organization by implementing the same daily schedule that the children had practiced at the Shonien: School followed breakfast and chapel services. After school, boys and girls studied and did homework, took classes in arts and crafts, and participated in organized recreation. Dinner was served at 5:00 p.m. Children and staff ate together at the Children's Village. The younger children went to bed at 7:30 p.m., and the rest of Children's Village had a curfew of 9:00 p.m.[65] As a result, even though the Children's Village was understaffed and less structured than pre-war children's homes, the Matsumotos and their staff were able to provide the children some continuity by keeping to a schedule many of the orphans were used to prior to camp. Altogether, Children's Village would ultimately provide a stable home for 101 children during the thirty-nine months it existed.[66] And like other Nisei children detained in one of the camps, the boys and girls of Children's Village formed bonds with each other that lasted a lifetime.

Leaving Children's Village: Finding a Place Called Home

For many of the former orphans, the trauma of incarceration started when it was time to leave camp, when the social welfare of the orphans took a backseat to child placement. According to social worker Helen Whitney who visited the Children's Village in 1945, one of the main legal issues regarding the orphans admitted to Children's Village was guardianship.[67] The War Relocation Authority refused to see itself as or act as guardian to the orphans at Children's Village and simply saw their role as "furnish(ing) necessary maintenance and supervision [...] no more than a boarding home for them until they can be properly placed or otherwise provided for."[68] As a result of the War Relocation Authority's stance, in the upheaval of moving to Manzanar from the various orphanages, the records for each child (such as staff notes about the child or family, birth certificates, marriage certificates of parents, and addresses of any living parent or relative) were unimportant to

[65] Lillian and Harry Matsumoto, Interview by Ford Kuramoto, 22 January 1972. See also Kuramoto, 45.
[66] Whitney, 29.
[67] Ibid, 41.
[68] Ibid. See letter from Dillon S. Myer, Director of the War Relocation Authority, Washington, to the California State Department of Social Welfare, 17 May 1944, Children's Village Collection, CSUF-Center for Oral and Public History.

the military authorities.

In addition, the three California children's homes specifically for children of Japanese ancestry had already closed as a result of the war, so finding these records for child placement was difficult and painstakingly slow. Among the seventy-five children who were sent to Children's Village during the first months of incarceration, "fifteen of the seventy-five children had no legal guardians," and "seventeen were wards of the juvenile court of California."[69] Because no one could fully claim guardianship for many of the children, no adult could fully speak or advocate for them at war's end, either. For children who were wards of the state, camp authorities merely returned them to the county where they came from originally; and for children with a living parent or relative, their parent or relative first needed to be located and contacted, or else they were "required to enter some county of some state."[70] As the last of the families left the barracks at the end of the war, many orphans were left stranded as staff members struggled over state and legal paperwork and then scrambled to find foster care placement for the remaining children. Consequently, many orphans at the end of the war were initially placed in families that were inappropriate for the child and, as some of the oral histories in this volume reveal, made life after camp more miserable than confinement itself.

Memories of Children's Village and the Documentation of Voices

As shown by the oral history interviews with former orphans, Children's Village was more than just a boarding home; rather, the Village was a place where the staff provided some semblance of structure and the children offered each other support and friendship. And in some cases, institutional life in an orphanage was a much better living situation than the foster or parental care that they received before or after they left the Village. In one interview, Celeste Teodor recalls, "I have no bad memories of Children's Village that I can think of. I absolutely loved it there. The only bad memory I had was when I had to leave. We all cried our eyes out."[71]

The oral histories presented in this volume are excerpts from longer interviews that have been abridged, without (for reasons of coherency and space) the customary ellipses to indicate cuts. Because many of the oral

[69] Whitney, 42.

[70] Ibid, 43.

[71] Celeste Teodor, Interviewed by Cathy Irwin, 9 August 2007, CSUF-Center for Oral and Public History.

history interviews took on a conversational tone in which interviewer and interviewee sometimes returned to a topic or question mentioned earlier on in the interview, some of the interviews have been reorganized for focus and clarity.

From the over one thousand transcribed pages of these oral history interviews, the different themes and issues that emerged have been organized into the chapters of this book. Chapter one focuses on interviews with brothers Tamo and Takeshi Isozaki as well as Mitsuru "Mitz" Yamasaki who recall life at the Salvation Army home and the Shonien before going to Manzanar. This chapter provides a comparative glimpse of what life was like for many of the Nisei children in orphanages before they were sent to camp. Chapters two through four focus on life at Children's Village from various perspectives. Interviews with Sharon Kodama, Robert Yamashita, and Clara Hayashi, former orphans who were four, twelve, and eighteen years of age, respectively, at the time they were incarcerated, provide accounts of life in camp from these different ages and developmental stages. Chapter three presents accounts of Children's Village from former Children's Village superintendant and social worker Lillian Matsumoto, child-care worker Taeko Nagayama, and storyteller Sohei Hohri, all former staff members who played different roles in the caring of the children at Children's Village. Chapter four presents oral history accounts of Children's Village from Takatow Matsuno and Mary Miya, who were two of nine children from the Matsuno family sent to Children's Village from Terminal Island.[72] Their oral histories tell of a remarkable family that struggled to stick together as a unit when the circumstances of war and prejudice tried to pull them apart.

In the final chapters of this book, the issues of family, home, and identity are emphasized to underscore the effects of war, internment, and separation on the children. In chapter five, former orphans, Ira Iwata, Herbert Suyematsu, and Sam Tanaka, share their memories of life immediately after Children's Village, specifically their reunions with one or both parents. Chapter six provides a unique glimpse of foster care home life after camp from not just former orphans Annie Sakamoto and Celeste Teodor, but from their foster care mother, Wilma Stuart, as well. In chapter seven, Ronald Kawamoto and Dennis Tojo Bambauer discuss the difficulties that children

---

[72] Before World War II, approximately 3,000 Japanese and Japanese Americans lived and worked in the fishing and canning industries on Terminal Island, located off of San Pedro in Los Angeles County [See The Terminal Islanders, Furusato: The Lost Village of Terminal Island Web site http://www.terminalisland.org (1 Jan 2008)].

of mixed-race parentage faced during and after Children's Village. In the last chapter, Lillian Bonner's inspiring pictorial autobiography covers her life, from Children's Village to today, as the wife of Dr. David C. Bonner, mother of two grown children, and grandmother of five grandchildren.

Through these oral histories, the coping and survival skills of each child are apparent, and yet what is also witnessed and cannot be ignored is the struggle. In *Years of Infamy: The Untold Story of America's Concentration Camps*, Michi Weglyn writes, "Though to all outward appearances the recovery of Japanese Americans has been good to remarkable, the rejection and social isolation of the war years have left scars which have not entirely disappeared."[73] Weglyn emphasizes the importance of documenting and listening to the voices of former internees when she concludes her book by acknowledging the Sansei generation's desire to know and understand their parents and grandparents' scars from the war years. The following oral histories give voice to former orphans of Children's Village, children of World War II who have been forgotten or ignored by "official" history. Through oral histories, their stories offer alternative points of view and perspectives on camp life during World War II. What these former orphans seemingly left behind have been contained in their memories and in the stories they tell; and in these stories is history waiting to be told, studied, discussed, and never forgotten, so that, as Weglyn writes, "people will be forever reminded that concentration camps and wholesale contempt for individual rights and lawful procedure are not the exclusive province of corrupt tyrannies and maniacal dictatorships."[74]

---

[73] Michi Weglyn, *Years of Infamy: The Untold Story of America's Concentration Camps* (New York: William Morrow and Company, 1976), 273.
[74] Ibid, 281.

Chapter One
Life in a
Japanese Children's Home

Most of the children who were sent to Manzanar's Children's Village had come from some type of institutional care or foster care family. Of the sixty-one children who arrived at Children's Village in June of 1942, twenty-four were from the Shonien, a Japanese children's home in Los Angeles, California, and nineteen were from the Salvation Army Home located in San Francisco, California.[1] Both the Shonien and the Salvation Army Home were originally built and founded by Issei who had converted to Christianity and had a desire to meet the needs of homeless children in their respective ethnic community in California.

Major Masasuke Kobayashi was born in Japan in 1883 and arrived in San Francisco in 1902. Shortly upon his arrival in California, Kobayashi moved to Ogden, Utah, where he was baptized as a Presbyterian. His conversion to Christianity led to his work with the Young Men's Christian Association (YMCA), and in 1905, he "established special YMCA services for the Japanese students and laborers in the area."[2] In 1918, Kobayashi traveled back to Japan to join recruits at the Salvation Army Training School in Tokyo and ultimately became a major in the Japanese Salvation Army.[3]

Returning to America as a "Japanese Salvationist," Kobayashi and the Japanese Salvation Army Corps provided not just "spiritual and legal services," but material needs as well.[4] To raise funds for projects, Kobayashi found donors to help him open different social services in the community, including "a dispensary, a children's home, a maternity hospital, the Eventide Home for the aged, and a Rescue Home for 'helpless Japanese girls.'"[5] According to Sandra C. Taylor, the Salvation Army Children's Home was built with dona-

---

[1] Helen Elizabeth Whitney. "Care of Homeless Children of Japanese Ancestry during Evacuation" (M.A. thesis, University of California, Berkeley, 1948), 28.

[2] Brian Masaru Hayashi, "The Japanese 'Invasion' of California: Major Kobayashi and the Japanese Salvation Army, 1919-1926," *Journal of the West* 23 (Jan 1984): 74-75.

[3] Ibid, 76.

[4] Ibid, 78.

[5] Ibid.

tions from not just concerned Issei in the immediate community, but from the emperor of Japan as well.[6]

Like Major Kobayashi, Rokuichi "Joy" Kusumoto was also driven by a desire to help his community. According to Ford Kuramoto, Kusumoto "was born in 1873 in Beppu, Japan, moved to Osaka after high school, and became director of children's education at the Episcopal Benevolent Children's Home."[7] The founder of this Osaka children's home, Utako Hayashi, was so "impressed" by Kusumoto that Hayashi's wife "arranged the marriage between him and her adopted daughter."[8]

Kusumoto immigrated to the United States in 1908, took business school and English classes in Seattle, Washington, and then moved to Los Angeles in 1912.[9] In both Seattle and Los Angeles, Kusumoto worked with community leaders to organize a Japanese Humane Society (*Rafu Jindokai*) that helped provide social services programs in the ethnic community. More specifically, in Los Angeles, the Japanese Humane Society "was established by concerned community leaders for the protection of young girls. These young girls (some were only teenagers) had fled unsuccessful picture bride marriages. Others sought refuge from the houses of prostitution."[10]

At this time, Kusumoto also became concerned with the number of homeless children in the community. He visited several Caucasian child-care institutions to observe their operation. A Japanese child who was found in one recognized Kusumoto as being Japanese and called him "*Oji-chan*," or grandfather. This Japanese orphan was unhappy in his unfamiliar surroundings. The incident moved Kusumoto to found the first Japanese children's home and day nursery in Los Angeles.[11]

Both Kobayashi and Kusumoto were able to identify some of the problems that Nisei children and their families faced as immigrants living in urban environments, and the children's home that each of these men founded is just part of their legacy. This chapter provides first-hand accounts of life at the Shonien and the Salvation Army Children's Home from three former orphans who lived at these homes. Mitsuru "Mits" Yamasaki, along with

---

[6] Sandra C. Taylor, *Jewel of the Desert: Japanese Americans Interned at Topaz* (Berkeley: University of California Press, 1993): 7.

[7] Ford Kuramoto, *A History of the Shonien, 1914-1972: An Account of a Program of Institutional Care of Japanese Children in Los Angeles* (San Francisco: R and E Research, 1976): 13.

[8] Ibid.

[9] Ibid.

[10] Ibid, 12.

[11] Ibid. See also Nisuke Mitsumori, "History of the Shonien," trans. Harry T. Kubo and Mitani Translation Services, *Kashu Mainichi* (October 18, 1963): 4.

his two brothers Isao and Hiroshi, lived at the Shonien for ten years and was placed in the Shonien by his father in 1932 after his mother became ill and was sent to a sanitarium.[12]   Takeshi "Tak" and Tamotsu "Tamo" Isozaki, along with their three other brothers and two sisters, were sent to the Salvation Army Home after their mother died while giving birth and their father became unable to support his seven children. Tak Isozaki was eleven years old and Tamo Isozaki was nine when they first arrived at the Salvation Army Home in 1936. They lived there and at other orphanages until they were relocated to the Children's Village in June of 1942. In the following interviews, Yamasaki and the Isozaki brothers recall some of the most vivid experiences of their Nisei childhood and of life in a children's home.

---

[12] Although they had been living at the Shonien, Yamasaki and his brothers did not move to Manzanar with the Shonien staff and children because Yamasaki was eighteen years old and had just graduated from high school in February of 1942. Instead, he and his brothers relocated with the Fujikawa family, first to the Santa Anita Assembly Center in California and then to Rohwer Relocation Center in Arkansas.

Mitsuru "Mits" Yamasaki[1]

Interviewed by Cathy Irwin

So when is your birthday and where were you born?

February 3, 1924. I was born in Caldwell, Idaho, but I don't remember anything. (laughter) It's what my birth certificate says.

Do you know where your family is from in Japan?

They were from Hiroshima. I guess I really wasn't that close to my dad. He put us in Shonien. During the first year, he came to visit us once. And then after that, we never saw him. I was there for ten years and never saw him, so I never did get that close to him.

Did you ever see him again?

We were both sent to the Santa Anita Assembly Center [located in the city of Arcadia in Los Angeles County]. One of our family friends, who knew my dad and was my mother's really good friend, saw my dad there and said to us when he saw us, "Hey, your dad's here!" For me, it was not that big a deal because I figured, I didn't see him for so long, it didn't matter to me whether I had a father or not 'cause it seemed like I didn't have one.

So the last time you saw him was when you were nine years old?

Yup.

And how old were you when you were at Santa Anita?

Eighteen.

Wow. It had been a long time. Do you have siblings?

I have two brothers, an older one named Isao and a younger one, Hiroshi.

Were they also sent to the Shonien?

Yes, they were. Hiroshi was. In the Shonien, supposedly, when you get to be sixteen years old, they send you out to work in a home as a schoolboy or

[1]COPH-Oral History 3592 was conducted on January 27, 2007, in Gardena, California.

schoolgirl. And you go to work, you go to school, you come home, you got chores to do. So, you get paid a few dollars. That's what they did.

The only thing is, when my turn came, when I turned sixteen, Mrs. Matsumoto, the one who was the superintendent at Shonien, asked me if I would stay and sort of act like an *otona*—an adult staff member—and help supervise the younger kids. So, I was really fortunate that she let me stay there because I finished high school there.

So you knew Lillian Matsumoto at the Shonien?

Oh, yeah, she came in 1935. And last time I saw her back then was February 1942.

So Mrs. Matsumoto was there almost as long as you were there?

Almost.

So she probably came maybe a year after you?

No, she came in 1935. I was there in 1932.

What was it like at the Shonien? You said that your siblings Isao and Hiroshi were also at the Shonien with you. What were the circumstances?

Yes, my mother was in a sanitarium. She passed away when we were there. But Dad couldn't take care of us. In fact, in 1932, it was a Depression year, and he had a hard time getting work. We got locked out of the house and went to live with some friends for a while. My mother used to go to L.A. [Los Angeles] Holiness Church, and I remember that because we used to go to that church. And the minister there found out about us, that my mother was in a sanitarium and that we were living with some friends of my mother's. So then, he got us into the Shonien. I guess it was the best experience of my life. I was really glad for that.

So you were already in Los Angeles?

Yeah.

Do you remember where you were living before you were in the Shonien? You mentioned friends ...

I know we were living on 10th Street near Central Avenue in Los Angeles. But other than that, I really don't know too much about it.

And so you and your brothers were sent to the Shonien. Do you remember where the Shonien was located at the time you were sent there?

Oh, yeah, 1842 Redcliffe Street in Los Angeles.

What was the area like in the 1930s?

Oh, the area was like an upscale neighborhood, I guess. I don't know.

Were there a lot of people in the area?

Yes, there were a lot of people.

Were they of different ethnic groups? Were there Asians? Caucasians?

No, I think there were very few Asians in that area. There were some, but not a lot.

Mostly Caucasians?

Yeah, mostly Caucasians.

Do you remember your first days in that area, at the home?

Well, even at that young age, I was glad that I was there! We had a bed to sleep in at night, we got food, we got clothes. So I was glad that I was there, really.

So you felt like the staff really cared for you?

Yeah, they did. I remember most of the ladies who took care of us from the time I was there. In fact, there were pictures that I had and I could still remember who they were! That's seventy-something years ago!

Do you remember any names?

Yeah, there was a Miss Wada, there was a Miss Yoshinaga, there was a Suematsu, Miss Miyamoto, Miss Sukimoto; in fact, Miss Sukimoto is still living. She's ninety-seven years old. I went to see her not too long ago. I remember the people there.

How did they help you adjust? How did they care for you? How did you know that you were cared for?

Well, I don't know. I guess, to me, there was never anything negative about being there. I really appreciated the fact that they took me there.

Did they get you clothes every year?

Well, we always had clothes. I really don't know where they got it from, and I really don't know where Mr. (Rokuichi "Joy") Kusumoto —he's the actual originator of the whole thing—got all the money! But I know it took a lot of money to feed all them kids and clothe them. It was amazing. He used to raise money by going to different churches. He'd take a movie projector, show a Japanese movie, and the churches would sell tickets. That was their way of donating. And I remember going with them, many a time.

Oh, really? So you got to watch movies?

Yeah.

He brought movies?

They were Japanese movies, and I really didn't understand too much. (laughter)

Did they ever teach you about the Japanese culture or the language at the Shonien?

Yeah, they had a Japanese school. We used to go to Japanese school. Only thing was, we never spoke Japanese. It was always English. So I learned how to read and write in Japanese, but I couldn't understand it. I still remember some of the words.

And so one of the staff members was a teacher?

Yeah, there were different staff members that taught Japanese.

Did the other children at the home help you adjust, when you first arrived?

Yeah, they were really welcoming. I never had any problems there.

What were your first impressions of the buildings?

How huge it was! And as I look at it today, I realize it was really huge. And when I think about how Mr. Kusumoto accumulated all the money to build that, I think, my gosh, that was really something! I guess you know the history? When they first started in, I think 1920, it was a two-bedroom, two-story house. And they moved from here to there. And then it kept getting a little bit bigger (looking at a picture of the Shonien). This was the final building, and it was huge.

So, we're looking at a picture of the Shonien from 1925 when it was on Redcliffe Street. And we're looking at one of the buildings. Can you tell me what these buildings are?

Okay. The building was shaped like a big U. It had a hallway all the way up and down. This was the sick room; it had about six beds in there.

The room to the left.

The next section was where the superintendent lived. Then after that was a living room. And then, next to that, was a girl's bedroom. They had about ten or twelve beds in there.

Oh, really? So there were ten to twelve beds in the dorms?

Yes, it was like an oversized dorm, I guess. Then, next to that, they had a baby's nursery. They had about ten to twelve cribs in there. Next to that, they had what they called a dorm for the younger girls. It's actually for kids that were five or six years old. They were already potty-trained, I think. Then the next section was where the boys' dorm was. They had about ten to twelve beds in there.

So that's where you and your brother stayed.

Yeah.

Can you describe what your room was like?

Yeah, it was one big, big room that had ten to twelve beds in there. And they turned the lights off every night around eight o'clock or eight-thirty. And the buzzer would ring every morning about quarter to six.

Quarter to six? Wow. And then, after you woke up, did you go straight to breakfast?

No, we got up and we had to make our bed. Everybody had a few chores to do. So, from quarter to six until quarter after six, that's when you had to do those chores, like sweep the hall, rake the yard, sweep the whatever. At a quarter after six, we went to a big playroom. It looked like an oversized gym. And we had chapel service there, just like a regular church service, in the morning.

What kind of church service was it? Was it Christian?

Yeah, it was Christian. We went to a Congregational church later, as we got older. They would take us there. For church services every morning, there were people who used to come, and that service lasted for half an hour, from quarter after six to quarter to seven. Then, we'd go eat breakfast. Then, after breakfast, you had to get cleaned up and get ready for school. So, we always left for school a little after quarter of seven or seven-thirty. Then, we'd go to school. And we went to Micheltorena School. Then for junior high, we went to Thomas Starr King.

Okay. Where did you go for high school?

We went to John Marshall.

Oh, you went to Marshall High?

I graduated from Marshall.

So you went to three schools. I'm going to get back to the schools later, but I want to get back to the schedule. Did you have to come back to the home, right after school?

Well, when I was in grammar school, yes. We'd go to school, and then we'd come home. And then, we used to go to a Japanese school for class for about an hour or whatever. Then, this is something a little different: We used to take our school lunch in a brown paper bag, and we'd always have to fold it up, put it in our pocket, and bring it home. So you'd bring it home, and then when you'd go to the office and give them the bag, you'd say, "*Todaima kaidimashita, oyatsu kudasai.*" "*Todaima kaidimashita*" means, "I'm home." And then "*oyatsu kudasai*" means "May I have my snack?" They'd always have a couple of pieces of those round Japanese candy that's wrapped for snacks.

So you would have this before Japanese school?

Yeah, right after you'd come home, you'd go through the office and you'd take your bag, 'cause, you know, you can't afford to be buying new paper bags for forty, fifty people every day. So, they'd use them as much as they could.

And what did you usually bring to school for lunch? What was usually in your bag?

In the lunch? You'd usually get a peanut butter sandwich, but I liked it because what they used to do with the peanut butter was they used to mix it with something sweet like caramel. Very seldom did we have bologna or meat. But they used to get this type of butter; it looked like lard. Then you'd put this orange powder in, and you'd mix it up. That's what makes it yellow. So we used to have butter and lettuce sandwiches. That was one sandwich.

As I got older, I'd say, "Gee, I need a sandwich." I'm coming home from school or something. So, they would accommodate you. You just tell 'em what you wanted and they'd give it to you. There were all different kinds of sandwiches that they would make. We used to get beet sandwiches. I guess you've never eaten one.

No. (laughter)

Cooked beet with a slice of onion. We used to get . . . Well, I would ask for sliced onion. I thought the food was good. I mean, I know you couldn't have all the fancy foods that a lot of the other kids used to bring, but it was adequate.

So you would have lunch at school. After lunch, you'd have more school, and then come back to the Shonien. Then you'd have Japanese school. Were you able to do other activities after Japanese school?

Yeah, we still had time to play. And one thing good about being at the Shonien was that there were a lot of kids, so you can make up different games.

What were your favorite games?

Well, we'd play softball. We'd play . . . we had a basketball court. And when it was raining, we'd have to go into the playroom, which was like an oversized gym, really big. And we'd play in there pretty much.

And so, what time was dinner?

Dinner was around five o'clock. We ate fairly early. Then, as you got older, you had quite a bit of homework to do or whatever. But, I don't know, I remember when we were kids, we sure did a lot of playing. (laughter)

What would you usually eat for dinner?

Yeah, well, I remember we used to get a spaghetti dinner. In fact, I loved the spaghetti dinner. You'd get spaghetti and they'd put it on rice. You know how most people make it? They make noodles, and then they put the goodies on top. But this was all mixed up in one big pot. So, they used a lot of water and lot of tomatoes, onions, whatever. Put that on top of the rice.

They would make stew. It didn't have much meat in it, but still it was good. I liked it. They had cooked turnips that I hated. (laughter) But that was the only thing I really didn't like. The food was actually good, probably healthier than I'm eating today. I liked it.

That's great. So when you were at Micheltorena School and Thomas Starr King Junior High, were there a lot of children of Japanese descent at these schools?

There was some, but not that many. Mostly Caucasians.

Mostly Caucasians. Do you remember other Asians, like Filipinos? Or Mexicans?

No, there was no Filipinos. There was . . . I didn't see any blacks either. Few Latino. There were mostly Caucasians.

Were most of your teachers Caucasians?

Yeah.

How did they treat you?

I think I was treated—*myself*—I think I was treated as well as anybody.

Did you like school?

Yeah, I really liked school.

What was your favorite subject?

Well, I liked math.

You liked math. What were your favorite activities? Did you play sports?

Oh, yeah, in grammar school, I guess it was kick ball. In junior high, we played softball, we played football, we played basketball. And at Marshall, I was really fortunate that Mrs. Matsumoto let me stay at the Shonien because, after school, I played football for Marshall High School.

Did you? Wow!

And if I had to go out and go to work, I wouldn't have been able to do those things. That's why I really appreciated Mrs. Matsumoto who let me stay there to graduate high school.

So you played football at Marshall. That must have been quite an experience!

Oh, yeah, that was really fun. I mean, I really enjoyed it.

What level did you play? Was there a varsity football team?

Yeah, I played two years on the B team because I was smaller. And as I got a little older, I played one year on the varsity.

Oh, you did. So you got a letter?

Yeah, well, I got three letters. Two years on the B, and one on the varsity. And Mrs. Matsumoto took me down to Albion Mills to get my letterman sweater.

Albion Mills?

They used to make these letterman sweaters. And she took me down there to get a sweater! And I thought, man, that's something because nobody else got one! And it's sort of special. I really appreciated what she did, so I wrote her a nice letter. The other day, she was telling me, "You know I still have that letter that you sent me."

Oh, do you remember what you wrote in the letter?

Oh, I just thanked her for all the things that she did for me when I was there.

So did you make a lot of friends on your football team?

Oh, yeah. In fact, when we had a fifty-year reunion—in 1992?—a couple of guys on the football team were on the committee. They found out where I lived and called me up and said, "Hey, Mits, you're on the reunion committee." And I said, "No, I don't know anybody." And they said, "Oh, yeah, you'll know everybody when you go to the meeting." So then they tell me, "Well, you know, you were the senior class secretary, so you have to be on the receiving line!" So even though I was an orphan, I wasn't looked down upon. I think they treated me just like anybody else.

So the teachers and the students never treated you differently, either in the elementary schools or at Marshall?

Nowhere.

So you had close friends on the football team outside?

Yeah, outside.

Were you ever invited to your friends' houses?

Yeah, well, I guess that's the only drawback. You know, you can't let everybody just go visit wherever they want. You can't keep track of forty kids, you know. So I realized that. A lot of my friends used to ditch school, go to the beach and things like that. I never went with them because, I don't know, I just knew that I couldn't do those kinds of things. So, that was one of the drawbacks, I guess, the fact that you really couldn't have that many outside friends to go to visit. I just had a few friends that I'd stop at the house on the way home from school.

Do you remember any great experiences, when you were playing football?

Not really. (laughter)

You just enjoyed the game.

Yeah.

And it seemed like the Shonien supported your activities . . .

Yeah, well that's the reason. If it wasn't for Mrs. Matsumoto, I would never have been able to play football. I'd have been out working as a schoolboy and wouldn't have done any of those things.

Did you ever date in high school or go to school dances?

Not really. I had to go to the senior prom because I was treasurer, and I had to be on the receiving line. So, there was this one Japanese girl and she was senior class secretary. I didn't really date her or nothing; I just told her that, well, I'd meet her at the prom and we'd sit together. But there was no such thing as dating her. (laughter)

So you had to attend functions because you were the secretary-treasurer?

Yeah, I did.

And the Shonien let you?

See, because Mrs. Matsumoto was there, I was able to do that. Otherwise, I would have never been able to. So I was really appreciative of what she did.

Did you ever celebrate birthdays or special holidays? How were they celebrated?

Not birthdays, but I remember the Fourth of July was one of our really good holidays. Before the war, San Kwo Low restaurant in Los Angeles was on First Street. I guess they are still there. They used to charter a bus and take us out to Brighton Beach. It's Terminal Island now. They'd have a box lunch for us. Then they'd bring us back and take us to the restaurant and feed us a big Chinese dinner. After that, they'd take us to the [Los Angeles] Coliseum for the Fourth of July fireworks show. Then, we'd get on a bus, and we'd go home. But I'm pretty sure that San Kwo Low paid for all that, so any time I go to a Chinese restaurant, I like to go there, if it's possible.

It's called San Kwo Low restaurant?

Uh-huh, yes. It's spelled S-a-n K-w-o L-o-w. Maybe it's o-o. I don't know.

And at Christmas, there was a Japanese Christian Church, and they used to have a big Christmas party for us. They'd come pick us up and take us down to the church. I think it was on Twentieth and San Pedro in Los Angeles. We'd have a party there and play a few games. The girls would go there with somebody, and the boys would go with somebody. They'd tell us stories. I still remember one of the stories that this Reverend Chuck Severen used to tell. He'd take all the boys and he'd tell us the story of Scarback, who was a deer.

Scarback?

Yes. And I'll never forget that story. There was a deer that he didn't want to shoot. He just wanted to get a picture taken of it. So they got a—I don't know where they found it—but they put a light on the deer, and the deer just sort of froze and they took a picture. But I'll never forget this reverend, Chuck Severen.

And so he told the story of the deer.

Yeah, I still remember. That's seventy-some years ago. Then, the Elks Clubs at Christmas time would get a bunch of presents and come down to the Shonien and have a party.

What kinds of presents did you receive?

Gee, I can't really remember. I just knew there were a lot of presents! (laughter) For everybody—boys, girls, kids. Then, another holiday was New Year's. There was Helms Bakery, a bakery before the war. They used to send over sweet rolls. There must have been a truckload of sweet rolls and stuff that we had for breakfast on New Year's morning. You know, little things like that, you can't forget.

That's great. So did the staff at the Shonien set high standards or have high expectations for each child?

Not really that high. They just expected you to behave, I guess. (laughter) They didn't want you fighting and things. I don't know. I think they were as fair as anybody.

So, if you ever did get into trouble, did they just talk to you?

Yeah, pretty much. Like myself, I never got in trouble or anything.

Did you ever hold an after-school job?

No, not really.

And you mentioned, as you got older, you cared for the younger orphans?

Well, you know, every once in awhile, the younger kids would play and I'd sort of referee a few things, but it wasn't really a big deal. They knew I was older, so they weren't going to be arguing with me. It was fun doing that.

Did you ever serve as a mentor or help out a younger child?

No, I don't think I did. I befriended a few kids that were picked on, I thought. One of the kids, in particular, was a Japanese kid that came from Japan. He lost his folks. He could hardly speak any English. I know a couple of kids used to pick on him, so I got after them and, in fact, had a fight with one of them. And since I was much bigger, they had no chance. But I guess, if he were here, he'd probably say, "Yeah, Mits saved my life," (laughter) so to speak, because they were picking on him all the time and, finally, I couldn't stand it anymore. He came up to me and asked, "Sam picked on me; he beat me up." I went, approached him and had a few words, and that was that. He was never bothered.

So, how did living at Shonien, being an orphan, affect you? Did it affect you and your attitude or goals in life?

No. Well, as far as affecting me, the only thing was . . . I guess when I was going to school, I always figured, I'd like to go to college or I'd like to do something else. But it never materialized because right after school, we got evacuated, went to Rohwer [Relocation Center in Arkansas]. Then, after we left Rohwer, I had nobody to support me. I had to go support myself, so I had to go to work. But that's still not really an excuse. I guess, I could have, if I really wanted to. It's just that, at that time, work was pretty important.

Mr. Yamasaki, thank you so much for the interview.

You're welcome.

Takeshi Isozaki[1]

Interviewed by Reiko Katabama

When were you born?

I was born March 15, 1925. I am sixty-eight years old right now.

So you went to the Salvation Army [Home in San Francisco, California] at the age of . . . ?

I was eleven. It was 1936 when my Salvation Army life started. We were not an English-speaking people. We just spoke mostly Japanese, even at the age of eleven. We didn't speak English too much. We lived at the Salvation Army until 1942, off and on.

At the Salvation Army, were your sisters and brothers separated?

Yes, life wasn't too good during a certain part of that time because we, the family, separated for different reasons. The longest we didn't see one of the brothers was six years or so. When we got together in 1947, that reunion was one of the happiest times for me.

Your father [Ichitaro Isozaki] had already left for Japan?

Yeah, he was already in Japan.

So after you went into the Salvation Army, you didn't have any chance to see him?

I didn't, but my oldest brother Sam and oldest sister Molly saw him. When my brother was in Korea for the war, he was able to see our father because our father came to see him in the hospital in Tokyo. He was able to see our father before he died.

---

[1] COPH-Oral History 2337 was conducted on July 21, 1993, in Gardena, California.

But all the children went into the Salvation Army?

Yes, all the children.

And then during the Salvation Army period, your father was already in Japan. So you didn't have any contact with him?

The only contact we had was just before he went back to Japan. I don't know what year it was, but it must have been about 1939 or so.

Do you know when your mother [Setsu Isozaki] passed away?

She died in 1934.

Do you have any memories of your mother?

The memories I have of her are all good. She was a really good lady. She took care of us. She always watched over us, so we wouldn't get into trouble, I guess. Like any other kids, we did things that we shouldn't have done.

In the Salvation Army, were the boys' and girls' dormitories separated?

Right.

So you didn't have a chance to visit your sisters in their dormitories?

Well, we always had church or playtime or eating time to see each other then. We were all together in the dining room to eat.

I see. Can you describe the staff members from a child's viewpoint?

Well, this is my experience: when I first went to the Salvation Army, we weren't treated very good because I don't know if it was a Japanese family or the Japanese people who were running it or what. But they had people who were not fit to run the home. The administrative people were okay because we hardly saw them. But the people who directly watched over us were not too good. We used to take beatings. When it was getting close to 1941, a lot of them quit the Salvation Army and went back to Japan. But the Caucasian people who took over started to treat us better. Life was getting better too. But the early part was pretty bad.

Then things we had no control over was bad because we were shipped out of San Francisco and then brought back to San Francisco and then sent to camp.

So the Salvation Army was a religious, Christian orphanage?

You know, I hate to say things that are bad, but the thing that happened to us ... for example, we got punished because they gave us money to put in the offering at church. And if the money didn't go into the offering total, they would get us together and say, "Who didn't put the money in?" We used to get beat up for that. That kind of stuff we didn't need. It's always the younger group that got beat up. The older ones could take care of themselves, so they didn't get beat up. I hate to talk about these things, but I think they should be told. The Salvation Army wasn't all good at that time. But togetherness in the home was really good because we did things together, played together. We did things together, which was important.

The children?

Yeah, so you remembered them, and what they were. Most of them were all good people. And they're good people now; they're my age and older. (chuckle)

The staff members were strict?

They just had to follow instructions and things. The food they gave us— for a guy like me—wasn't enough to take care of us. We were hungry until somebody started giving us more food! (laughter)

Were you hungry after not getting enough food?

For me, yeah. I'm a big eater.

Were there other kids who were like you?

Oh, yeah. There were many who were hungry. So, we did things that we weren't supposed to, like I said before. Some of those people who watched over us were good, others weren't. When we had the reunion, we didn't invite them to come. That told the story to them. A lot of them were hurt because we didn't invite them.

Do you know the name of the person who didn't get invited?

The person who didn't get invited? He's dead now.

Before the Salvation Army, you went to school. Was it an English [speaking] school?

Well, we went to public school.

And you had to speak English?

We started to pick it up. They put us in a special class. Things you were good in like math were pretty good because you learned it in Japanese school. So that part wasn't hard. We had to learn the other part, so we didn't get the education that we should have had. That's why some of us didn't do what we really wanted to do. If we had good, proper learning, I think . . . well, we did well anyway, but we would have been much better, if we had gotten the education.

Did you have difficulty with the English language?

Yeah, even now I have difficulty trying to explain things.

Was the school mostly Caucasian students?

Well, yeah. There was quite a few Japanese where we lived. We lived near a Japanese town, and there was quite a few Japanese. But I got into trouble at school because I didn't know English, even with the teachers. You get angry when someone says something like "dumb" to you. That would get me angry. So you get into fights, and you get into trouble with the school. So our education was very poor. Mine was.

So the students were mainly Caucasian students and some were Asians?

Oh, yeah, there was a mix.

Which ethnicities?

The people we ran around with were all mixed. We had Blacks, Filipinos, Spanish, Chinese, and Japanese. They were all a mixed group.

But mainly Caucasian students?

Yeah, like now, we didn't have that kind of feeling. We went by how a person was. If they were good, they were good! So we treated them like anybody else. In fact, we didn't even separate each other for being a different race.

So when someone told you that you were "dumb," did the name-calling happen among students?

Most people if they're good to you, you're good to them. But some of them like to say bad things without any good reason. That's the kind of people who we used to fight. In San Francisco, we didn't have a problem the way they do now. We didn't have gangs. If you fight, you fight your own battle. You fight with your fists. We didn't pick up sticks or knives or guns or whatever. We never did that. The first time we heard that was when we came in touch with southern California people. Otherwise, we never had no problem with that kind of thing.

So during your school-age years, were there any racial conflicts?

No, not at the time. Well, to a degree. The school I was going to had enough Japanese, but, to me, they did play favoritism. Before I went to Lytton orphanage, I was on the basketball team in junior high school, and we took the championship in San Francisco. Then when we went to Lytton orphanage, I went from junior high to high school. We went to school in Healdsburg [Sonoma County, California]. We tried to get on the basketball team, but they didn't want us because it looks bad for the people that lived there, that their kids can't be playing on the team. So a lot of the kids from the home couldn't play sports with kids in Healdsburg because there was favoritism anyways. They were country players—it's not that country players aren't good; it was just that they weren't good and couldn't make the team. So those things show up. You feel that kind of thing. You try to avoid those things. I don't think people like to get into problems; they try to get along.

But these things come up, and you have to cope with it. Do what you can. You probably would fight.

So you first went to the Salvation Army and then, for some reason, you were sent to Lytton orphanage?

Yes, that was because of the war.

For three months?

Yes.

And then you came back to the Salvation Army?

Yes.

So that second time you went into the Salvation Army, you couldn't make the team?

No, when we went to Lytton, we went to Healdsburg High School. And that's where we couldn't make the team because of the people or the big bosses around town—business people thinking, if their kid's not in it, they wouldn't support the team. So we couldn't go out for the team. It hurts you because you can't show it.

But we joined other teams after—just the home kids. When you take home kids, there are just so many kids. At the high school and the towns that you played in the league, they had choices of good players, better players, than we did. But we still did well.

Would you describe what kind of kids were at Lytton orphanage? Were they bad kids?

Well, I guess they couldn't get along with the people at certain places. Or they weren't really bad, so that you had to put them in prison or a real bad boy's place. This was a sort of mild kind of thing that they used to do. They were slightly hard-to-handle people, but they weren't criminal types.

Were they in between extremely bad and extremely good?

Yeah, in this home, they were pretty good. They were trustworthy. They could go out, and they would come back. At other places like juvenile hall, if they go out, they won't come back.

So Lytton orphanage was a . . .

Well, we called it "bad boy's school," but we were in there too. We were there because of the war. When we were there, they gave us duties to do. If you do certain things, you get paid for it. You get a dollar per week for it. I used to sweep the gym every day.

How much did you get?

A dollar. Some got seventy-five cents. Some got piecework to cut wood, what they call a chord so high, you have to cut that much to get whatever they are paying for that.

So while you are staying at Lytton orphanage, you got pocket money.

Yes.

Were you satisfied?

Well, we had no choice. (laughter) It was better than nothing. At least we didn't do bad things like we used to when we didn't have any money at the Salvation Army. So if we wanted something, you just have to take, and that's what we did. But most, in fact, almost 100 percent of the kids that was in the Salvation Army—we used to . . . when we went camping, we didn't have any fishing supplies. So we'd go take from the stores. (coughing)

So when you say take, do you mean buy?

Doro botsu [Japanese for steal].

Ah, steal! (laughter)

That's the only way you could have anything.

So you think . . .

It's better to give kids spending money by having them work. The Salvation Army wouldn't give you anything.

They wouldn't allow you . . .

No, they don't give you allowance; you just took care of the property. You'd sweep, clean the *benjo* [bathroom], take the wax off and put the wax on. Things like that. They didn't pay you for those jobs, but the Lytton home did. I don't know if they later started giving kids something for their labor. Like us—before we used to steal, but we stopped stealing because we had money to spend for a show or something. At least you had your own money.

Now you're satisfied.

Yeah, I mean if you're hungry, you're going to steal to feel full. You're not going to steal something you can't eat. If you're hungry, you're going to steal for food. That's what we were doing, stealing for food and things.

And did you have any trouble? Did anyone find out that you stole?

They—the people who caught us—usually let us go. They didn't put us in juvenile hall or something like that. They knew we were in the Salvation Army.

So the other kids also stole?

I would say 100 percent stole!

So after school, you came back to the Salvation Army and were given something to eat?

Yeah, *ohatsu* they called it.

Snack.

Yeah, a snack.

And still, you had to steal something when you went to that summer camp?

Well, what they give you was like bread that they would chop up, put it in an oily thing, and then put sugar on it. That's *ohatsu*. But after that, I think they were giving five cents an hour for certain jobs. During the week, you have enough to go to a movie. So that was enough for us. We have other entertainment that we could do without stealing, like play baseball or football. Different things. But when you have to pay and you don't have the money, you either sneak in or you got to get money some place if you want to go see it. Somehow, we used to go to the show.

Did some of the older kids have a chance to work outside?

No, that's it. You can't even work outside!

But some kids delivered newspapers or something like that?

No, you can't do any of those things. That's why you just didn't have any money. If you could deliver a paper or something like that, you have a job. You get money.

But no kids were allowed to work outside?

Yeah, but we would go to a different place. They have samples; they'd give out samples for you to sell and they pay you for it. Or we'd sell newspapers at a football game or things like that. That kind of money. We weren't supposed to do it, but we did it. Otherwise, the kids are pretty straight to me.

Compared to the high school in Healdsburg, were the teachers at the public schools in San Francisco Caucasian?

Oh, yeah.

No Japanese?

I don't think so.

And how about the racial make-up of the students?

There were always more *hakujin* [Caucasian] than Asians. At most schools, the majority was Caucasian.

And at this time, were they also Spanish?

They're from all over now. The Spanish, Chinese, Vietnamese. They are all going to one school.

And blacks as well?

Yeah, blacks.

Jewish?

I assume. They're all mixed groups.

What was school life like for students?

Oh, school life is the same as any place. Kids are kids.

Did you have the same type or typical experience as other kids?

I'm sort of an exception. I was getting into a lot of trouble because if I believe a certain thing is right, and then they didn't do it, I'd go to juvenile hall. See, if they were fair to me, I could take that. If they're not fair, I'll fight for it.

This one time, I wanted to play basketball. They said I was too small. They kept saying I was too small. And then the last year that I was there, they said, "We want you on the team." But by then, I had already been to juvenile hall because, when they wouldn't let me go out for sports or for the team, I wouldn't go to school. So I told them, as long as you keep me in this school, I'm not going to school. I told them that if I could go to another school, I would go back. When they told me I could go to another school, I said okay, I'll go back to school. So that's what happened. And that year, like I said, we took the championship.

The coach was good to you?

The coach was fair to everybody. He told you from the beginning that if you were good enough, you could make the team. And if you were one of the better of the people who made the team, then you might be first-string. So at least I had hope.

How long did you play basketball at this school?

For one year or half a year, I transferred to this school where there were hardly any Japanese, maybe two or three. There were two from the home and another one. I don't know where he came from, but it was mostly Spanish or Mexican at the school because that's the area. I don't remember seeing too many blacks. I remember that Roosevelt Junior High School had mostly blacks on their basketball team.

So you were the only person from your family who transferred to another school?

From my family, yes.

How was that school?

Well, when I went to that school, I had no problem because I was on the basketball team. I was doing what I wanted, and I got to take the courses to graduate from that school. There was no problem after that. Kids are kids. They either make friends with you or they don't. So if a guy wanted to be friends with me, okay! If they don't want to, fine. We stayed away or whatever.

So while you were staying at the Salvation Army, you graduated from elementary school?

Yeah.

And then you went to junior high school?

Yeah ...

And you took a bus?

No, the grammar school was only a block and a half away. The junior high school was about ten blocks away, so it was close enough for you to run or walk to school.

Can you tell me the daily routine at the Salvation Army?

Well, the daily routine at the Salvation Army was: you'd get up early, get ready for breakfast, eat your breakfast, and then get ready for school. And grammar school was [at] 9:00. I think junior high started at 8:00. Then, you'd come home to the Salvation Army and get *ohatsu*. They'd give you *ohatsu* up to a certain time. If you came later than that, you don't get it. Then after that, you're on your own. You could go out and go to school and play basketball, baseball, whatever. Then, you had to be home by 5:00, I think. That's when we had dinner. We ate our dinner. Some people would study from after school and do their homework already. Some people did it late; after dinner, they'd study.

At one time, they had Japanese school at the Salvation Army, but not many were interested so they quit that. That's basically it. You'd go to bed pretty early. They didn't have television or anything. You could go to bed and listen to the radio, if you had it.

And then you had to get up early?

Yes, same routine. Then, we had chores when we got up. You had to make your bed. All your clothes had your name on them, so they had a slot where they put your clothes after they finished washing them.

And some kids helped in the laundry?

Yeah, usually girls do that. The girls had certain chores, and the boys had certain chores. And the girls had to do the laundry. I don't know where they did the actual laundry. Some might have helped, but they had a laundry lady who does that. Then they had to have so many people to fold the clothes.

What about the washing of dishes after eating?

I think we boys did the dishes. At least I think we did! (laughter) The girls helped with setting the table and getting the food ready. They had their chores.

Did you enjoy doing it? (laughter)

I don't know about someone else, but I didn't mind.

What did you have to do?

Well, you had to wash, clean, and then wipe the dishes. Mop the floor. Those things. We had bathroom chores. They rotated many of us in a group that cleaned the toilet and things like that.

And then after school, you came back to the orphanage and then went to play basketball?

We had a small area where we played baseball. We'd get a tennis ball and a small stick or hit it with your fist. You'd throw a tennis ball, let it bounce, and then you'd hit it.

With your fist?

Yeah, with your fist. That's our baseball. They had all the windows covered with wires, so it won't break the windows. Then they had a basketball court. If you played basketball, then you can't play baseball because it takes up all the space. That's all we had as far as entertainment. If we wanted more, we'd go out to the playground or parks.

Do you have any memories of the dormitories? Was there a girls and infant section?

Yeah, they had separate rooms.

How did they take care of any babies?

Well, there was a lady who took care of them. They'd get help.

How many ladies?

Well, I don't know. There weren't too many babies. There were very few infants. They didn't have too many. It was mostly boys.

Did you visit the baby dormitory?

No, I don't remember. When we went in, they were ready to break up the building and put in a new building. And this person named Major [Masasuke] Kobayashi was the one who ran the place. And he used to go out and talk to people to donate money to build this place. Anyways, before that, we lived in different places, so everything was not in one place. It was maybe a block away. The eating place was some place else. Then, after they built it, they had a dining room, a sick room, and different places.

So before you moved into the Salvation Army, it was a different facility?

Yeah, when we first went in, the girls were in one section and the boys were in another building or apartment. They rented the whole floor, so you had only so many kids there because of the fire regulation.

So Kobayashi-san raised the funds?

Yes, Major Kobayashi used to go to different places like New York to raise funds to build. It was terrible that the war authorities took it away from the Japanese people because he built it. Now, it's a Chinese consulate. While we were there, they were sort of changing to a Salvation Army training school for Salvation Army officers. So they moved all of the kids to one side of the building, and the other side was for training people. I think the third floor was for boys, the second floor was for girls, I think. And in between was something like a hospital, where they take care of the sick.

So your orphanage was partly occupied by the trainers?

Yeah, after a while.

Before you moved to Manzanar?

Yeah, maybe two years before or something like that.

Oh, long time.

Well, when you're kids, the only thing you are interested in is your area.

In the Salvation Army, did you see the training for two years?

Yes, maybe it was less than that, but it seemed like that.

You saw officers being trained?

Yeah, that place began to train people for the Salvation Army.

So you saw adults?

Yeah, we saw adults being trained.

What was your reaction?

Well, it was just loss of space! (laughter) I guess we didn't interfere with them because the only thing they were doing was learning whatever they had to learn. For us, we went outside for any activity. If you wanted to play on some basketball team or baseball team, we'd go outside to these parks and form a team.

Was the new building constructed for the training of officers?

It was an orphan home, period.

Well, thank you very much. I really appreciate your cooperation, enthusiasm and patience.

Well, thank you! You're very welcome.

Tamotsu Isozaki[1]

Interviewed by Lisa Nobe

You didn't tell me when your birthday was, unless maybe you don't want to tell me.

(chuckling) Oh, no. My birthday is June 17, 1926.

Okay, 1926. What generation are you?

I'm the second generation.

So you're Nisei.

Yes. Actually I look Issei. (laughter)

Both of your parents [Ichitaro and Setsu Isozaki] were born in Japan, then?

Right. They're from Kanagawa-ken.

They married here?

Actually, I think they got married in Hawaii.

Oh? Did they go to Hawaii first?

Yeah, they lived in Hawaii for a short time, and then they came to California. I think it was a picture marriage. I'm sure my mother was a picture bride.

Do you remember when they came to California?

I don't remember.

So, I know that you have four brothers and two sisters.

Right.

Can you tell me how your relationship is with them now and how it was when you were growing up with them?

---

[1]COPH-Oral History 2332 was conducted on March 13, 1993, in Monterey Park, California.

Our family, all the brothers and sisters, was pretty close because, age-wise, we're close. We're a year-and-a-half apart—at the most, maybe two years apart. We had lost a sister, the oldest sister. Do you want the names of everyone?

Sure.

The oldest one is a sister and her name is Molly, and the youngest one is Haru. My oldest brother's name is Sam, the one next to him is Kiyoshi, then Tak, then myself Tamo, and then Aki. The boys are all in between; we're sandwiched between the two sisters.

Going back, you said that one of your sisters had passed away?

The oldest one drowned.

Molly?

Before Molly, but I don't remember her name, though. In those days, a husband and wife both had to work out in the field. Even if there were little two-year-olds running around—they were just supposed to be around their mother—they'll drift away, and somehow the child fell in a ditch and drowned. The oldest one passed away that way.

Was that in California?

Yes, the same place.

All of your siblings were born in California?

Right.

Can you tell me where your birthplace was?

I was born in Stockton, California. Actually, the birth certificate gives Stockton [San Joaquin Valley], California, but the actual place is Mandeville Island. In Stockton, there are a lot of man-made islands, and Mandeville is one of them.

In those days, way back in the 1920s, there were midwives. You couldn't go all the way to Stockton to have a baby; it would be too late. Then the second most important thing: they didn't have money to even go to a hospital, so families used all midwives. I was born that way, and I was the last one born on the islands. From Mandeville Island, we moved to a town called Exeter [Tulare County, California] near Visalia [Tulare County, California], and my parents had two more children. A boy and a girl were born in Exeter. Then we moved to Visalia, where my father ran a restaurant.

Was it a Japanese restaurant?

Yeah, a Japanese restaurant. Then, during this time, my mother passed away giving birth. We were too young, so Father actually couldn't take care of us anymore. It was too tough on him, so we went to an orphanage in San Francisco. That's the Salvation Army Orphanage Home in San Francisco. It's on Geary and Laguna. We were there in 1935, around May of 1935. We were there until the war broke out.

How old were you when you went to the Salvation Army?

I was about nine years old.

How did your father tell you? What did he say to you about going to the orphanage?

It wasn't a matter of saying, "Oh, you're going to an orphanage." The welfare (people) said that he wasn't able to handle us, to take care of us, so the welfare (people) sent us to the San Francisco orphanage at that time.

You didn't have any other relatives to help take care of you?

No, we don't have any relatives in the United States.

When you went to the Salvation Army, did your father still have his restaurant?

No. After that, he was sick too, so he wanted to go back to Japan. They asked us if we wanted to go back to Japan with him. We said no, we didn't want to because we had nothing in Japan. So we stayed in the orphanage.

Is your father still alive?

No, he passed away around 1947.

While he was in Japan, you really didn't have any contact with him?

No. I just went to Japan one time with my wife. We went to the family cemetery.

When your parents were running the restaurant, would you help them out?

Very little. I was too young yet.

How about schooling?

Oh, yeah, we'd go. We had a hard time in school because our folks only spoke Japanese, and they didn't want us to speak English at home because they didn't understand what we were talking about. It was worse for us because we only spoke Japanese at home, and then we would go to school and have to speak only English. We didn't understand it. So I flunked kindergarten, I guess. And my behavior did too (chuckling). I probably flunked both ways!

You flunked kindergarten?

The kids nowadays, at two years old, they know their ABCs. I didn't know my ABCs until at least third grade, so that was really slow, very slow. Plus, there are so many boys in our family. We used to get into trouble quite a bit. We were city boys in the town of Visalia, and the country boys would come to Japanese school on Saturdays. We used to go out there and tease them and get into trouble and have fights and stuff. We were more mischievous than studious.

You would tease other Japanese?

Yeah. On Saturdays they had Japanese school kids from the country come out. The city people go to Japanese school, Monday through Friday, like for one or two hours. But the country people would come on Saturdays for eight hours. They'd come in the morning and leave about 4:00 [in the afternoon]. We used to go and tease them and have fights with them. We were very mischievous. We weren't sweet little boys. (laughter)

Was the conflict because they were from the country?

No, we were just mischievous little boys, that's all.

You would go to Japanese school during the week?

I didn't.

You didn't, but some of the Japanese children would?

Right.

But then you would go to regular school?

Yeah, English school only. I didn't go to Japanese school at all.

For the English school, was it mixed? Were there white children in your class as well?

Oh, yeah.

Were there Hispanics in your class?

I just remember white people and Asian people. I don't remember too many black people or Hispanics. There might have been, but very few. It wasn't very noticeable. I don't think I remember any. Plus, my brothers and I did so much together that I guess we kind of kept to ourselves. Then, in town, the rich boys would keep to themselves. They don't want to be rubbing shoulders with the bad boys, and I don't blame them. (laughter) We depended on each other quite a bit.

In the area where you lived at the time, did you live among other Japanese?

Oh, yeah, we were in a Japanese area, a Japanese community. That was the Japanese business area at that time.

Did you feel it was kind of segregated, that you had to kind of stay in that community?

The only time we used to go beyond our area was to go to the movies or go play sports or go watch sports. Then we'd go out of the area. We weren't scared to go to the white area. There was no problem, but basically we were around the Japanese community.

Do you remember any experiences of prejudice or discrimination from whites or any non-Japanese?

Not so much then, no.

When you were in the Salvation Army orphanage, were your four brothers and two sisters at the orphanage too?

Yeah.

At the orphanage, did they separate the boys from the girls?

Right. They did that, so we didn't see the sisters too often because the girls did their things and the boys did their things. Sometimes we would see them at the dining room or outside. There was a play area where we'd play with tennis balls or something like that. They might come out then. You're not restricted in that area, but we were not allowed to go in the girls' area. They divided that, so we didn't see the sisters too often.

Then, at the orphanage, once you're out of high school or you are eighteen years old, you move out. A lot of the girls went to do housekeeping jobs or something like that, unless they had relatives to go to. My sister Molly did that. She went into housework and got paid minimum wages — less than minimum wages, actually. You'd get room and board. I think it helped her to be there because she learned English. She also learned how to cook and bake, so it kind of helped her out that way. But financially, you're always broke.

You only had one sister that turned eighteen who left the orphanage?

No, my brother Sam went out too.

So one sister and one brother?

Yes.

What did your brother Sam end up doing?

Sam went to a cannery in Alaska. He did farm labor work; he did cleaning. I guess, at that time, it would be called laundry work, plus they had cleaning, pressing, and that kind of stuff. He did manual labor-type jobs.

Then, if you don't behave yourself, they'd send you back to the county where you came from, and then they would place you into some foster home or something like that. One of my brothers, Kiyoshi—the second oldest brother—left and went to a foster home where they had a grape winery, and he stayed with an Issei couple there. When war broke out, he went to Amache [Relocation Center in Colorado]. When he was old enough, he volunteered for the 442nd.

He was not interned?

He was interned at Amache. People from Livingston [Merced County], right around central California, were in Amache.

What happened to your brother, Kiyoshi? Did he do something that got him kicked out of the Salvation Army?

Because Kiyoshi wasn't quite behaving, the staff figured they'd send him back to the county. And the county decides what they're going to do.

Do you know what he did that got him kicked out?

No. Actually, my oldest brother Sam was going to be kicked out, so Kiyoshi, the second one, said, "Well, if he's going, I want to go too." When they would go to the county, the county would split my brothers up. Sam was sent to another orphanage run by the Salvation Army but with *hakujins* [Caucasians] and other races. It was not a *nihonjin* [Japanese] orphanage.

The Salvation Army orphanage was all-Japanese?

Ninety-eight percent or 99 percent.

Who were the other 1 or 2 percent?

Oh, they'd be *hapa*, mixed race.

The hapas *that were there—what mixture were they? Half-Japanese and half-white?*

Hakujin, usually. *Hakujin*.

When your sister left and then with your two brothers gone, did you keep in contact with them at all?

I saw one brother, Kiyoshi. It was so many years. Before he went overseas, he came on a furlough to visit us.

While you were in camp?

When I was in Manzanar.

While you were at Manzanar, Kiyoshi came to visit you?

Yeah, because he was going to go overseas. He had a furlough. Then I didn't see Kiyoshi until after I got discharged. I got discharged from the army in 1947. He got discharged in '45.

Did you see your sister Molly, the one who left the Salvation Army and was doing housekeeping?

Oh, yeah. Molly and my brother Sam eventually came to Manzanar. They went to Santa Anita Assembly Center [located in the city of Arcadia, Los

Angeles County, California]. They were there for a while, and then I guess they said, "Hey, my brothers are in Manzanar." So the authorities allowed them to go to Manzanar. When they got a section in the barrack, my older brother Tak eventually got out of Children's Village and lived with the two.

So they weren't in the Children's Village. They had a regular barrack at Manzanar?

Yeah, right. Sam and Molly. Tak was in the Village. He was in the Easter Sunday, 1944, picture; but afterwards, he left.

At the time that you were at the Salvation Army home, culturally, how Japanese would you consider yourself, in terms of how much Japanese you spoke?

When we went to the Salvation Army, they only spoke English except for the oldest Issei workers who were there. We were able to converse with them. Eventually, we started moving away from the Japanese language because all our playmates spoke English.

In terms of the staff at the Salvation Army—

There were a lot of Issei workers there.

Were they all Japanese? Or were any of them white?

In the beginning, when I went in 1935, I think it was a 100 percent Japanese operation. Eventually the older staff passed away; then they had *hakujin* come in.

Did you consider yourself close to your siblings at that time?

Oh, yes.

You were only about nine years old or so. At your oldest at the Salvation Army, did you have any dreams or aspirations?

No, we had no dreams—at least I didn't have any dreams. Sometimes I wished I was adopted because it's nice to be able to have change in your pocket, it's nice to have a bedroom of your own, and that kind of stuff. I used to see some people getting adopted or taken in by some other people, and I actually wished that. But I didn't want to leave my brothers and sisters either.

You wanted to all be adopted?

Yeah, but it was impossible.

The Shonien orphanage had adoption inspections. They would have days when couples would come in and view the orphans. Would you have those at the Salvation Army orphanage?

No, I don't remember anything like that.

While you were at the Salvation Army orphanage, did you go to regular school at the orphanage or would you leave the orphanage and go to a school?

Yes, we went to public school all the way through. Do you remember I told you that I went to high school and junior high and grammar school at the same time?

That's right. Go ahead and tell the story, so we have it on tape.

Okay. In 1941, there were winter graduates and summer graduates, so I was a midterm, which was a winter graduate. When the war broke out, I was in junior high school in San Francisco. I was in the eighth grade, just about to go into ninth grade. When the war broke out, our Salvation Army orphanage in the city sent us to the country, to a Salvation Army orphanage near Healdsburg [California] called Lytton. When I went there, I had to go back to grammar school because I was an eighth grader, and, in the country, they only had grammar school and high school. I protested and told them that I should go into the ninth grade, and they said, "You're right." They let me go to high school. They checked my records, and so I went to high school. A month later, they said, "You're going to go back to the same orphanage you came from in San Francisco." So I went back to junior high school again because junior high school is from the seventh to the ninth grade in the city. We stayed at the Salvation Army orphanage in the city until school was out in June 1942. Then we went to Manzanar.

Why did they move you to Lytton orphanage in the country?

I don't know. I can't understand it because they only sent some of us from the city; some of the children stayed in the city, so it didn't make sense at all.

Were any of your brothers and sisters moved with you?

Yeah.

All of them?

All my brothers and sisters went to Lytton.

Did all of you end up going back to the Salvation Army as well?

Right. Not only our family; some other families went too. They went to Lytton and came back.

And you have no idea why?

No, it didn't make sense at all. It made it difficult for us because now we were the minority over there, because there was a mixture of other children there. Actually, that home was not really an orphanage home; it was for little bad boys, you know? They were a little mischievous, the ones that were sent over there.

Did you do something wrong?

No. In our case, it wasn't; they just moved us out. Of course, I can't speak for everybody, but I know that by talking to the children at Lytton that they had problems at home.

What year was it that you went to Lytton?

It was 1941, December—a little after Christmas, actually. Between Christmas and New Year's, we left.

It was already after Pearl Harbor?

Pearl Harbor was on December 7th, so within three weeks, we were moved out.

When did you return to the Salvation Army?

The end of March or the first part of April.

Of 1942?

Yes.

Do you think that the Pearl Harbor incident is the reason why they moved you back to the Salvation Army?

No. They sent us to Lytton a little after Christmas 1941. I stayed there for part of December, January, February, and March; and then we came back to San Francisco again.

Were the children from the Salvation Army home the minority at Lytton orphanage?

Yes.

It was mostly what, whites?

Mexicans. That's when I learned about Mexicans. Whites, Mexicans, and blacks.

There were blacks there as well?

Not many, but the majority were whites and Mexicans, and then we were next. Compared to blacks, there were more Asians, which is us.

Were there conflicts between the groups?

We had more conflicts with the Latinos than the other races.

Can you remember any specific incidents?

Well, we used to fight. We fought each other.

Physically, you mean?

We wanted to protect ourselves. We were like the intruders because they had been there, so they wanted to cover their territory. That's what happened there. It's slightly racial, but it was a man-to-man thing, so it wasn't so bad. It was not all of the Mexicans fighting all of the Asians. It wasn't that way. It was individuals fighting, so I wouldn't call it a racial thing. But it is slightly because we were the minority. It's hard to explain, I guess, but you know it without explaining it. I mean you feel it.

But there were some good points about the place. They used to give us an allowance if you did a job, so we used to take care of chickens. Every day, we'd go there and get the eggs and feed them twice a day, morning and evening, and pick up the eggs. If we did that, we used to get something like seventy-five cents a week.

How would you spend it? Could you go out anywhere?

We used to go to school, and then, at the home, there was a place where you could buy things too. When I went to high school, there was a cafeteria.

In high school and junior high, were you the minority as well? Were there a lot of other Japanese there?

No, I don't remember any Japanese at all.

It was mostly whites?

But then, most of the Japanese were out of California anyway, so it would be whites and the kids from the orphanage going there.

You were at the Salvation Army [Home], when the Pearl Harbor attack happened?

Right.

How and when did you learn about Pearl Harbor?

That same day.

How did you find out?

Through the radio.

At the orphanage, you had a radio that everyone shared?

Yes, right. That's all we used to listen to, radios, the "Lone Ranger" and all that. I used to work for a short time delivering a Japanese newspaper.

While you were at the Salvation Army?

Yes. That was just maybe for three or four months. I used to carry the paper and deliver it, like the *Rafu Shimpo* [Los Angeles-based Japanese vernacular newspaper], you know. If you delivered so many, you got paid so much. I forget how much it was a month. We used to get paid monthly. When the war broke out, Pearl Harbor was on a Sunday. So on Monday, I went to the newspaper to see if I could keep working because I wanted the money they owed me, but it was boarded up already. We couldn't get in, so that was it.

You could go to school and get a job? You weren't confined?

No, this was at the tail end of the Salvation Army orphanage, when the Caucasians started taking over it. Before then, when the Issei were running it, they didn't want us to go running around doing things like that. They worried that people would think we were kind of begging. The Japanese community would say, "Well, why are these kids doing that when we're supporting them?"

They were donating money to the orphanage, and it looked like we were running around begging. That's one of the reasons that they didn't want us to work. Later on, when the heads passed away or left, the Caucasians took over. Then it got lenient. They started giving a little allowance.

Do you mean the Caucasians took over the orphanage?

Yes, so it was a Caucasian way of doing things. We went to work, and they didn't mind.

When you heard on the radio about the Pearl Harbor attack, what was your reaction? What was the reaction of the other people around you?

We really didn't like it because we knew what the problems would be. We were going to be called "Japs," and it came out that way too. The Chinese right away put a badge on or a pin saying, "I'm Chinese." There's no way we're going to put our name or "Chinese" on to protect ourselves. If they wanted to fight, we were ready to fight.

There was name-calling. What a lot of the *hakujin* would do is, when you walked by or passed them up, there might be four or five of them and one would say "Jap" or something. You can't fight four of them, so you just keep walking. That's the kind of sneaky stuff they were doing to hurt our feelings. We weren't feeling good either because now, with the Japanese fighting the United States, it was not a good deal for us. From then on, everyone was looking behind their shoulder. I didn't think we had too many friends, like guys in sports or something didn't come say, "Hey, I know you're American and I'm with you." Instead, a lot of them kind of shied away from the Japanese.

Kind of ignoring you?

They'd kind of drift away from you. That's why you felt uncomfortable. They didn't say anything, but they didn't have to.

Did you have any white friends before Pearl Harbor?

Not real good, close friends. I think the only friend I remember who wasn't Japanese was one black guy. Even the Issei in the Japanese community weren't so fond of us orphanage kids. I think they didn't care for their children to associate with us because they would never come to our orphanage or say, "I want to come and see Tamo. He's my friend." They might see us, but then they don't come in and visit us. I think that's why the orphanage kids were pretty close to each other. It was like, if you fight him, you're fighting me too because he's my brother. It was that kind of attitude.

Even before the war, can you remember prejudice from the Japanese community against the orphans?

Oh, yeah, I felt that. At school, they'll play with you, but that's all. They'd never say, "Hey, Tamo, why don't you come over to my house?" "Hey, have some cookies at my place or something." We'd be happy to go eat cookies at their house, you know? (chuckling) But I can't remember anybody inviting me, or I don't remember anybody else being invited to their classmates' home. Japanese were prejudiced too.

That's why I was always hoping my kids didn't feel that way. It doesn't mean I'm not prejudiced; I'm prejudiced too. (chuckling) But I try to set a little example of, hey, we're all human beings. You don't like a person because he's not a good person; you don't *not* like him because he's Japanese. That's the way I look at it. So we're kind of intermingling. When I started out, the community was saying, "Our kids have got to all marry Japanese." But at the end, not all got married to Japanese. It didn't matter. I don't have any hatred. Everybody's a human being.

Thank you very much for taking this time out for the interview.

You're welcome.

(above) Shonien campus
(below) Shonien orphans

社團人南加小兒園兒童及職員

Chapter Two
The Road to Manzanar:
Life Behind Barbed Wire

While the majority of the orphans at the Children's Village had lived in orphanages or foster care before the war, their experiences at Children's Village varied because of age, sex, and circumstance.[1] Each child's age and circumstance impacted the length of time he or she spent at the Children's Village. Clara Hayashi, for example, was six and one-half years old when she and her father moved to Los Angeles, at the urging of her father's minister. Reverend John Yamasaki recommended the Shonien to Hayashi's father, and her father paid for her expenses there by working as a carpenter at the Shonien and as a gardener in different parts of Los Angeles. When she turned twelve, Hayashi was able to leave the Shonien and live with her father, who by that time was able to buy a hotel in downtown Los Angeles. In 1941, however, Hayashi's father died and she returned to the Shonien. As a result, Hayashi accompanied the Shonien children to Manzanar; but, because she was eighteen years old, she lived only temporarily at the Children's Village and soon transferred to the Young Women's Christian Association's (YWCA) barrack for single women located in the Manzanar camp. In this chapter, Hayashi remembers the days after Pearl Harbor and her experiences at both the Children's Village and at the YWCA barrack at Manzanar.

---

[1] According to Lisa Nobe, "The age range of the Village children was newborn to eighteen, the mean age upon admission to the orphanage being eight years old. Records indicate that fifty-four of the orphans were boys and forty-seven were girls." [See Lisa Nobe, "The Children's Village of Manzanar," *Journal of the West* (38 (April 1999): 67.]

In terms of social circumstance, Helen Whitney's 1948 master's thesis shows that 63 percent of the Village children were Nisei and 37 percent were Sansei; of the twenty-four children who were Sansei, fourteen were children of mixed-race. In addition, Whitney adds that out of the 101 children who were placed at the Children's Village between 1943 and 1945, 50 of the orphans were either whole or half-orphans (i.e., one or both parents dead); 21 came from broken homes; 14 were illegitimate; and 16 were at the Village because of temporary difficulties in the family (i.e. a brief illness or confinement of mother or father). [See Helen Whitney, "Care of the Homeless Children of Japanese Ancestry during Evacuation and Relocation," (Diss. University of California, Berkeley, 1948): 34-35]

In contrast to Hayashi, Robert Yamashita was nine years old and the youngest of six children when he was sent to the Salvation Army Home in 1939. His father had passed away and his mother, who had gone back to Japan for medical treatment in 1938, was never able to return to America. In the excerpt from his oral history, Yamashita recounts his experience at Children's Village from the perspective of a twelve-year-old boy who has an older brother and a sister living in the barracks.

Unlike Hayashi and Yamashita who had experienced institutional care before Children's Village, two children became orphans after they relocated to Manzanar. Born in 1938, Sharon Okazaki Kodama was three years old when her parents died in their barrack apartment, and she and her older sister Helen were sent to Children's Village.

While both of her parents' families were from the Wakayama-ken area of Japan, Kodama's mother, Frances Skaye, was a Nisei born in Davenport, Washington, where her parents (Kodama's grandparents) ran a restaurant in nearby Harrington, Washington. Kodama's grandparents, like other Issei, sent their daughter Frances to Japan to get an education. Kodama's mother and other Nisei children in America who were sent to Japan for their education and returned to the United States as teenagers or young adults were called Kibei.[2] According to Paul Spickard, by the early 1940s, approximately 50,000 Nisei had been sent to Japan as children, and 10,000 of them migrated back to the United States before World War II.[3]

While Kibei usually struggled to fit in when they returned to the United States, they usually had in their favor family members already in the United States to help support them. Kodama's grandparents, for instance, had already established a restaurant business in Washington. Kodama's aunt, Buni Kinoshita, who would later become her guardian, helped run the family business with the help of Tom Tagami, who had been married to the sister of Kodama's father until she died. With the families merged by business and by marriage, Kodama and her sister had relatives in America outside of the military exclusion zones who could care for them after their parents' death. In the following excerpt, Kodama recalls moments with her parents at Manzanar—from the family's first days in camp to the night of their death— as well as her aunt's struggle to become her guardian. Her story reveals the community silence surrounding her parents' death and the trauma she experienced as a child in suddenly becoming an orphan.

---

[2] Paul Spickard, *Japanese Americans: The Formation and Transformations of an Ethnic Group* (New York: Twayne Publishers, 1989): 89.

[3] Ibid.

Clara Hayashi[1]

Interviewed by Reiko Katabami

When and where were you born?

I was born March 17, 1924, in Livingston, California.

You went to Manzanar when you were—

Eighteen.

Before that, you told me that you kept going in and out of the Shonien.

Yes.

Could you give me the age at which you left Shonien and then went back in again?

Well, I was six and a half years old when I went into the Shonien with my father, and then I was about twelve and a half or thirteen when I came out, and then my father died when I was seventeen. So I went back because they didn't know what to do with me. They didn't want to send me to my aunt in Hawaii because she was Buddhist. My cousin was Christian, but he had his own problems. He had gotten married. So they didn't know what to do with me, so they just sent me back to the Shonien. At that age, they didn't want me living by myself in Los Angeles.

During your stay at the Shonien, when did you find out about the Pearl Harbor attack?

We went to church, and when we came home the staff were whispering. It was over the radio.

So you knew through the radio, through the conversation.

Yes.

On the same day, December 7th [1941]? It was Sunday?

---

[1] COPH-Oral History 2334 was conducted on July 12, 1993, in Redondo Beach, California.

Yes. That night they took Mr. [Rokuichi "Joy"] Kusumoto. The FBI came. They were banging on the door at midnight. They scared us because they made so much noise.

Okay. Were you scared when you found out about the Pearl Harbor attack?

Uh, no, I wasn't scared, but I was really—I think you have mixed emotions.

After the Pearl Harbor attack, did you experience any prejudice or segregation or discrimination?

Not really. We went to school. We were going to school, and the students would treat us just the same. Then when they started the relocation and the newspapers said that all "the Japs" are gone, we couldn't go to school anymore.

So you stayed at the—

We had to stay within the area, yeah.

At the Shonien?

Yes, because we might get shot at or something.

Do you have any memory of the curfew?

Yeah, I remember.

You didn't go anywhere.

We didn't go anywhere. We didn't go outside of our boundary, not even to the sidewalk, because we were supposed to be unseen.

So you knew about relocation. How did you know [about it]?

The newspaper. They had no place to put us, so we had to stay until they made a place for us, and that was in June [1942]. We were at the Shonien for about two or three months after everybody else was gone.

So what were your feelings when you heard about the executive order?[2]

[2]Executive Order 9066. On February 19, 1942, President Franklin D. Roosevelt issued Executive Order 9066 which gave the secretary of war and the US armed forces the authority to define military areas along the West Coast and to exclude from these areas anyone who was considered a threat to the United States. This order eventually gave the military the power to send 120,000 people of Japanese ancestry to concentration camps.

Yeah, I felt it was wrong because, like you said, we were citizens. But in those times, Japanese, Nisei or whatever, it was bow down, *ah so*. That's how we were pictured, always obeying.

Did you have a feeling of solidarity at the Shonien?

I think we did, yeah.

Like brother and sister?

Yeah.

If something happened, everyone took care of each other?

Mm-hmm, yes.

Were the Shonien staff like father or mother figures?

I don't know. They were—what would you call it?—more like, I think, teacher figures, responsible. But I think a lot of the way I felt was because of what I learned from my father. He was very liberal. He really didn't have the Japanese way of thinking. Because he would remind me, "You're American. You got to stick up for your rights." He doesn't say bow down and say yes, *hai, hai, hai*. He says, "You're American, you stick up for your rights. I'm Japanese, so I have to follow a different authority."

So you arrived in Manzanar in June the next year.

Yes.

Do you remember when you arrived at Manzanar? In the morning or in the nighttime?

I think it was in late afternoon.

Did you see gunmen, military, barbed wire? What was your reaction at that time?

I knew they were there for a purpose. In fact, I knew a lot of them. We used to talk to them.

So when you arrived in Manzanar, you were the first to go to Children's Village. How about the Maryknoll orphans? Do you remember?

I was just wondering if they came with us. I think Maryknoll closed and sent their children to us, and then we had people from Terminal Island—or well, San Pedro [Los Angeles]. They had to leave first. They moved to L.A. [Los Angeles]. A lot of them were fishermen, and the FBI took the fathers. We had the Matsuno family come to Shonien from San Pedro because their father was arrested. So more people were coming to the Shonien, and others were leaving because their parents came to take them with them to the camps.

How did you go to Manzanar from the Shonien?

Bus.

How many buses?

Two buses, I think.

When you were on the bus, did Lillian Matsumoto encourage singing or—?

I think whenever we did ride buses and stuff, we always did sing. I can't understand kids now; they don't sing. Whenever we got in cars and stuff, if it's a long trip, we'd start singing.

So it was like a happy mood?

Yeah.

When you left the Shonien, what did you bring with you?

Your clothes. Whatever you can carry.

You were given a bag or something?

Yeah, I think so.

And then you packed everything, whatever you have?

Yes.

Did you leave something?

I left something in storage. Before I went to Hawaii in 1946, I went to get my things, and they said, "Well, it's way in the inside there. We can't get it out." Reverend [John] Yamasaki went with me to get my things out of storage.

Who looked after the Shonien when you left for Manzanar?

I don't know. I think they had a committee or something to decide what to do with it. I went and they said they couldn't get to my things. Then, when I came back from Hawaii, they said that it's too late. They burned it all up. And there were important books that the church wanted. My father had two bookcases and about three shelves with Bible study, all the books of the Bible, study books.

Oh, your father's books were also there?

They were all stored there. And my mother's things. Well, everything. And my father's tools.

After he died, you kept your father's legacy.

Mm-hmm. They were all stored there, and everything was gone. I had kept a few pictures. I was able to take a few pictures and stuff home with me.

So the other Shonien orphans, their stuff was also burned?

Most of them didn't have things because it was with their family. But, see, my father died, so I had all of his things and everything.

When you first saw the Manzanar landscape, what was your impression?

What kind of place? Desert.

How was the climate?

It gets very hot in the summer and very cold in the winter. The wind is very —if you got caught in the windstorm, you had to get down and cover yourself because the sand hurts you. It just pierces.

And were there also Issei or Nisei staff at the Children's Village?

Staff? Uh-huh.

Do you know the names of them?

At that time it was all Japanese. The only time they had *hakujin* [Caucasians] is when I first went there. There was Masayo Deguchi and Ruth Takamune.

So you remember the Matsumotos [See COPH-OH 2494]?

The Matsumotos, I think Miss Takamune, and I think Alice Kaneko. And then, of course, Taeko. She was one of the kids, and then she stayed there and was elevated.

Taeko Nagayama [See COPH-OH 2494]?

Kajiwara Nagayama. She married one of the guys there.

So the staff are from the Shonien.

Yes. I think those are the ones that went from Shonien. Then, of course, the Salvation Army brought their staff.

Okay. Regarding the counseling and the casework, do you have any memory about counseling? Did the staff members counsel you?

No.

So when you had a terrible experience, whom did you talk to?

Oh, you could go to one of the staff members.

Did you feel free to go?

Yeah. It was like going to a big sister or something.

Would it happen frequently?

No.

So were the orphans well-behaved?

Yeah. Most—I think everyone was well-behaved.

So the Maryknoll orphans and the Salvation Army orphans and the—

We got along, uh-huh.

So you mostly mingled with each other.

We got along, and the Shonien girls would kind of have their eyes on the Salvation Army boys and stuff like that. I think one couple did get married.

Did you know of any romance?

That was about the only one. You know, some girls are more attractive to the opposite sex than the others.

How about you?

Couldn't be bothered with guys. (laughter)

Did the Children's Village have three sections [or buildings], with a boys' barracks?

 Yes, and a girls' barracks and a kitchen.

And infants? Would you describe those?

Uh, let me see. I don't know if the infants were on the other side or not, but I know the—

I think the infants were on the other side of the girls' section.

Girls, yes. The infants—I really didn't pay much attention to any other barracks except our area and the kitchen area and laundry. At first we had to wash by hand, and the water [was] so soft [that] you couldn't get the soap out of the diapers. We rinsed and rinsed and rinsed and rinsed.

 You mean the older orphans were helping with the laundry?

Yes.

But some person was in charge of the laundry?

Yeah, there was somebody in charge. But the equipment didn't arrive yet, so we were just washing diapers.

How about in Children's Village, other informants say that it's very difficult for boys to visit the girls' dormitory because it's restricted. So they didn't see each other much.

Well, you see each other every day. It's just that you didn't go in each other's —it's just like when you're at home, you don't want your brother in your bedroom. And people who had brothers and sisters outside, they were always over to visit the younger ones. The older ones would come visit.

In the girls' section, would you describe how many orphans are in one room?

Each one has a bed. We made our own little dresser with crates. Maybe twelve. I don't know.

And there was an older girls' section and a younger girls' section divided into two?

Let me see. This was more or less the teenage section. Then I guess the younger ones were with the babies, I guess.

So did you have any privacy in your room in Children's Village?

No.

Did you have any inconvenience?

Not really.

How many people were in your room?

I don't know. There could have been about twelve maybe.

Can you give me names, if you remember?

I can't give you all of them. There was Sumako Tanaka, there was Mary Matsuno [See COPH-OH 2489], Hatsui Kodani, Nakako Kodani. Oh, what's their name? I can't think of her name, from San Francisco. Mary and Jane Honda.

Did you notice if the siblings were close to each other?

Yeah, they kind of hung around together.

Did they defend each other when some problem happened?

Mm-hmm, yeah.

So, generally, you felt in Children's Village that you were safe, you were protected.

Yeah.

How was the food at the Children's Village?

Children's Village was lucky that the cook that they had was from the Clifton's Cafeteria in downtown Los Angeles.

Did you enjoy the food?

Yeah. His food was different from the other barracks; they had like amateur cooks and stuff.

So you visited other barracks?

After I left.

So you knew the difference?

Only one thing I didn't like was the horsemeat.

Did you eat horsemeat?

I didn't eat it.

They served horsemeat?

They had it once.

But everybody knew it was horsemeat?

They knew it after I hollered, "Horsemeat!"

Oh, after you ate, you knew.

I cut my meat; I looked at it. It wasn't meat. And, you know, you kind of hear about things, so I said, "Horsemeat." All the forks went down. I wasn't going to eat horsemeat.

But nobody tells you—

No. They said it was cutlets. They didn't say what kind of cutlets. It was horse cutlets.

Do you remember everybody not eating then?

I think after I said it, most of them didn't. But the little ones, they don't understand. They ate it.

You were eighteen when you went to Manzanar. Did you get to stay at the Children's Village?

Yeah. But then I left the village and went to the YWCA [Young Women's Christian Association].

Oh, you went to the YWCA after Children's Village?

Uh-huh. They had one barrack for single women. Our cook was from Little Tokyo, and they made *shochu* out of our rice and sugar.

You mean the shochu, *as in sake?*

Yeah. Our block and the next block. When our food was bad, we'd go to the next block. When their food is bad, they come to our block. Sometimes we meet halfway, and then we don't know what to do. My friend lived on the next block.

But you can choose where to eat?

No, not really.

So at the YWCA you didn't like your food?

So we'd just sneak over to the next block.

But somebody would check?

They don't check.

You can eat other food?

Yeah, you could go and visit friends and eat.

Did you do that while you were staying in Children's Village?

At Children's Village, you ate there. They had the best food anyway.

Okay, so you went to high school, while you were at Manzanar?

Yes.

Would you give me a brief description of school? Who was the teacher?

They had teachers from the Los Angeles School District because Manzanar was part of Los Angeles, technically. So they had L.A. schoolteachers.

Caucasian teachers?

Caucasian teachers, yes. A lot of them were . . . well, like one was just out of college and wasn't really that good at it. Well, she was more like a friend than a teacher. She was a sewing teacher. At that time, all Japanese girls learned how to sew by their parents, so the students knew more than the teacher. (laughter) As far as sewing is concerned, she came from a rich family, and she could tell you about color and stuff. We could tell her about sewing. But then you had certain courses you had to take to graduate. So we had regular courses.

Did you have any other classes, teachers?

There was one teacher nobody liked. Her name was Miss Stump, and they used to call her everything else. She was all right, but I don't know. I never had her for a class. She was my study hall teacher, and people didn't study in study hall. They just played and stuff, and she had no control of the class. I found out, though, when I was there I used to kind of struggle in school. I didn't get as good grades as others because I never studied. I later found out that I was smarter than most of the students. They used to get all *A*s in school. Because I studied less in Manzanar, it was easy for me. I didn't have to study.

Nobody cared?

I got good grades, but I didn't have to study. It was just easy for me, whereas a lot of students found it hard.

About how many students were in one classroom?

About twenty maybe. I think it depends upon what class, though.

So, ability-wise, the teachers were good?

I think most of them were.

How about the enthusiasm?

I don't know. Our class was something else. We told them when we wanted to graduate. They said, "No, you can't. You have to wait 'til June." We said, "We don't want to wait until June. We've prepared our own graduation. We ordered our own cap and gowns." We told them, "We're not going to wait 'til June. We're through with school; why wait to graduate?" So, like I said, our class was something else.

So there was a conflict between teachers and students?

Well, not the teachers, just whoever was in charge.

Like an instructor?

The administration wanted to make just one—like they do now—graduation. But in those days they used to have graduation twice a year, and we were what they called winter graduates. But they wanted us to wait until summer. So they wanted us to wait like one semester after we're through with school to graduate, and we didn't want to.

So you graduated in winter?

Yeah, we graduated. Well, we didn't graduate in February when we finished, but we graduated in March because we planned our own graduation. The teachers chose the valedictorian, but we more or less planned what we were going to do and stuff. Luckily, at that time, the great photographer Ansel Adams was taking pictures in Manzanar, so we had him take our graduation picture.[3]

Do you have that picture?

No.

So you graduated in 1944?

In 1943. Like we had to wait. There was no school. So everybody was more or less put behind in school, so the thing was to get out of school, to get your diploma. I don't even know if they gave me a diploma or not. I don't remember. I don't have one.

Was there any prejudice or discrimination towards you?

No, I think all these teachers volunteered.

Did they live outside of camp?

They had the area for them to live. Outside. I don't know if they lived in town or what.

Did you perceive any prejudice from the Japanese community? I mean at the barracks, did families look down on you?

No. Maybe some of the Issei did, but it didn't bother us because we didn't communicate with the Issei. The Nisei, I think, treated us like anybody else.

Were you ever invited by families living in the barracks there to visit?

---

[3] See Ansel Adams, *Born Free and Equal: Photographs of the Loyal Japanese Americans at Manzanar Relocation Center, Inyo County,* New York: U.S. Camera, 1944.

A couple barracks away, I used to go visit a family all the time, until I found out the brother liked me, then I—I didn't like him. (laughter) But, yeah, I had certain friends that I'd visit, but not too many.

Psychologically, what was the general mood? What feelings did you have?

Well, I know—take all the young people. The Issei used to tell you, "You people take this like a picnic, but it isn't a picnic." We just carried on as usual. The only thing is that it's all Japanese. There's nobody else. But we played, we went to school, we did whatever.

So any serious complaints?

No, not so much, not in the young people. You made the best of what you had, you know.

Did you make any close friends there?

Yeah, the Matsunos, from Children's Village. And Sue Tanaka. She was right across the street from the YWCA, and she was my boss when I was working.

She was at that time living with family?

Yes, she was with her family.

How many people lived in the YWCA barracks?

That one? About a half a dozen, I think. We all had our own room.

All single women?

Yeah. There must have been about ten women.

Was it better than other barracks, or something like that?

No, it's just like any other. You have your little room, and you have your army cot with straw mattress like everybody else, nothing special. Then it's up to you to furnish it.

In terms of the facility, was it a poorly constructed barrack?

Yeah. It was a regular army barrack. They put a bunch of boards together, but you can see the holes in the floor and on the side. And then they covered that up with—being that people complained—they put linoleum on the floor and they put tarpaper on the walls, on the outside. I think they did put plasterboards inside, because the wind would blow and all the dust would be inside the house.

Did you have a fan in the summertime?

I don't think so. We had stoves for the winter, though.

Was it warm enough?

Yeah.

So did you frequently visit barracks when you had free time?

No, I don't think I was really interested because in the family barracks, you were allotted so much room, and if you have a big family, you have no room to move.

Oh, you mean you have no room to visit, then?

And so we usually met friends outside instead of going into people's barracks.

Did you have any privacy?

Yeah.

Oh, really? But it's open space.

No, each room is closed space.

Oh, partitions.

Yeah, partitions. It's more like cubicles.

Did you watch movies in the camp?

Yeah. It was outdoors, and you'd take your blanket and lie down and watch the movie. We also had concerts, records, and we'd watch the shooting stars. You'd be looking at the movie and all of a sudden everybody would go, "Ooooooh!" "What happened?" (laughter) Because the stars would distract us.

So you were generally satisfied with the facilities and food at Children's Village?

Yes, when you compare it with the others, yes. They had a good cook. When I went to the YWCA, our cook got fish. They didn't clean the fish. It's frozen. They don't clean the fish. They just take the frozen fish and throw it in the oven, and then they take it out and put it on top of your rice. Then they put your Jello on top of the fish. You can't eat that. They're feeding you fertilizer in the first place.

Do you have many complaints about food?

Yeah. But it didn't do any good.

But later it was amended?

I don't know because I didn't wait that long. I said, "I have to get out of here."

Thank you for the interview.

You're welcome.

Robert Yamashita[1]

Interviewed by Art Hansen

Was there a family feeling at the Salvation Army in comparison to the Children's Village?

For the families that stayed together after Children's Village, there was more desire to keep in touch with other family members. Whereas in my family, that wasn't the case because, even before I left Children's Village, our family was already pretty much separated. All of my brothers and sisters [Grace, Frank, Kiyo, and Mits] who were in Manzanar had left before I did, and I personally never had that close feeling.[2]

Even though I went to the reunions, I was still working at the time, living my life. It was nice to go to the reunions and see some of the kids that you grew up with when you were young. But I didn't have any strong feelings about keeping in touch. Everybody was kind of living his or her own life in those days, you know? In my case, I never went back to Manzanar until only less than a year ago. The only reason why I ended up there was because a guy I've known through my job for over thirty years who lives up in Sparks, Nevada, was nice enough to drive me.

After Executive Order 9066, did you have conversations among yourselves, within your family group, your siblings, and maybe others about what's going to happen to you, especially after all the Japanese people from the area and your school had left?[3] Because they were classmates of yours and all of sudden they were gone, and you were still around.

Well, I was twelve and a half. I don't remember even thinking about that. Of course, we didn't know anything about Children's Village. I don't remember anybody telling us what was going to happen. All I remember is that some

---

[1]COPH-Oral History 3502 was conducted on March 3, 2006, in Alameda, California.
[2]One brother Jack Yamashita was sent to Rohwer Relocation Center in Arkansas.
[3]On February 19, 1942, President Franklin D. Roosevelt issued Executive Order 9066, which gave the Secretary of War and the US armed forces the authority to define military areas along the West Coast and to exclude from these areas anyone who was considered a threat to the United States. This order eventually gave the military the power to send 120,000 people of Japanese ancestry to concentration camps.

of the kids were sent to Lytton orphanage, but they came back and went to Manzanar. I'm not sure of the exact reason why some of these kids went to Lytton; maybe at the time [it was] because new kids were coming in or maybe there wasn't enough space at the Salvation Army—I'm not sure.

Now, you had some classmates that were going to the same school as you were going to who left San Francisco and then went off to Tanforan [Assembly Center, in San Bruno, California, south of San Francisco]. Did you know anything about Tanforan? Did that increase your consciousness at all? Or were you just oblivious to where they were, and where their parents were going, or anything like that?

Yeah, I would say I was more oblivious to it. Except that my sister [Grace] who had left the Salvation Army ended up at Tanforan.

You never visited [her] at Tanforan, did you?

No. Maybe at the time I didn't even know [she was] at Tanforan.

When did it start pressing upon your consciousness that you were going to be leaving San Francisco and going someplace else to live?

Well, I think probably a very, very short moment. It wasn't like somebody saying, "A month from now you're going to be leaving."

Do you remember being told that you are leaving? Being gathered up? That must have been reasonably traumatic, to pick up and go someplace else.

Yeah, I remember. I guess none of us had much to carry. But from what I remember, we were taken to a train station. It seemed like it was in San Francisco because there were trains going across the bridge. As far as I know, I think the train must have gone to Union Station in Los Angeles and from there we went by bus to Manzanar. I don't have too good a recollection of that.

Do you think you remember where you were going to go? Did somebody say we're taking all the kids from the orphanage and we're going to move up to this place out in the desert in California? Did you get any kind of preview of any coming attraction, or not?

No, I don't remember any kind of advanced notice of exactly where we were going to end up.

So you were going, but you didn't know where, right?

Yeah.

Then as you were going on the train and then on the bus, you must have been getting somewhat curious as to where you were going. Do you remember that experience very well? I mean the actual trip itself, or not?

The train trip more than whatever the bus trip was, yeah. I don't remember too much about what I was feeling.

Do you remember getting to Manzanar? Because here all of a sudden you are out in the middle of nowhere, except that camp was almost completely populated by the time you got there, because you got there kind of late. Towards the end of June, many internees had been there for a while, probably close to eight, nine, ten thousand people. What did you think when you got there at Manzanar?

I guess because we were a little bit isolated where Children's Village was, I had no idea at the time how many people there were or anything. Within a couple of months, of course, we started to go to school, and the school was closer to the main gate area, and we were kind of at the opposite end.

Did Children's Village and Manzanar make any kind of impact on you of being different from what you had been doing for three years before in San Francisco?

Yeah, I think at that point I realized that the Japanese were evacuated or whatever. You didn't stop to think about how long you'd be there. But I never gave much thought about wanting to get out until some of my brothers and sisters left. I don't recall many kids in Children's Village who left before me. I know my brother [Mits] did. My brother [Mits] left in March of 45', and I left in June. But the last year that I was in camp, I really wanted to leave bad because my brothers [Frank and Mits] and sisters [Grace and Kiyo] were all gone. Even though I was around a lot of kids, people ask, "Well, what was the reason why you wanted to leave so bad?" Even when I was asked if I wanted to be adopted, I wanted to leave so badly that I would have said yes. I really didn't want to get adopted. What I really missed was going out and playing sports against all kinds of kids, instead of just Japanese kids, because I used to love to play sports, and I wanted to play baseball. I played a lot of softball; I played a lot of basketball, in camp. That was one of the things on my mind. I wanted to go back to a normal school and play sports with kids of all different nationalities.

Like you had done in San Francisco?

Sure. Like I said, it started probably the last year I was there, I remember, but it wasn't anything I ever talked about. But I remember how badly I wanted to leave.

When I was young, when I was that age, I could hardly think of anything but sports. So when you are talking about playing sports, you are talking about mostly the different elementary schools playing against one another?

Right, yeah.

That's where you played kids from other backgrounds. Even at your own school, you had kids from other backgrounds. It wasn't just Japanese and American kids, right?

Well, what I remember is that I know that if the camps didn't happen, that I would have been going to high school. They had John Foote High School, and they asked us what kind of musical instrument we wanted to study at John Foote. I know that the older kids used to play soccer and other things at John Foote, and those things were on my mind. It would have been nice to do that.

Did you feel any sense of a stigma for being in an orphanage, that you felt that somehow you were a compromised person in the eyes of other people if not in your own?

Sure. When I was in the Salvation Army, I knew that there were a lot of kids who didn't want to be friendly with kids in the home because they think you are a bad influence, or you always want to fight and do bad things. Well, part of that is true. When you are in an orphanage like that, you have your meals, a place to stay, and you're taken care of, but you don't have any money. You know, kids are going to get in trouble. So that's one of the reasons why I think every summer we used to go to camp.

Oh, where did you go?

Well, the first couple of years that I was in Salvation Army, we used to camp out in tents by the American River near Sacramento. I think some Japanese people—I found this out later—owned the property used by the Salvation Army for the kids.

Would you just go up there for a couple of weeks?

Oh, no. We were there for the summer.

The whole summer? Oh, wow!

Because this gets the kids out of the city, and you don't get into trouble, right? Some of the people you talk to from Salvation Army, Children's Village, say that they'd get in trouble. But I think when you don't have any money, and you want things, you're going to end up doing some bad things.

I'm kind of curious about this news because you said you used to go to camp every summer, and now all of sudden it's summer again and you're going to another camp, except it's a different kind of camp. Did it seem that different? Or did it seem a lot like the camp you used to go to up by the Russian River?

No, you mean Manzanar? Oh, it was much, much different because you knew that you couldn't leave. Even if you could go beyond the fence that was on the perimeter, you couldn't go out very far. I remember going beyond those fences very few times. But I don't remember there being much of anything other than just desert. I think people were able to go toward Mount Williamson [mountain peak located behind the Manzanar camp, second in altitude to Mount Whitney in the Sierra range], but I don't know if they had to get a permit. We never went that far. Like I said, if there were any creeks or any kind of river where kids could fish, I know there were some kids in Children's Village who would have loved to go fishing and liked to fish.

Now you said that you felt some stigma attached to being in an orphanage. Did you feel some stigma attached to being at Manzanar?

In the Children's Village?

Well, not necessarily just in Children's Village but in Manzanar as a whole, because Children's Village was a camp within a camp. But in the general camp, you are there because of your ancestry, because you are Japanese American. Did you feel some stigma attached to that?

Yeah, I don't think I gave much thought to it. It seems once I left Manzanar and I was going to school and after I went in the service, I don't remember hardly ever talking about being in camp. The few times that the subject of internment camp came up especially in the Midwest and the East Coast, people that I came in contact with through work or whatever didn't know anything about the camps, and I got "Well, we didn't know about it" reactions and the subject kind of ended there. So for most of my life, I just didn't talk about it.

Now you were at Manzanar during the Manzanar Riot that occurred in December of 1942. You would have been in there for six months by then. Two people [internees] got killed, and [nine] other people [internees] were wounded. Did that bring home to you that this was a little different kind of place?

I remember the kids in Children's Village, when I remember the riot. I do remember that somebody did get killed. They just told the kids in Children's Village to stay home and don't go out. I don't remember how many days the school was closed, but we didn't go out until school started up again.

Well, one of the big action points on the night of December 6th when the shooting occurred was the hospital. There was a whole gang, thousands came over to the hospital, and you were pretty close to the hospital.

Right, but here again, I don't remember seeing anybody because we were told to just stay home.

Okay. So you knew what happened, but you didn't really witness much, right?

Right, right, and probably didn't know as much about these things until years later when I read about it in the book, especially that *Years of Infamy* [*Years of Infamy: The Untold Story of America's Concentration Camps*, by Michi Weglyn, New York: William Morrow and Co., 1976] that goes into a lot of details.

Well, tell me a little bit more about the Children's Village. How did it compare physically as a place to the Salvation Army [orphanage]? Was the place a better sort of facility than what you had experienced when you were living in San Francisco?

No, the Children's Village was not because we were sleeping in a large dormitory area, not just small rooms. Even though sandstorms did not happen all the time, they had sandstorms when you're going to school, or coming home from school sometime. The overall conditions were not as good as San Francisco.

How about the food at Children's Village?

The food was okay, but I think the food at the Salvation Army was probably better. I just couldn't get all the things I wanted. I don't remember, but I wasn't always drinking fresh milk at the Salvation Army, but I don't remember that I was having fresh milk or skim milk at all in camp.

So the standard of living for you went down?

Well, sure.

You're talking about how in San Francisco you had a separate room?

Yeah, with maybe two other kids.

So you had greater privacy. At Children's Village, you had a cot or something in a dorm, rather than having a separate bunk bed. Then the sports facilities you described as pretty bad in San Francisco, and I know you were really interested in sports. Were the sports facilities better in Manzanar?

Yeah, in that regard we had our basketball court and a softball field, and we had a grass area if we wanted to play football. But they wouldn't buy the kids any equipment, so they weren't too keen about that. They didn't want kids getting hurt.

So when somebody who was not in the Children's Village as you were looks at the comparison between what your living situation was and the situation of people like in Block 29 or the rest of the thirty-six blocks that made up Manzanar, it looks like your facilities are better. Did you feel at the time that you had an advantageous situation, compared to your schoolmates whom you would meet at school and came from these other barracks?

No, not really because I saw where my brother [Frank] lived. My sister [Kiyo] was living at the YWCA [Young Women's Christian Association] at another block after she left the Children's Village [and joined our eldest sister Grace at the YWCA].

They had a YWCA at Manzanar, and she moved there? And the bachelor one is where you're brother was, right?

Yeah, my brother [Frank] was at the bachelor one. They did have a YWCA, but I don't know if they had it from the very beginning. But my sister [Kiyo] and some other girl stayed there, after they left Children's Village.

So you had a chance to compare because you had siblings who were in the camp?

Yeah, having a basketball court and having the nice grass, and having our own mess hall, I think it was better. But in the barracks, these people at least had partitions; we had a couple of big rooms: the older kids and the younger kids.

You know, your chef at Children's Village was a person who had worked at Clifton's Cafeteria in Los Angeles, and they had really good food there. But you didn't feel that way, huh? (laughter)

No, you see, we learned at the Salvation Army that we had to eat everything whether we liked it or not. So by the time I got to Children's Village, even if the food wasn't the best, I always ate everything. (laughter)

So you were very good at that. What did you think of the superintendent and his wife, Harry and Lillian Matsumoto? What did you think of them as sort of surrogate parents for you at the camp?

Well, I remember them both. But the boys were probably dealing with Harry Matsumoto more, and they were a fairly young couple. Harry Matsumoto used to play softball with, not the young kids, but the older kids who had a softball team. He used to play; I forgot whether he played first base. Yeah, I thought they were fine. Here again, I think they were probably strict like the people running the Salvation Army. They had to be kind of strict. But by the time I went to Children's Village, I didn't need any supervision. People could leave me alone. But when I first went to Salvation Army, I was only about nine years old.

So you needed more affection, sort of nurturing.

Yeah, you know, people a lot of times think that people who grow up in orphanages or foster parenting don't get much love at all, [so that] when they grow up to be adults it's more difficult for them. But I'll be very honest with you. In my case, living in the Salvation Army when I was really young, maybe even more so than living in the Children's Village, I've always felt that there were people that did care. Even after I left Children's Village and lived with five different families, I had some pretty good experiences. Not all good, but most were pretty good; people showed me that they cared.

And that was true at the Children's Village too, right?

Yes, I would say yes. Except when Ms. [Eva] Robbins took over, it was kind of different.

Oh, could you talk a little bit about that? How did that change?

Well, first of all, I just assumed that she was a widow or something because she had no husband. But we didn't know that she was a federal government employee, and that her job was to find families for us. After I found that out, I realized why I was asked if I wanted to get adopted.

Was she a cold person as opposed to say, the Matsumotos?

Yeah, she didn't seem to be as close because here again, maybe her . . .

Well, she wasn't Japanese American for one thing, right?

But I think more because of her job was different in some respect. I got the feeling that the best interest of the kids was not the main point. The main point was to get them out.

And did you think that was a generally shared feeling?

The kids? I'm not sure because see, in my case, I felt that way because of them asking me if I wanted to get adopted and then how I ended up in Milwaukee [Wisconsin]. I didn't know anything about foster parenting. Even if I did, that was the only way that I was going to be able to live good. Here again, Ms. Robbins must have gotten in touch with the Children's Welfare Society and made those arrangements, I'm sure.

Do you remember when the Matsumotos left, and your feelings about that?

I think my first reaction was that I was really surprised they were leaving so early. I think they were there about two years. I just remember being a little surprised that they were leaving all of a sudden. I guess I knew that people were allowed to leave; I didn't think they had someone who was managing Children's Village. Maybe a kind of a feeling of abandonment, I don't know. Maybe these are things I never talked about with other kids; but maybe some of the other kids had similar feelings.

I asked you earlier if you felt a sense of abandonment when your mother went to Japan. It sounds like you found more abandonment in terms of the Matsumotos leaving than you did with your own mom, right? Maybe that was just a reflection of your age difference.

Sure, I was pretty young when my mother went back. I guess I knew that it wasn't a permanent thing.

Of the two Matsumotos, you spent more time with Harry because he did things with the boys and was a younger person and played sports and stuff. Did you have a relationship with his wife, too?

No, no. I don't remember talking to either of them one-on-one when they were there, because maybe I wasn't getting into any trouble. Or maybe my school grades were good enough, so that they didn't have to talk to me.

So you weren't particularly close to them?

No.

Now I think Lillian Matsumoto was a trained social worker, and her husband was not, although her husband held the position of superintendent and she was the assistant superintendent. Who did you think of when you thought of who was the boss of this place? Who did you think was the boss of the Children's Village?

Well, I think I thought Mr. Matsumoto, Harry Matsumoto.

So you looked towards him as the leader. Did you become close to other staff members who were more hands-on, working with the kids and different kinds of activities?

Well, John Sohei Hohri [See COPH-OH 3786] was the only one that I can remember. Also, I remember another teacher—I don't know if the wife was teaching the girls—but they stayed at the Children's Village for a while. I can't remember the name of the husband. I don't remember where they were from.

It was a husband and wife then? Were they the Nielsons?

I'm not sure. Anyway, the husband used to play softball with us. But other than those people, John was the only one, here again, because I was already twelve or twelve and a half years old, and I didn't need somebody to take care of me. The reason why I got to know John so well is because he used to tell stories to the younger kids, and I used to sit in and listen to his stories a lot, because he was a good storyteller.

Well, that's interesting that you mention that because the next question I was going to ask you was about the same fellow, John Sohei Hohri. One of the things that was legendary about him was that he was a great storyteller, and the kids at the Village liked him because he told those stories. I was going to say maybe you were too old for the stories, but maybe you listened. (laughter)

He was also a good artist. He sketched.

When you were at Manzanar, would you say that the center of your existence was the Children's Village or was it the public school that you went to?

Well I think, because having kids your age that you are seeing more, I would have to say Children's Village was more central than going to school.

Would you participate in any after-school activities? Or would it be a case that you went home right away because you were doing these recreational things at the Village rather than at the school?

The only after-school activity that I got involved in sometimes was softball or other games that were played after school. I'm not sure, but it could have been part of the physical education program. I never got involved in any other clubs or things at school.

When they had sports, they sometimes had block-based teams and stuff. Did the Village sport their own team to play these other blocks?

We had our own team, and we used to play kids from some of these other blocks. I don't think that every block had a basketball court. I know there were some, but there again I remember that the kids that came from regular families didn't specifically like playing with the kids in Children's Village. They didn't want to lose to us either.

Did you make use of the facilities in the general camp, like the dojo *for different kinds of martial arts sports?*

No. I don't remember any of the kids in Children's Village taking up judo or other things. I don't know why that was, whether we were not allowed. I didn't even give it a second thought. Most Nisei kids take up judo and kendo, but that was more when they were living as a family. But the Salvation Army didn't have any of that.

Yeah, because it was really big in the camp as a whole. What about use of the libraries in the camp? Did you go to the library to get a book, or did you have your own library within the Village?

No, we didn't have our own library. But I don't remember going to the library at camp either.

Were you encouraged to stay in your own area, or were the Villagers sort of enjoined to sort of stick, except for going to school, pretty much close to home there?

Yeah. Unless you had friends in other blocks, there was no restriction about visiting them. But, here again, I don't remember kids in Children's Village visiting other kids in other blocks because most kids with families probably didn't want to associate with kids in Children's Village. The kids that were living in Block 29, the Satos and the Neos, used to come over, but I don't remember us going over to their house.

The average age of the Nisei who went to Manzanar was not fifty, it was not forty, it was seventeen and one-half. That's because there were so many kids. You were a bit younger than that, so you would have been a young Nisei and then you have siblings who were in that sort of age group. What was life like for them? Was there, for instance, the same kind of propensity to figure out places where you could be private? At that age, you sort of learn about the other gender, but you also learned about how to be a man or something in those days.

In my own case, it seems like it revolved around school and sports, so I didn't think about it. First of all, I don't remember I had friends I used to visit outside of Children's Village. The only guys that I got to know really well were the guys that used to come over from Block 29: Gordon Sato and his brother [Wilbur] and some of the people who worked there like John [Sohei] Hohri. My brother [Mits], who is a couple years older than me, got into weight lifting. So he used to hang out with some of the Nisei kids close to his age who lived in a block where some kids from Venice, California, used to be. My brother left camp when he was about seventeen and one-half.

So he was just like the average age I was talking about. Now the high school and junior high are periods when there starts to be reaching out to the opposite sex and things like that—if not having torrid love affairs, at least having sort of boyfriend-girlfriend [relationships]. Did you see a lot of the boyfriend-girlfriend thing going on within the Village as opposed to kids from the Village having relationships with people in the other blocks, and people that they met at school? I'm trying to see how closed-off a society the Village was, in terms of social relations and things.

Within the Village itself, I didn't notice any of that, whether it was boys and girls. Of course we would see them in the mess hall and things. I don't think, as far as I recall, we had any assigned seating in the mess hall. We could sit wherever we wanted. But there were very few close relationships between somebody not in Children's Village, but in the Salvation Army. I know one couple in Chicago that ended up getting married.

But you know there are photos of Manzanar having these Jitterbugs and these dances. What did you do for that?

I wasn't into that yet. I don't even recall thinking, "Gee, I'd like to go to that!" I just wasn't, maybe because I was more just into the school and the sport thing.

Did the Children's Village have their own dances, or not?

No, they had a small recreation room, which was in the building where they had the mess hall, a small recreation room, and a room where the Matsumotos or Ms. Robbins stayed. I don't know but I think the older kids—maybe not inside the barracks but outside, where they had a little space—might have had or done a little dancing. Nothing organized.

They would go to the dances in the general camp?

I don't know because I never did. But maybe some of the older kids who were fifteen or seventeen maybe did. I know some of the older kids got involved with some of the school plays directed by Lou Frizzell.[4] He used to come over because I think some of the kids at Children's Village were in some of his classes. But I remember him coming around. In fact, I think I may have a picture of him and my brother. I wasn't in any of his classes, but I only remember him from coming to Children's Village and the fact that he put together some of these plays that were held in the auditorium, where the museum is now.

Thank you very much, Robert, for the interview.

My pleasure.

---

[4]Born on June 10, 1920, actor Lou Frizzell served as the music and drama instructor at Manzanar High School, located in Manzanar camp during World War II. Frizzell went on to become a Hollywood actor best known for playing the character Dusty Rhodes in the 1970s television show, *Bonanza*. In 1976, he played himself in the television movie *Farewell to Manzanar*. Frizzell died on June 17, 1979.

Sharon Kodama[1]

Interviewed by Richard Potashin

Can you tell me what year you were born and where?

In 1938, in Long Beach [Los Angeles County], California.

And your father's name?

Fred Tetsuko Okazaki. And my mother's name was Francis Skaye.

Do you have any particular remembrances about your father? What kind of person was he?

I don't ever remember my parents yelling at me. It was an easy childhood, and I think we had a really good childhood with our parents. I remember, one time, when I cut my head, my dad ran in the sand with a handkerchief on my head to take me to the doctor.

In my mind, I remember a train right off the pier off of Pacific and Ocean Park in Venice [Los Angeles County], California. We used to really love going on that train. And then, I can remember the train ride going to Manzanar. I remember it was dark. I think it was from Los Angeles. Where is that train station now?

Union Station.

Union Station. I remember getting on the train [with her parents and sister]. I don't remember crowds of people. I just remember getting on there. And there was a black porter, who picked up my five-year-old sister [named Helen] and me, with one [of us] in each arm. I just remember looking at him, with he being so big and in this white jacket. And my sister was looking at him and crying because he scared her. But I was just quiet, when I looked at him. And he put us on the train. And I remember the soldiers being on the train with us.

And then I must have fallen asleep on the train because I just remember waking up to the itchy blankets around our necks. I think my sister said she had to go to the bathroom, so we had to go to the bathroom in the dirt,

[1]Manzanar National Historic Site (National Park Service) Oral History Program-Oral History 1041 was conducted on September 9, 2005, in West Hills, California.

because there were no bathrooms around. But I remember her saying the blankets were those army blankets. They were up against our necks because it was cold. It must have been somewhere in March when we were relocated, and it was very cold. So we had those blankets that were itching my sister's neck, and she was crying about it. So our mom put towels around her neck. I remember that.

And I remember things at camp, like sitting out there that summer with my parents on the steps. Here in Los Angeles you don't see the stars that much; you see fog. You look up and you don't see the stars like you do at Manzanar. At Manzanar, you looked up and the stars were so bright and so clear. I remember sitting on that wooden step in front of that little shack and looking at the stars with my mom. And I remember faking falling asleep, and my mom would carry me in. I just remember that.

And then I remember there was this show, this Japanese show. I don't remember what the show was about, but it was something Japanese. When we went home, we couldn't find our place. Everything was just pitch black. I figured we must have lived somewhere around the end of a block. When I see that little map of the camp today, I think we were on the end because our dad just walked and walked. We went in the wrong direction, and we couldn't find our place. So we had to turn around and walk another way, and I think my dad went to the very end and then counted the buildings backwards to wherever we were because we couldn't tell which was our house. We were just lost out there.

Very disorienting environment out there. All the buildings look the same, especially if you add that darkness to the picture. Then it's really difficult.

And we were just lost out there anyway.

What did your father do for work in Manzanar? Do you recall that?

I think he was a cook because I saw his picture in one of the museums, I think, here in Los Angeles. I saw a display one time and saw his name. I would think that's what he would do because he had a restaurant.

I don't remember going to any school. I think we stayed with our mom. That was only a short time. If we were there in March [1942] and they died ... Was it October? Was it September? That wasn't too much time.

September 25. And here it states that your block address was 35-13-1 [Block 35, Barrack 13, Apartment 1]. Block 35 would have been on the end.

It would have been on the end?

It would have been way off to the north end of the camp. There were two blocks...

I think I saw the map somewhere, when I was at Manzanar once. I think that's when I discovered where we were. I remember being lost that night, and it being pitch black, and I felt like we were walking and walking and walking.

Were you scared?

Well, no, because my mom and dad were there. I figured that they're the ones who would be afraid; they're the ones who took the brunt of everything. But I do remember the night they died. I can remember.

What do you remember about that?

I can remember the night before. I saw that my mom had put a little wire across the room, and this side was my sister and my side, and the other side was my mom and dad's side. And there was this little sheet going across the room. And on this one night, my mom said, "Oh, Helen can sleep with me, and you can sleep with Daddy, okay?" So that's how we went to bed: my sister in my mom's bed and I in my dad's bed.

But when I woke up in the morning, we were both in the same bed, where we usually were. Then Helen said that she had to go pee. She said, "I have to go to the bathroom," so I could hear her running over to wake my mom up. And she's trying to wake my mother up, and our mother does not wake up. And then, I ran out there and I was trying to wake my dad up. And he wouldn't wake up. And there were all kinds of people crowding to the screen—well to the door—and you could hear them rapping. And I think my sister went over there and opened the door because I could see out and I could see the screen. On the screen door, there's a little hook on the screen and one of our neighbors said, "Open up the door! Open up the door!" But we wouldn't go there. So he got out a matchbook out of his pocket and flipped open the thing, and stuck it through, opened the cover of it, and flipped up the latch, and then the neighbors came and took us out. But I could hear my dad breathing. I could hear him gurgling.

They took us out. And no one ever told us that they died. I mean, no one tells little kids anything. No one said anything, and I didn't know what the funeral was about. I remember going to the funeral because I heard the gongs. I smelled the incense, but no one said, "Hey, you're never going to see your mother and father again."

So nobody ever tried to sit down and explain to you that your parents were dead?

Nope.

They were just not there anymore?

No one said anything. We were just led out of our place where we lived and went to the neighbors. It was in the Buddhist Church. That funeral meant nothing to me: the gongs and the incense meant nothing. Does that tell you that your parents are dead, when you've never seen a funeral before? After the funeral, I think we stayed with a neighbor, and then we went to the orphanage and lived there for three years. Three years is forever for a child!

So moving to the [Children's Village] orphanage happened quickly after the funeral?

Yeah. Another thing that was traumatic to my sister and me: my sister always worried about us being separated. You know, she would always shove me in the back whenever somebody would come in and look at the kids for adoption. And at the time, I just thought, what is she doing? Later on she told me, "I was always afraid that you were going to get adopted." She thought that she was not as adoptable because she was not as friendly, and she thought that I was too friendly. She thought that somebody would just pick me up and adopt me. So that was her fear, but I didn't know that at the time. She told me that later, which is kind of a sad thing. I do know that my aunt was trying to get hold of us through correspondence with a lady. That was Mrs. Tanaka.

Mrs. Tanaka? And she was the woman who kept you for a while?

No, Mrs. Tanaka did not keep us. I met her when we were in Children's Village. She came over to visit and said that she corresponded with my aunt. She said that we were going to live with my aunt later. And that was the only explanation that we got during the whole time, through her. She took us home and told us. She showed us a picture of my aunt, which was a big relief to my sister. My sister was just so happy to hear that we were going to be together. I don't know why we were staying there in the orphanage for so long, when there was somebody [Kodama's aunt Buni Kinoshita and her uncle Tom Tagami] wanting us there in Harrington [Lincoln County,

190 miles east of Seattle], Washington. I mean, we were there at Children's Village for three years. Half of my life, at that time! So that part I don't understand, and I don't think my aunt or uncle ever understood either. But part of it might be a guardianship thing.

So she had to spend lots of time and money to prove guardianship?

Yeah, I'm not sure how that worked. I know my aunt had to get a lawyer. I'm not sure if she hired these two ladies who came to get us after the war. Then during the war, she had a difficult time. I think just to be out of camp, you had to get permission. It took a lot of work just to go anywhere past a fifty-mile radius. So there's no way my aunt and uncle could travel to Manzanar when my parents died. I think they were telegraphed that my mom and dad died.

Correct, I just saw that . . . There are a couple of telegrams here from your Uncle Tagami, trying to secure permission.

And they say go ahead with the funeral . . . But from this you would have thought that the WRA would have corresponded with my aunt and uncle about our property, and about us leaving the camp because we were out of the area.

Right, it took so long. They were communicating with [Uncle] Tagami about the funeral and how if he wants to come down to the funeral, he needs to get a military permit.

That would probably take a year or so—

Are you certain, one way or the other, Tagami didn't come down for the funeral?

No, nobody came down for the funeral.

Nobody from the family came down because of this burdensome paperwork, most likely. It took a lot to get a permit because they were entering an exclusion zone. They would have had to have escorts to take them down to Manzanar. And at that point, if they came down, it would seem that they would have wanted to leave with you.

Yeah, you would have thought that. You know, part of their problem was my aunt and uncle both spoke Japanese. They didn't speak English very clearly; they had a hard time. You know, they spoke English and they read English.

And conversation-wise, they could get through what they were saying, but it wasn't easy.

It might have been intimidating for them as well.

I think so. I think it was very intimidating, even to talk to a lawyer and to talk to a lawyer about us. I don't think this lawyer my aunt hired did anything for us, except take the money.

Going back just a little bit, did you ever get any correspondence from your aunt while you were in the orphanage? Any letters from her or from anybody?

No, no. Why would she write to us when we were three and five, or four and six? I don't think we could even read or write, but she did send a picture of herself to Mrs. Tanaka, so she wouldn't be a stranger to us.

What are your first recollections of being in the orphanage?

I remember being in there and seeing these kids all pass us, just looking at us, while my sister and I were standing there in a room. I think we were just brought in. I had never seen so many kids! I had never been to a school. In fact, I had probably never seen so many Japanese! I remember seeing all these kids, and I think that we spoke Japanese, and I don't know if a lot of things registered in my mind because I think my mother and father spoke Japanese to me, and everything at Children's Village was in English. It was very disorganized in my mind. I don't know what was said in the conversations, and I think it was because I didn't know any English.

And maybe even not knowing where you really were?

No, I did not know where I was. And no one told us anything. No one told us where we were. I didn't even know the place was called the Children's Village or it was an orphanage until much later, until I was older and looked into it. And I didn't realize that there was only one orphanage in all of the camps. When you think about it, 101 children going through the Children's Village isn't very many for the number of people that were in all the camps. Most relatives—most Japanese people—take care of their own. So it's really amazing to me to think that my aunt had to sit there for three years without us, and knowing that she was going to get us, and something wasn't done sooner.

That added to an already very traumatic experience.

See, but I didn't know these things that were so sad at the time they were going on. Basically, my sister and I were protected because we were children. Maybe it was a good thing that no one said anything; but then, I think we did deserve an explanation or some sort of hopeful message, like that one from Mrs. Tanaka who was there.

What else do you recall about the Children's Village and your time there?

I remember the little children; the babies' quarter was right next to my bed. I would see this little baby who was in his crib and he would be rocking back and forth and saying "Ah, ah, ah." I remember little things like how the teenagers would come and play with us. There was one girl who was very, very nice to me. She used to come sit with me and talk to me. I don't remember her name, but I just remember she wore a sailor hat, a white sailor hat. She'd come over and talk to me. I remember there was a chair right beside every bed, and every day there would be clothes, you know, folded neatly: underwear, everything all stacked up, and then one little sock on top. The sock would be balled and put together, sitting right on top of the clothes, everyday. And I think I remember seeing women sewing over there, and they would be making clothes for the kids. I remember a picture taken. I think we were all dressed up in the same outfits for Easter, and everybody at this age would have that little pinafore dress on. I looked at that picture and I recognized the outfit I was wearing in that picture.

After we left camp, I remember when my aunt saw the clothes from the orphanage in a big, boxed crate. She just looked at them and threw them away because they were "so shabby," she said. She couldn't believe how poor and shabby these clothes from the orphanage were! She said that she wouldn't send them to even the poorest people in Japan. I can remember her saying that. And I don't know how we got the clothes, or maybe they were just the leftovers from the orphanage, but she looked at them and couldn't believe it.

So was your sister in the bed next to you in the orphanage?

No, I think they did it by age.

By age? There were just beds lined up along the wall there?

Yeah, there was one huge room. There was a room for babies, and then there was the huge room for younger kids. I think that's where the majority of children were, and then there was a bathroom in between. There was a bathroom, a storeroom, and then there was a room for older girls. That's all

I could see. I mean, I never went to the boys' area. It was like a little prison! We could go outside to go to the bathroom, but I think that was my whole life for three years.

That's it? You don't remember ever going out to any other parts of the camp at all?

I went one time with this lady who was trying to be nice with me, but I didn't like that lady. I remember going out with her once. And I remember going out to see Mrs. Tanaka [person who was receiving correspondence from Kodama's aunt regarding the Kodama sisters] once. And then, we did go to school everyday. But I didn't go to school until I was five, and I was four when I entered Children's Village. I was there a whole year before I ever got out of that room to go to school. So I was confined to Children's Village for at least, I would say, a year until I got to school, just a regular, public preschool. At five, six years old, I went to kindergarten.

I didn't realize it at the time, but the children stuck together. All the children in the village did stick together. I remember that, when it was really snowing and cold, the older boys would give us little kids a piggyback ride back to the Children's Village. I don't know how far the school was from the Children's Village, but we went to regular public school.

Right, yeah. Well, originally, I think the school was scattered in a number of different little recreation rooms on each block. And then they consolidated the school into block sixteen, which wouldn't have been very far away from Children's Village. It would have been pretty close. Do you remember the grounds at all around the Children's Village—the gardens or trees?

I remember the tea garden. The tea garden was somewhere where we could sit. I don't know if it was for the children or whether we were free to go in there. But I think we called it the tea garden. There was a gazebo and benches at each one of them. I remember running on the benches and trying to jump to the next one.

And I remember the butterflies. There was a man there who used to catch butterflies and pin them on something and display them. I remember trying to catch the butterflies without harming them, and then he would put a drop of something on them to kill them. Then he would stack them. I don't know who he was or what.

So you were trying to collect them?

He was collecting them, and we were helping him catch them. But I don't know what he was doing there, but I just remember that

What games do you remember playing amongst the kids?

I remember the games; they did have games. Oh, racing! Racing. I remember my sister was a really good runner; she would even beat the boys. She was very proud of that. And I don't remember if it was in school or if it was at the Children's Village, but we used to jump rope. They had jump rope, they had little hop-scotches, and things like that. But I think it was at the school because I think we played with the regular children.

So you don't recall any really good, steady girl friends that you hung out with?

No, isn't that funny? I never got attached.

Do you recall any special holidays or things that happened on Christmas or Thanksgiving or special occasions that were celebrated by the kids?

Nope, I don't remember any special occasions. I don't even remember anybody having a birthday celebrated.

How about your birthday?

No, I did not. I don't think I had a birthday there. I don't think anybody celebrated anybody's birthday. I don't remember. Because I remember the day I arrived in Harrington, Washington. My birthday had just passed. After my first day of school, I got home and there was a birthday cake. I don't remember having a birthday cake at Children's Village, so it was the first time I ever recall having a birthday cake and blowing out candles. And that was when I was seven years old.

One of the questions about the area around the Children's Village was an orchard of pear trees and apple trees. Do you have any recollections of that?

I don't, although when I went back and I saw them, I just realized that they were there. But I did not actually have any memories of them. I just remember the cotton falling down off those one trees, the cottonwood trees. I do remember the cotton. And when I went back to visit Manzanar and saw the cotton falling down off those trees, I said, "I remember these trees." It was hot summer, and you would feel like it's snowing, you know, so I remember the cottonwood trees.

Do you recall the day that you left camp?

Yes, I do.

What was that like?

We got on a bus. We didn't know why, but we just got on the bus. And then, you know, coming into the camp it was dark, or I maybe I was asleep or something. I didn't remember having been outside the camp. Period. So coming out was like after somebody's been in prison. When you were three yours old, you don't remember a lot of things on the outside. So I remember getting on that bus, and I hadn't been on a car or bus or anything for all that time. Then I saw the mountains; they stuck with me. I could see the mountains in the background fading away, as we went to Los Angeles. I've done the trip many times since and have tried to picture what I must have seen when I was leaving camp.

But it was going to an orphanage in Los Angeles that I really remember. At the orphanage, I saw bricks and I saw ivy. At the time, I didn't know that it was ivy. The orphanage building was maybe a three- or four-story building, and it was brick, made out of brick. There were also sidewalks and a lawn. And I remember looking at that building and saying to myself, "Oh, my gosh!" I probably had never seen a building like that before going into the orphanage. Then I don't know how I didn't get lost without my sister there next to me. I don't remember how many kids went to the Los Angeles orphanage, but I remember being by myself and walking through a great big, front double door and seeing furniture. I mean just seeing furniture and carpet! It was a big, fancy, huge room, and I just had to stare because it was just like, "Wow!" And I saw a big roll-top desk with a lady sitting in front of it. And she scared me because when she saw me, she turned around and she looked. I just bolted out of there! And I saw a staircase, and I was just thinking, "Oh, my gosh!" You know, you don't remember those things. It's just an ordinary thing, but when you are seven years old and you have never seen it before ... At camp, we didn't even see movies. We didn't even have TV. So I guess it was like being in a foreign world after being in prison.

And suddenly being "out"!

Out! Yeah, that's the way to describe it.

I know it was a long time ago, but can you recall any of your emotional reactions to the feeling of not only leaving the Children's Village—which to you was like a prison, or a confinement in itself within another confinement, which was the camp—but then going to Los Angeles. Like you said, suddenly the world is open to you, but how about any emotional connections? How did you feel at that time?

Well, the surprise of seeing overstuffed furniture, the stairways, and things like that. As a child, you just look around and you can't believe what you're seeing. But we weren't at the Los Angeles orphanage very long. We must have been there just a very short time, and then these two ladies, Margaret and Elizabeth, came to pick us up there.

Do you remember anything about them?

Oh, yeah. One thing that they did was change our names. We were sitting on the train and one of them she said, "We have to get new names for you. You can't use these Japanese names. They are just too hard to pronounce, and in the little town you are going to, it would just be easier to get an American name." So she named Helen "Himeko Helen," because it was close. And I was named "Shizuko Sharon." We kept those names for the rest of our lives. But the funny part of it is, all the rest of the people in my family, like my cousin, my aunt's son Josho, and Sidal always use their Japanese names, and no one ever had a problem pronouncing them. And they lived in Harrington all their lives.

We went with Margaret and Elizabeth back to the same train station that we used to go to camp, at Los Angeles's Union Station. We got on a train that would go to Spokane, Washington. Then we went to Harrington. I think we spent at least one night on the train. Compared to the train to Manzanar, we had a really different trip because it was very luxurious! We had berths that folded down, and we were sleeping in beds. And we were in dining cars and had really fancy food and drank from glasses, which we didn't have in either the camp or in the children's orphanage in Los Angeles. I don't think we had that. But getting on the train, we had these luxuries like napkins you know, and sheets—well, we must have had sheets in camp. But just looking at the world through this little window in the train was just amazing!

Then when we arrived in Spokane and got off the train, we went to a dime store, a ten-cent store. And my sister and I were both to buy a present for my aunt. My sister picked out a pair of blue plastic earrings for my aunt. I saw what she picked out and said, "Oh, that looks good!" So I picked out a pair of pink ones. She just gave me this dirty look and said, "You picked out the same thing that I picked out," and I said, "Yes!" We had all this stuff to pick from, and I could have really picked out something different. But those were our presents to my aunt, and I think they both cost ten cents! The funny part of it was, because we didn't know my aunt, we didn't even know that she had never worn a pair of earrings in her life! But she kept those earrings all her life. And when she died, I found the earrings, the pink ones and the blue ones.

Do you remember anything else?

When we arrived in Harrington, I knew my cousin—[the] Tagamis' son—because when we first got to camp, he was there working on a crew. Takagi had also babysat me when I was a year old; he was like eighteen years old when he took care of me! So when I went to Harrington, there he was! I had one familiar face that was just really happy to see us. And they were all just so overjoyed to see us. But we didn't know the joy because, except for my cousin Takagi, we were actually meeting strangers. It was a new beginning.

Sharon, thank you so much for telling your story.

Thank you.

Harry and Lillian Matsumoto with Sarah who lived at Children's Village
for approximately one year before Lillian returned her to her mother,
who was at Heart Mountain Relocation Center in Wyoming. Baby Sarah was
"exchanged" by Lillian via a social worker from Heart Mountain in Ogden, Utah.

Harry and Lillian Matsumoto with the infants on the Village lawn.

March 1943, diapers are floating between Building 2 and Building 3. Part of the Gazebo can be seen directly behind Building 2.

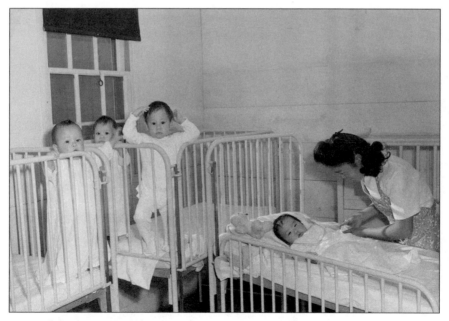

Some of the nursery residents.

Mrs. May Ichida with pre-schoolers on seesaw and
wooden horses made by the gardeners.

Toddlers with staff on the
swings made by gardeners.

Baseball field within
Children's Village area.

The orphans ranged
in age from infants to
eighteen years.

Chapter Three
The Staff
of Children's Village

In the months leading up to the removal of orphans of Japanese ancestry, the California State Department of Social Welfare, along with other public assistance agencies had recommended to the War Relocation Authority (WRA) that "the best plan for the children would involve continued association of the present staff with the children both during the interim and at the permanent relocation center."[1] As a result, while most individuals relocated to Manzanar camp with their immediate families, the Nisei staffs at the Shonien and the Salvation Army Home had to decide before removal whether they wanted to remain in their jobs and continue caring for orphan children. Since Shonien staff members Lillian and Harry Matsumoto were appointed assistant superintendent and superintendent of Children Village, and the majority of orphan children sent to Children's Village were from the Shonien, the entire Shonien staff was approved to continue working as staff at Children's Village.[2] Besides the Shonien staff, three staff persons from the Salvation Army Home also continued their work at the Children's Village.[3] The Matsumotos' staff would ultimately grow to thirty-six workers and would include not just child-care supervisors, but child-care "helpers," maintenance and utility personnel as well.[4]

Harry and Lillian Matsumoto were both university graduates with the special training needed for their job as superintendents of Children's Village. Harry Matsumoto had graduated from UCLA with a major in business.[5] While still a senior at UCLA, he began assisting Shonien Director Rokuichi

[1] War Relocation Authority. "Report on Children's Village" (February 1946), 3. See also Helen Whitney, "Care of Homeless Children of Japanese Ancestry During Evacuation and Relocation" (M.A. thesis, University of California, Berkeley, 1948), 15.

[2] Ford Kuramoto, *A History of the Shonien, 1914-1972: An Account of a Program of Institutional Care of Japanese Children in Los Angeles* (San Francisco: R and E Associates, 1976), 44.

[3] Ibid. See also Whitney, 19.

[4] Whitney, 19.

[5] Lillian Matsumoto and Taeko Nagayama, Interview with Lisa Nobe, 12-13 May 1994, CSUF-Center for Oral and Public History.

"Joy" Kusumoto and "was being groomed for the superintendent's position."[6]
Lillian Matsumoto, who had graduated from UC Berkeley's Graduate School
of Social Welfare in 1935, was also hired to assist Kusumoto at the Shonien
and "joined the staff as the first graduate trained social worker" hired by the
Shonien.[7]

Born in 1913 in Salt Lake City, Utah, Lillian Matsumoto was the
daughter of Hiro Iida, the publisher and editor of the Japanese language
newspaper, *Rocky Mountain Times (Rokiji-ho)*, who had immigrated to
the United States in 1906 to help his older brother with the newspaper.
Matsumoto's mother, Isa Mary Tomida Iida, was the daughter of one of Japan's
first Episcopalian ministers; she came to Salt Lake City in 1912 to join her
husband after their arranged marriage. Lillian's family moved to Berkeley,
California, in 1929, where she attended UC Berkeley and became a social
worker. Lillian and Harry Matsumoto met while they were both working
at the Shonien and married in February of 1942.[8] In the following excerpt,
Lillian Matsumoto shares some of her most vivid memories of administering
and working with the staff and children of the Children's Village.

According to Lillian Matsumoto, the Shonien staff members who
accompanied the children to Manzanar "were all young, unmarried women
in their mid-twenties. One of them [Taeko Kajiwara Nagayama] had been
raised in Shonien from the age of ten and had returned to become one of our
staff."[9] Like other Shonien staff members, Taeko Nagayama was also a high
school graduate. She continued her education at Woodbury Business College
until she had to leave as a result of the war and relocation orders. When she
was ten years old, Nagayama and her four younger sisters were placed at the
Shonien after their mother and father became ill with tuberculosis and were
sent to a sanitarium in Los Angeles. She and her younger sister Fuji went
with the group from the Shonien to Children's Village, with Taeko as a staff
worker and Fuji as one of the orphan children (her other three sisters were
adopted, while at the Shonien).[10] In the following excerpt, Nagayama, who
left Manzanar in 1943, recalls her experience as a staff member at Children's

---

[6] Kuramoto, 28.

[7] Ibid, 28.

[8] Lillian Matsumoto and Taeko Nagayama, Interview with Lisa Nobe, 12-13 May
1994, CSUF-Center for Oral and Public History.

[9] Lillian Matsumoto, "Memories of Manzanar: The Story of the Children's Village"
(unpublished memoir/manuscript, 2007), 7.

[10] Lillian Matsumoto and Taeko Nagayama, Interview with Lisa Nobe, 12-13 May
1994, CSUF-Center for Oral and Public History.

Village and then her courtship with former Children's Village staff member John Nagayama.

One of the Village children's most beloved staff members was Sohei Hohri, who told stories to the boys at night in their dormitory. Hohri's Issei father Diasuke was a Christian clergyman who decided to move his family to the United States to help minister to the Nikkei community in California. Hohri and his younger brother William lived at the Shonien temporarily from 1930-1934, after his parents were sent to a sanitarium to recover from tuberculosis and his four other siblings were either sent to live with families or to also recover from ill health.[11] In this chapter, Hohri shares details of his two-year experience at the Shonien, as well as his memories of working as a storyteller at the Children's Village.

---

[11] Hohri's brother Wiliam would grow up to become a leader in the Japanese American Redress Movement, and in 1986, was the key figure in the movement's class action lawsuit *William Hohri, et al, v. the United States of America.*

Lillian Matsumoto & Taeko Nagayama[1]

Interviewed by Lisa Nobe

Could either one of you tell me how the two of you met?

TN: Well, I went to the orphanage when I was about nine or ten years old. Lillian wasn't there yet, but she came later on. I can't recall what year it was. Do you remember, Lillian?

LM: Nineteen thirty-five, right after I finished my training at Cal [University of California, Berkeley].

TN: Nineteen thirty-five? So it must have been about five years, because I think it was about 1930 when I went into the orphanage.

And when you say the orphanage, do you mean the Shonien?

TN: The Shonien in Los Angeles [California], right.

And how old were you?

TN: I was about nine or ten years old.

And Lillian, when did you first start working at the Shonien?

LM: I was hired by the Shonien to be their caseworker. That was probably in the fall of 1935, right after I had finished my training at Berkeley.

And do you remember how old you were then? (chuckling)

LM: How old was I? (chuckling) I was born in 1913, and it was 1935 when I went there. So how old would I be? Twenty-something? (chuckling)

So, Lillian, you were born in 1913. And Taeko, when were you born?

TN: In 1921.

Are you both Nisei?

---

[1]COPH-Oral History 2494 was conducted on May 13, 1994, in El Cerrito, California.

TN: Yes.

LM: Yes.

Do either of you speak Japanese at all?

TN: I speak very little.

LM: The same. (laughter)

Lillian, at what point did you and Harry [Matsumoto] get married?

LM: The war started in 1941—wasn't it December of 1941? We were married in February of 1942.

How did the two of you meet?

LM: I met him at Shonien. He was a volunteer worker. I went there in 1935 to work, and he was there. He's a Los Angeles boy—man. (laughter) He graduated from Hollywood High and then went to UCLA [University of California, Los Angeles]. He passed away in 1988, just before his eightieth birthday.

Taeko, in the Shonien, once you became eighteen, did you have to leave? I mean, were children then seen as adults and had to leave the orphanage?

TN: I think the majority had to leave after they graduated.

But you stayed on as a staff member?

TN: Yes.

Stepping off the bus and seeing Manzanar, what was your general impression?

TN: I can't even remember that part, stepping out of the bus. I don't know why. I don't know. (chuckling) I can't remember. It's terrible how there's different times I just can't remember.

LM: Even to me, the recollection isn't too clear. The only thing I do remember: as the bus pulled through the gate and up to where the Children's Village was located, the people who were already in Manzanar sort of stared. They probably knew who we were and probably looked at us rather strangely. I kind of sense and remember that. But once the bus stopped at the Children's Village building, I think we were just too busy getting the children off and getting them settled. I know I remember it being very, very hot. (chuckling)

And the children were tired. I remember that. But I don't think there was actually anything out of the ordinary.

So, seeing the desert and everything didn't really hit you in any way?

LM: We just came through the Mojave Desert, and when you see this picture of the children, there are so many that are under ten. So I think to them—and we sort of explained it to them—for many of them, it was a new adventure that we were going through. I think they were very eager to see Manzanar and the new place where they were coming to live.

Do you remember approximately how long the ride was?

LM: We left probably around 8:00, 9:00 in the morning, and there was one stopover someplace where they had a chance to go to the bathroom. But we didn't take anything to eat or anything on the bus or stop anywhere for a meal. Did we?

TN: I don't recall.

LM: But I think it was probably mid-afternoon when we arrived there.

And were the shades drawn on the bus? Did they put something in the bus so you couldn't see out?

LM: Oh no, there was nothing. But there was a military police [MP] sitting in the front of the bus next to the driver.

Of each bus?

LM: Yes.

And was one bus for boys and one for girls?

LM: Yes.

So were you on the bus with the girls?

LM: Yes, the girls. I have to tell you this one experience. For the children to be entertained, different girls would get up and sing or do whatever. This one little girl—her name escapes me—but I can still picture her coming up and saying that she was going to sing. She must have only been about four years old, three or four years old, and she started singing "God Bless America." And then, whenever she didn't know the words, she'd just hum a little, and that was the way she would sing it. (chuckling) But this young MP was a very young soldier, and he put his head down. He was crying. And I noticed that because I was sitting in the aisle criss-cross from him. I remember that. But when the bus stopped and we got out to use the bathroom and take the children to the bathroom, this MP had to stand up and be on guard with his bayonet. (chuckling) And what the children would have done . . . (laughter)

Did you feel that it was kind of ludicrous to have an MP on the bus? I mean, the bus was just a bunch of kids?

LM: Yes. I was, I think, surprised. I don't know at what point the MP joined us, whether he came up to the Shonien, because that's where we were loaded on the bus. I don't remember whether he came to the Shonien and started from there or whether the bus picked him up someplace in downtown Los Angeles.

You were talking about the time when one of the little girls sang "God Bless America" and the MP put his head down and cried. In general, do you think among the white administration at camp and the MPs that there was a general sense that there was something wrong about internment, and they were just carrying their orders out?

LM: I really can't say because, at least in my work, I didn't have that kind of contact with the MPs or soldiers that were assigned there.

How about the white administration?

LM: I think some of them felt that internment was an injustice; and the others probably thought it was a job they were carrying out.

Lillian, let's talk about choosing the site of the Children's Village. When you and Harry went up to Manzanar, did you actually get to choose and say, "This is where we would like the orphanage to be?" Did they agree with that?

LM: I think, at the time, the project director agreed with us; but of course the final say would have been the army engineers, or whoever was in charge to build it. We didn't want Children's Village to be put in some corner, isolated from the rest of the community, but it was near enough. We were part of the community, but not right in the midst of it. And then we were next to the orchard, which I thought gave a setting for the Village. And then the other consideration was that we would be near the hospital. And they did pick the site that we more or less hoped they would.

When you first got to Manzanar, what was it like being among so many Japanese Americans, so many others of the same ethnic group as you? What was that like?

LM: I don't think it made any particular impression. It just seemed like a natural thing to us. Maybe it was because my work and my contacts were always with the Japanese, socially, in business, and in my work at the Shonien. So being with so many other Japanese Americans seems just a natural thing.

Taeko, how about you?

TN: I don't really have that much of an impression. I just took things as they came. I don't know why. I know I was there in my late teens, but it was just kind of hazy. I just kind of took things as they came.

Was it exciting, in a way, to be around so many other Japanese Americans?

TN: I guess, sort of, yeah.

How about in terms of the Caucasian staff? Do you remember Margaret D'Ille?

LM: Yes, because the Children's Village came under her supervision. Wasn't the title she had Director of Community Affairs or something like that? We were directly under her, so what we needed or anything would go through her. We would present it to her. But she was a very cooperative and understanding person, a much older person. I think she was from a missionary family, and she had lived in Japan a long, long time. So she understood and spoke a little Japanese herself.

Did she actually have an office in the Village?

LM: No, she was down in the regular section where all the offices were.

Did she come to the Village regularly to check up on it?

LM: She'd come, but I think her visits were more like friendly visits. They didn't seem to be official or to check up on what was being done or anything. I think we held a weekly meeting with her down in her office to go over whatever was necessary and give her reports.

When she came to the Village, would she interact with the children?

LM: Oh, yes, she was a friendly person.

TN: I think so. I remember meeting her.

LM: She was a large person, a big person, and a very friendly person. I think the children would come to her.

To what extent did you deal with Ralph Merritt [the director of the Manzanar Relocation Center]?

LM: Very closely, as far as the Village was concerned. We also got to know him on a social basis.

Did you have dinner with him on occasion?

LM: No, not too often, because Harry and I felt that that might work against us with the Japanese, and so we didn't do that, going to the point of having dinner with him. I think we had dinner with Mrs. D'Ille in her apartment.

Would Ralph Merritt come over to Children's Village and visit?

LM: Oh, yes, I think he would always bring every visitor of any distinction who came to Manzanar camp to Children's Village. I think Children's Village was sort of his pride and joy, too.

Did he ever play with the children or interact with the children in any way?

LM: Oh, yes. Very friendly.

When he came to visit the children, were his visits frequent?

LM: If he was ever in the area where Children's Village was, he quite often stopped by just to say hello. And he would go into the kitchen and shake hands with the kitchen staff or talk with some of the staff members. He made himself known in a very friendly way.

Taeko, what would you say was the major difference between the Shonien and the Children's Village? Or what similarities can you draw from the two?

TN: Well, the thing I noticed most when we went to Children's Village and merged with the Salvation Army children [those who lived at the Salvation Army orphanage in San Francisco prior to World War II] was that, boy, they were rough! (chuckling) The children from the Salvation Army, or the boys I guess you would say, were much bigger, older teenagers. They were big, and our kids were more or less younger.

LM: Under ten years old. (chuckling)

TN: Yes, and I thought, boy, what a rough bunch! (laughter) But they seemed very friendly after we got to know them. I don't know if I ever gave it a thought, if there was that much difference. I guess we met a lot of new people. In camp, you don't just meet people at the Children's Village. You meet people from outside.

LM: I think we encouraged the older children to make friends with other children in Manzanar.

Outside of Children's Village?

LM: Yes. And they were going to the same schools, attending church, and so forth. But we did restrict one thing. At every meal, the children should come back to the Village. See, one of the problems that I think many of the families had was that they didn't know where their children were. They were gone, and then they would eat in other dining halls and so forth. Their family life kind of disintegrated there. But we had a strict restriction that the children could go and make friends and everything, but for every meal, like lunch or dinner, they would have to be back in the Village. And they kept that. They were very good. And I think with that, we had cohesion of children being together. They weren't scattered. So, I hate to use the word control, but at least I think we were able to stay together.

In instances where the children misbehaved, how would you handle that? I know, for instance, from talking to some of the kids that were from the Salvation Army that they were physically abused; in some instances they were hit.

LM: We didn't discipline like that. I think most of the time, discipline was through talks with them and so forth, but I don't think there was any kind of physical handling of the children for disciplinary purposes. Certainly not at the Shonien and not at the Village. The Shonien never did it that way.

I know this might be a tough question, Lillian, but can you describe or explain your philosophy, in terms of what you felt your responsibility was towards orphan children at the time of the Shonien and at the time of internment? What did you feel were your responsibilities to them?

LM: Well, to me, after I finished school and I got the job at the Shonien, it was just a job. As they said, "We need a caseworker and we have nothing here, in terms of a record for each family." So I had to establish a record for every family, and I thought it was a job. But then, I think it was Mr. [Rokuichi "Joy"] Kusumoto's [founding director of the Shonien] philosophy and his attitudes. He was a very strict person in the Japanese sense, but he was also a very kind and gentle and understanding person. I don't think he liked to show that, but he was that way. I think I got to know his feelings about these children, children that didn't have parents, or if they had parents, couldn't be with them, and what we had to give these children in place of their parents, in how we took care of them and so forth. I think his philosophy sort of grew into me. I felt that that was part of my job, to not be a parent, but somebody older than the children that they can lean on for help. I think this just carried on at the Village, and I think the workers that went with us from Shonien were all workers with that kind of feeling. I don't think they would have gone with us, if they didn't have that feeling that these children needed help and that we could give it to them.

Did you feel that your position or role in administration wasn't necessarily to spend time with the children as much as, let's say, for Taeko or Alice [Kaneko]? Or would you say that no, your position was that you needed to spend time with the children as well as do the administrative type of work?

LM: I think so. I didn't do any hands-on direct care of them, you know. They had to feed the babies, change and bathe them, and all the other things; but then I felt that my presence should be known, be shown that I care, and that I'm there if they needed me. So I had some of the children that, after they'd come home from school and they had problems, they would come up and talk to me, even though they were only ten, twelve years old. So I think this was my plan and my feelings, that I establish some kind of . . . I don't want to say like I'm a mother to them, not that way, but then that I was someone that they could come to.

So the physical affection wasn't really there between you and, say, the orphanage kids? I mean, would you hug them?

LM: No, you don't show physical . . . you know, like embracing them or something, because you've got so many that you don't want to show to one or to the other. I think that was my feeling, but I felt their needs, not just physical needs but their needs for attention or love or whatever.

I think, consciously or unconsciously, I think part of it is the way I was raised by my parents, that it just fits my personality, my attitude towards the children. I don't think my mother ever hugged me like a mother would do now or give me a big kiss or anything, but I never ever felt that she didn't love me. I always felt that she cared for me and loved me, and I thought she gave me that feeling in some other way. So I think it's that kind of a feeling that I always had towards the children there. Each one meant something to me.

Taeko, how about you? When you were staff at Children's Village, how did you feel about the children and your role towards them?

TN: I learned better later, but at the time, I just kind of took it as a routine matter of taking care of them, that I should be doing this and so forth.

What kind of duties did you have or do?

TN: I'm surprising myself that I can't remember so many things in detail. I can remember helping to take care of the little ones, the little toddlers, saying goodnight to the girls, but I can't remember the regular routine. (chuckling)

What were your feelings when you got to Manzanar, coming with the orphans? Were you self-conscious that you were coming as an orphanage? Or did you feel that you were just like the rest of the internees?

LM: No, I don't remember if I had any special feelings that I was different because we had all these children and we were bringing them there. I think my concern was to get them established and into a feeling that this was their home now, probably just trying to keep the same feeling we had with the children of Shonien. I didn't want them isolated from the rest of the Manzanar community. We liked to have the older ones participate. We naturally had to have the younger ones, of course, the toddlers and a little older, with us. Those that came from the San Francisco [Salvation Army] orphanage were high school age, and I think we tried to have them participate in anything.

Taeko, how about your feelings when you first got to camp, first as an orphan and then coming on as staff?

TN: When I think back, it almost seemed like a dream. I mean, it didn't seem like it was a reality. I don't know. I went along with the orphanage group, and I just did what I thought I should do. I didn't really have any special feeling. I just kind of went along. (chuckling)

The reason I ask that question is because I have spoken to other internees that were outside of the orphanage who said that prejudice existed among internees against orphans, just for the fact that they were orphans. Did either of you get that feeling from other internees?

TN: I had the feeling afterwards, not so much before, because I was always with the orphans group, but it was after the war, living day-by-day and meeting different circumstances. For a long, long time, I was very inhibited. I didn't want to really meet people. I just wanted to kind of stay away, I guess, just to isolate myself. But after I married John [Nagayama], I gradually started meeting people and being a little more vocal. And I surprise myself. (chuckling) I'm a little more open than when I was small.

Did being Japanese American make you feel that way?

TN: Well, I just found out through different circumstances how different Japanese did look down on orphans. I had that feeling.

But not while in camp?

TN: No, not while in camp.

How about while in the Shonien? Did you get that feeling from the Japanese community?

TN: No. Well, we didn't have that much contact with the outside, but I don't know, I guess it's just the feeling or the thought that would come to me every now and then that, oh, we're kind of underprivileged. We don't have parents like some people do. It kind of gave me that insecure feeling, I guess.

Lillian, did you get a sense of that?

LM: Well, when I was at the Shonien, there were a lot of people I knew that I talked to who would tell their children, when they were disciplining them, "If you don't behave, if you don't do this, we'll send you to the Shonien," making Shonien a place where the children were all bad children or problem children.

So after I started working there and I learned that this was the type of thing that people said in the community, when I got a chance to speak to the church groups or the women's club or when groups came to visit Shonien to see the place, I think one of the main things I always tried to explain to them and dispel was that they shouldn't say those things because the children in the home are not bad, problem children. In fact, I don't think we had children that were there because of any juvenile problem; they existed, but they weren't sent to Shonien to be cared for. So I tried to let the community people and church people know to try to dispel this kind of idea and tell them that Shonien children are just children as good as their own children, but they have problems beyond their control and they have to be cared for.

I think, even in the Village, I'm sure people at Manzanar must have said the same thing: "If you're not good, we'll send you to Children's Village." And maybe there were parents that didn't want their children to be in contact with people in the Village, but it never came to my attention directly that any of our children faced discrimination because someone's parents said, "No, you can't play with them," or anything like that. I don't know if any of them told you that.

Yeah, I have, I think a lot of times it was just subtle.

LM: Oh, I'm sure.

They would just say, "You can't play with them." Or if you know that you're not allowed inside their barrack, then it could be because you're an orphan. I know that you didn't want the children to feel isolated. Around the Children's Village, was there an actual fence?

TN: No, no fence.

LM: The fence that was built was not a fence to keep children in or keep outside children out; it was a fence that was built by the gardeners as a decorative piece. They were made out of wood, and they planted vines and so forth, so it was part of the landscape.

Did it circle the whole village?

LM: No, I don't think so.

TN: No, it was only on one side because we had buildings.

LM: The backside was all lawn that the gardeners fixed, and then we had a little, covered gazebo. And then the fence was built behind that. And it was made out of twigs and things like that, not boards.

TN: Then we had a big lawn.

LM: You know, I think in some ways people envied us.

TN: Yeah, because it was really (chuckling) landscaped, and we had a lawn. Other places didn't have lawns.

But those were put in after you came in?

TN: Oh, yes, afterward.

LM: Because we hired women to help. The staff that went with us more or less acted as supervisors, and then we hired women to help take care of the children. We hired a few women who did the laundry, because all of the laundry had to be done by hand, and then we had a number of men who were gardeners who took care of and planted the lawns and everything. I think the administration was happy because they didn't have to do any of that. (chuckling) We were able to do that.

Now, is it true that you had a Clifton's cafeteria [a famous Los Angeles eatery] chef in the mess hall? (laughter)

LM: We didn't hire him because we thought he was a Clifton's chef, but because he was very good. He was among the applicants. He had a good understanding of the children and helped. And then Manzanar got pretty hot, and so in other mess halls, the cooks and kitchen help would take their shirts off and so would be completely bare-chested. We didn't want that kind of appearance in our dining hall and kitchen because of the children, and we asked the head cook if he could tell his men that they at least put their shirt on, at least when they were serving the children or were in view of the children during our mealtime. And they were very cooperative, very nice that way.

Do you remember the chef's name? Was he Caucasian?

LM: He was Japanese. Do you remember his name?

TN: I don't know that. Oh, I can remember an experience in the dining hall. It was at breakfast time and I was drinking a cup of coffee and something got stuck on my teeth as I was drinking. I took it out, and it was a cockroach! (chuckling)

LM: Oh, really?

TN: Oh, yes! Oh, my goodness! (chuckling) Oh, I've never had the experience since then, but I tell you. You don't see it because the coffee is dark. It was probably floating down on the bottom then, and when I drank, it didn't go through my teeth. (chuckling)

What about the rest of the staff?

LM: I think we had a staff that understood the children. I have to tell you one of the most memorable times we had at the Village was our first Christmas. We decided to have a Christmas program, and different age groups prepared a program: songs and skits and different things that we would present. At that time, we received some money from the administration that they told us to use for Christmas presents for the children. So we used that money, and we ordered a lot of things from the Sears Roebuck catalog. (chuckling) I remember the teenage girls got a mirror set with combs and different things. We got them a mirror that they could put by their bedside.

A retired Episcopal bishop, who was *hakujin* [Caucasian], used to come up about once every two months to give Episcopal services to those of us who were Episcopalians. He told a lot of church groups, not just in California but back east, about the Children's Village. So that Christmas, many of them sent lots of gifts for the children. Our children were very fortunate and got lots of Christmas gifts. And they gave a very memorable program. Do you remember?

TN: I don't remember at all. (chuckling) Isn't that terrible?

LM: They had the program on Christmas Eve. Of course, the recreation room wasn't very large, so we just included the children; the administrative staff, who were *hakujin* [Caucasian]; and then our staff, the gardeners and cooks and their families. Some of the children asked if they could invite their friends. Sure, they could come. So it was a very nice program. One of the most memorable was this boy. I think he came to Children's Village when he was about thirteen. He came to us from the Maryknoll Children's Home.

TN: That must be Kenny. I remember him singing. He had a really nice voice.

LM: He had a beautiful voice, the voice before it changes, you know, like a soprano voice. I think one of the girls from that group played the piano, and he sang a solo. Do you remember which one that was?

TN: I don't remember.

LM: It was one of those Christmas hymns that is difficult to sing as a group, but as a solo, it's beautiful. And Kenny sang that, and, oh, it was beautiful! The Caucasian staff was in tears, so I always remember that.

And then Jackson Takayame, who later became a minister and was one of the staff workers, was Santa Claus. He had a way of giving presents to the children. So to me, that Christmas Eve was one of the most memorable things that happened. That was early, just six months after we arrived, the first Christmas. It was really something.

On a personal level, how did that make you feel? I mean, here's Christmas and then you're in a camp.

LM: Well, I think Harry and I tried to prepare early. We thought that we got to do something for Christmas. It just can't be, you know, "this is Christmas Eve" kind of idea. So I think we worked on it. The staff helped us, and we worked on it. That's why it was such a successful one.

How about personally, for yourself? How did you feel about being in camp, sitting there at Christmas?

LM: Oh, I think I felt then that it was all worthwhile for Harry and I because Harry and I debated too, whether we should leave Shonien and go on our own as a family of two at the very beginning. I think it didn't take us much time to decide no, we're going to stay with the children. That's our work. We made the decision to be with the children. So I think that first Christmas, too, I really felt that we were right in doing what we did.

So it gave you a sense of self-worth or it legitimized the decision you had made.

LM: Yes.

So instead of seeing it in a negative way, you saw it in a positive way?

LM: Yes. I don't think there was any regret once we came to camp and started working with the children. It was the thing we were supposed to do. Years ago, many people who went into social work felt that social work was the type of work that was self-sacrifice. You were a different kind of person, that you sacrificed your whole life for this. But I didn't have that feeling, that I was sacrificing myself, or we were sacrificing, to do this job. I think we knew that it was part of our life, part of what we were supposed to do. I think at that time we really realized that it was the right thing to do.

Do you think that you got that sense because the children were Japanese Americans?

LM: I think at the time it was because they were Japanese Americans. They needed someone, and no one was really there to take care of them.

When you and Harry accepted to work at the Children's Village, did the administration tell you, "This is what your responsibilities are"? Or did they just leave the running of the orphanage up to you and Harry?

LM: I think they left it very much to us. I think when people heard that the Children's Village was coming to Manzanar, several people had applied to the administration, to the project manager, saying that they would like to run the place. But I think they were told that we were coming and that we would be in charge, so I think the administration had already made up their mind. No one told us or appointed us, when we got there. I think they took it for granted, and we did too. (chuckling)

And you and Harry were each getting only sixteen dollars a month?

LM: We got nineteen dollars.

I was reading that fourteen of the children at Children's Village were of mixed ancestry. Did they have any problems because they were mixed?

LM: The only one I would think of is Dennis Tojo [Bambauer. See COPH-OH 2335]. He stood out because he was blond. He must have been about ten, twelve years old. His surname was Tojo, which wasn't a popular name then, so everything was against him at that time. And I guess even the children teased him. But many of the mixed-race children were the babies and the small ones, so I don't think it affected them.

Some of these children were born out of wedlock. Was there a sense of shame for not being married and having a child, especially among Japanese Americans at that time? Would the majority of children born out of wedlock just be turned over to the Village, or did some females actually raise their own kids?

LM: I don't know. I have no idea. Some of the children did come to us after we were established there. They came from other relocation camps, so they may have been children of unwed mothers and then arrangements were made to bring the baby to Manzanar right away.

Would a person then from one camp bring the baby across to Manzanar?

LM: There was a courier, a Caucasian. I think the meeting point usually was Reno, Nevada, because beyond Reno would be the restricted area. So I think that probably a social worker from the other camp would bring the baby to that point, and then the Caucasian courier would bring the baby into camp.

How about the kids in camp? For those with parents or siblings, would their families come visit or write them?

LM: I don't think we had any children whose parent or parents lived right in Manzanar. Usually, if a child had only one parent, the single parent was a father and couldn't take care of them. He would leave the child in Shonien or Maryknoll or the Salvation Army Home. If they were one of the men picked up by the FBI on the night of Pearl Harbor, then after things were settled and they were released, these fathers usually asked to be sent to Manzanar, if they knew their children were there. Then we would reunite them and the father would take them.

When the children would leave, would you throw parties or give presents or anything? Or would they just leave?

LM: I don't think there were presents, but we had little parties if children or when staff members left.

In the Children's Village barracks, was there any privacy for the children?

TN: Oh, it was all open. Each bed lined up right next to the other.

LM: The only privacy was that each child had a little box-like thing where children kept their personal things. And there was a closet where they could keep their things.

Did they just sleep on cots like all the other internees?

TN: Yes.

LM: Now, by looking at the pictures of the orphanage barracks and comparing them to the regular barracks, the orphanage barracks seem a lot nicer.

TN: Oh, yes, much nicer.

LM: See, the regular barracks were built very close to the ground. You can tell that Children's Village barracks is built much higher because there are steps leading up to them. The floors were solid. I think everything was better built.

Do you know why the barracks in the Village were built higher than others?

LM: I have no idea.

Now, was there a request to make the barracks in the orphanage nicer?

LM: Well, some of the things we asked was that they be suitable for staff and for the children, so that we could care for them. We didn't want to have to take them to an outside toilet, so we asked them for showers and toilet facilities in each of the buildings. And then, if it was one large room, we might have asked to have the room separated so that one of the staff could have a room. Like in the girls' building, one staff member, Ruth Takamune, had a room there, and the other room was the diet kitchen where the babies' formulas were made or whatever.

Did it make you feel in any way guilty to have more than other internees had, or did you feel privileged?

TN: I felt fortunate (chuckling) that we were able to live in so-called barracks or whatever which were nice.

LM: I think it would have been very hard to take care of a hundred children in facilities that the others had. I think we emphasized that a lot to try to make it, so that it would be easier for us to take care of that number of children. We knew, I think, at the time that we went up to talk with the authorities about approximately how many children would be there. I think we had heard from the Salvation Army about how many they were bringing, so we knew about how many would be there right at the beginning. Then, if other children were going to be brought in, and the authorities thought there would be, I think we asked that the buildings and facilities be built so that it would be convenient for all of us.

Taeko, as a staff worker, were you involved in helping out with the birthday parties or any kind of parties or activities with the children?

TN: I can't remember the parties so much, except for just taking care of the children. I can't remember helping out with birthdays. There might be others that helped out, but I don't remember doing it myself.

LM: I think quite often Mrs. May Uchida was the one because she was sort of in charge of the recreational activities, especially for the girls.

How about movies? When the camp would put on movies, would the children be free to go to those?

LM: The older ones, probably.

Do you remember the Village kids playing with non-Village kids?

LM: I think the older ones did; the little ones probably wouldn't, no.

TN: The little ones wouldn't; they stayed there at the Village.

Would any of the non-Village children come to play there at the Village?

LM: That again would be the older teenagers, I think. I don't think we allowed non-Village kids to stay to eat at the Village dining room. We knew that one of the problems that families were having was that their children would be scattered. They couldn't eat together. Of course, we always made it a rule for our children to come back to the Village for their meals, unless there was some special occasion when one child would ask if someone could come and stay for dinner or something like that. But no overnight stays or anything of that kind.

Were there other areas in camp that had swings and other toys or slides?

LM: I think so. It depended on the blocks, what the block people did for their block. I think they had swings and things like that, whatever they would make for them.

Could other children come to the Village to use the swings or slides or something?

TN: I don't remember others coming in to swing.

But they could have, right?

LM: I guess so. But there might have been sort of a prejudice on the part of the rest of the community. You know, parents might say, "Don't go over there and play with those children." Maybe that was the reason they didn't come, I don't know. (chuckling) But then that was no problem. If they came, why certainly we wouldn't have chased them out or anything. (laughter)

Did you have trick-or-treating for Halloween?

TN: I don't think so.

LM: I don't know whether the camp ever had that or not. I don't remember at all.

But there would be Christmas parties?

LM: Yes, we always had a Christmas party. We had parties, and sometimes the cook would have something special in the way of dessert for a special occasion. Like if it was Valentine's dinner, he would have special heart cookies or something that he would make up. So in that way the children were fortunate that the head of the kitchen was a very understanding person.

Did you have better food at the Village than the rest of the mess halls?

LM: Well, I don't know whether we had better food because the same basic food was passed out at all the mess halls. I think our chef's menu at the Village was more interesting. He didn't have to serve as many, but he made it. (chuckling)

You mentioned that the Children's Village was located close to the hospital. How often were children sent to the hospital? Did they get sick often?

LM: No, no big need. I don't think we had any serious injuries. I don't think we even encountered a broken arm or broken leg or anything like that.

I think Tamo Isozaki [See COPH-OH 2332] said that he had appendicitis though, while he was in camp. So he went to the hospital for surgery.

LM: Did he? I don't remember that.

Were there any deaths of any of the orphanage children?

LM: No.

Were there any pregnancies or anything?

LM: No.

No fights? No fist fighting or anything?

LM: No real big fights. Sometimes there might be shouting and a tear and something, but—

It sounds like a good bunch of kids. (chuckling)

LM: See, the older boys, Tamo Isozaki and his group who were the older ones, really looked after the little ones, the younger ones. At the fiftieth anniversary reunion, I think the younger ones who are now grown up mentioned how they looked up to Tamo and the other boys and how good they were to them. So I think that was one of the reasons why the children were happy to stay there.

Taeko, as a staff member who was only a few years older than some of the teenage girls there, would the girls come to you when they needed to talk to someone about boys or personal things?

TN: No, I don't remember any of them coming to talk on any kind of personal matter.

And they would all be educated outside of the Village, so you didn't have to worry about schooling, except for the nursery school children, right?

LM: Yes.

Would you allow other children outside of the Village to come in for nursery school?

LM: No, it was just the children there. Mrs. Uchida was in charge of that.

And how about in terms of having a group of males and a group of females living so close together without parental supervision all the time? Did you have any problems between males and females, in terms of sex or them wanting to go off together?

LM: No. I had several girls who came to me because they were older ones who were interested in one of the boys, non-Village boys you know, who they met in high school or something and they wanted to go to the movies together. They usually came and asked permission; they didn't just go off on their own.

So they would usually come to you or Harry to ask for permission to do something like that?

LM: Yes.

So in a way, you and Harry were kind of the parental figures?

LM: I guess so, yes.

And it was your sense that they could come to you freely if they wanted to talk?

LM: Yes.

Did you and Harry spend the majority of your time actually in the office or was a lot of time spent out in the orphanage with the children?

LM: I think for 50 percent of the time, we would be interacting with the other staff and with the children.

What did you do during your spare time?

LM: Well, what did we do? (laughter)

Did you have any spare time? (laughter)

TN: I guess we just walked around camp, went to the co-op store, bought a little something. Or there were times when we'd order from the Sears catalog and wait—anxiously wait—for the item to come.

LM: What you could buy for sixteen dollars! (chuckling)

TN: We just walked around, I guess, and watched people play baseball or . . . I don't remember volleyball. I remember baseball.

LM: We had a team. The boys had a baseball team that was part of the Manzanar league, or whatever it was. I think we let the girls join a club. There was a YWCA [Young Women's Christian Association], and I think some of the girls took part in the activities there.

Did you and Harry have any free time to spend together, to do whatever?

LM: I suppose there was. (laughter) We went to the movies together or something.

When a child became eighteen, did that mean that the child automatically had to leave the Village?

LM: There was no automatic rule that they had to leave, but many of them wanted to. They felt that they were old enough to establish themselves outside of the Village, and we encouraged that. With the administration, we helped them find a barrack that would be close to the Village, so that if they needed any help, we were close by. Then they established themselves in one of those barracks. Now some of them, like from the San Francisco Salvation

Army group, had some older brothers and sisters that came with them, but we considered them too old to be living in the village, so we got them assigned barracks nears the Village. But they had their own quarters, so they went to the dining room on their block. But when we had holidays or something special, we'd ask the cook to make something special and we'd invite them to join their brothers and sisters. Like Tamo Isozaki's family, his older brother Isamo and his older sister Molly, lived outside.

And Tamo Isozaki himself?

LM: He lived with us. I don't know if he later joined his family, but he lived in the Village. He never was ever a worker with us, but he was one of the older children who helped John [Nagayama] and Dick [Akagi].

TN: I can recall when Fuji, my sister, and I went and took a little apartment across from the Children's Village.

LM: Did you later?

TN: Yes.

Were you still a worker at the Village, even though you lived outside?

TN: Yes.

And your sister lived with you?

TN: Yes.

So, Lillian, you and Harry left Manzanar and Children's Village in 1944?

LM: Yes, September 1944.

How did your leaving come about? Was it a personal decision?

LM: Personal, yes. We decided. And I think the project director may have encouraged us. They said, "The end of the camp is coming" and they would start making arrangements to slowly close us. Also, I think the administration finally wanted the closing of the Children's Village for the records and so forth. I think they wanted someone from Washington [DC] to do that. So we just decided it was a good time.

Taeko, were you still in camp at the time that Harry and Lillian left?

TN: Oh, no, I had left before. Was it 1943? I think it was not quite two years. I think it was 1943 that I left. I went with Ruth Takamune and my sister. The three of us relocated to New York City. My sister had taken up cosmetology in camp and got her certificate for that, so she found a job there in New York as a cosmetologist.

Ruth and I were accepted at the Saint Mary's Hospital for Children, a high Episcopal hospital and the teachers were all nuns. It was the first time I had seen a nun in her habit, and I thought it was rather strange. A lot of these things, it was the first time for me, you know? (chuckling) But I went there. The course was only one year, and I worked for a year, and then I relocated to the West Coast and got married in 1947.

You and John [Nagayama] met . . .

TN: In camp.

Did you meet because you both worked at Children's Village?

TN: He worked at the Village, yes.

How did he start working for the Village?

TN: Well, I guess to help take care of the boys.

Did he have any affiliation with the orphanage beforehand? Did he just apply?

TN: He used to lead the Sunday school, and I used to play the piano for him at the Sunday school. (laughter) What little piano I knew. I took up piano at the orphanage, and I had received my certificate for it. I learned from a missionary who taught me to play hymns, and if I could play a hundred hymns perfectly, then I'd get a certificate. (chuckling) When I went to Saint Mary's Hospital, I played the organ there. And then afterwards, after John was in the ministry, I played the piano at different churches. (chuckling)

So how did you and John Nagayama end up getting married? Where did he go after camp?

TN: While I was still in camp, he went to Wheaton College [Illinois], and he was there when I relocated to New York City. We always wrote to each other. He was to go back to the West Coast because his parents were coming out of camp, and he wanted to help them settle down. So he came over to New York City to visit me, while I was training out there. I can remember we had a green nurse's uniform, with black stockings and shoes. (chuckling) When we graduated, then we had our white caps and white shoes. I remember John came to see me before he went back to the West Coast. Then after I worked for a year, I went to the West Coast in 1946. Then we were married in 1947.

LM: And Harry gave you away! (laughter)

TN: Oh, yes! Harry gave me away, right. I almost forgot about that. (chuckling) We were married at the Christian Missionary Alliance in Santa Monica, California. I remember.

Thank you, Lillian and Taeko, for this interview.

LM: You're welcome.

TN: You're welcome.

Sohei Hohri[1]

Interviewed by Cathy Irwin

Where were you born?

I was born in Salinas, California. The actual locale was Natividad. It's still on the map, but the official locale is Salinas.

And when is your birthday?

My birth certificate says February 4, 1925, but I was actually born on January 24, 1925. My wife always laughs that I get to celebrate two birthdays. (laughter)

So just in case we miss your January 24ᵗʰ birthday, we can still sing happy birthday to you on the fourth!

Yes. (laughter)

So how old were you when you were sent to the Shonien?

I was five and a half years old. We arrived November 15, 1930.

Do you know what the circumstances were?

My father and mother had tuberculosis, so they were sent to the Olive View sanitarium that at the time was on the northern edge of the San Fernando Valley [Los Angeles County, California]. I think it may no longer exist.

Were your five other siblings and you sent too?

No, my oldest brother Sam, since he was in his late teens, stayed with a family in Sierra Madre [a small community near Pasadena, California]. This was before child labor laws, so my oldest sister Saeko worked as a live-in house girl for a family. They provided a roof over her head, three meals a day, but no wages. They did allow her to go to school. She says that she was terrified the whole time she was there. She was only nine years old.

And your brother Takuo?

[1]COPH-Oral History 3786 was conducted on January 27, 2008, by phone (the interviewer in Claremont, California, spoke to the interviewee who was in New York City).

At the time, everyone had to get a physical check-up. Ieko had apparently also contracted tuberculosis, and she was sent with our parents. Takuo was found badly malnourished, so they had these health camps that were up in the hills of Los Angeles with fresh air, a cure-all for all things. He wore khaki shorts, would get three square meals a day, which was important, and a regime of exercise. He stayed about a year, and then he joined us at the Shonien. So it was only me and William who went directly to the Shonien.

What was it like to be sent to the Shonien? What was your first reaction?

It was absolutely the worst experience of my life! After the first week I was there, I lost my speech. I couldn't say a word. And then at school, I think it was first grade or kindergarten and I was learning to read, I remember that I could understand the words. But when it came my turn to read, I couldn't say a word. The teachers were understanding, and I think they had special classes for slow children.

But I think at the Shonien, I don't fault these people as far as malice or evil, but one thing they didn't want was to be taken advantage of. So a little child is scared to death! And in a work environment, the adults have to get things done and they are in charge of fifty children and they don't want to show favoritism or anyone to take advantage of them or trick them on the sly. So they would crack down a little bit. I can say that I hated every day of it.

Did they ever crack down on you?

What I want to underline is that there was no malice or anything like in a Dickens' novel. But the staff had to run things orderly. Everything is semi-military. Everything is—they ring the bell, you line up in the halls to go to breakfast, everyone eats at the same time, you line up to go to school for inspection and get lunch bags. These little rules. If an infraction occurs, an adult is always watching. As far as I could remember, it wasn't a loving relationship but one of control. In a normal family, the parents really enjoy their kids.

Did you miss your parents, while you were at the Shonien?

That's hard to say. I think when you're young and something happens, one of the emotional reactions is you blame somebody. You don't blame the United States or the mayor, but if you strike out, you strike out at somebody you know. And the people you know are your parents. Someone says to you that they have a terrible disease and they're being taken somewhere far away, but a little child doesn't understand this and wonders: what's happening to me? The only thing I knew was that we were placed in a terrible, frightening environment. My younger brother William, who was about three and a half when he went into the Shonien, remembers that when he was seven and came back to live with our parents, he had the feeling that he was being adopted. The emotional ties had been completely broken. He thought his real mother and father were his foster mother and father.

Was there anyone at the Shonien who made you feel okay? Made it bearable?

I can only tell you that I lost my speech. I couldn't say a word for at least a whole week and developed a stammer that remained with me until the summer of 1967. For some reason, my stammer disappeared in 1967.

The only thing I can say is that, when I started grammar school, there was a big brute of a boy who started picking on me in class. At that age, I had just left my parents and moved into the orphanage and was terrified. Anyways, this boy came up and defended me. He told me later that he had to fight the whole thing after class in the schoolyard. Anyways, I met him in 1960. I found his name in the phone book, and he's been my oldest friend ever since! He and his wife live in Hawaii now. I correspond with him and talk to him about once a month. But I wonder why I can't dig up any recollection of the boys who I lived with for three years.

How old were you when you left the Shonien?

I was just three days short of turning nine years old in 1934.

Did your parents get better?

Well, yes. One thing I do remember is that when it was almost time to return home, at Micheltorena Grammar School, the principal called me out to the yard and my mother and father were standing there. I remember I ran to my mother and I hugged her! To this day, it's hard to explain what happened. I'm not sure I recognized her! It was an overpowering, spontaneous thing! And then we carried on for a few more weeks, and then we returned to Sierra Madre.

In terms of the Shonien, it's a complete wipe out. I can't remember any of the boys who were in my age group at the Shonien even though I lived with them for three years. I do remember one boy who ran away. Of course, the police found him and brought him back. We all ran to the window.

Was it hard to readjust to parents?

The years I spent in Sierra Madre from 1934 to 1936 were the happiest years of my life. There were lemon and orange groves. I can still smell them and the pepper trees. And there was the grammar school. It was the first time we went to church.

So there was a big difference between being back at the Shonien and being with your family. It sounds like you were happier after you left the Shonien, being with your family.

It was nurturing; it was like a garden, you know. You pour water and let the sun shine, and it will blossom. You really don't have to do much work! But when you treat it like a lawn, you keep mowing. There's no natural growth; it's constantly being trimmed and washed over and sure it doesn't get out of line. With the family, it was: feel free! Do your best. I trust you. I am not worried.

Do you think having lived at the Shonien affected you and your attitude toward life? Did it have a great impact on you?

How it fits into or affects my memory. At Manzanar, there were ten thousand people. Today, I can only call up about two hundred people from Manzanar. But about Shonien, there's a wipe out. I remember so well the non-Japanese students at the grammar schools. I can remember so many details of Sierra Madre.

Were you old enough to remember when you heard about Pearl Harbor?

By then we had moved to North Hollywood in 1938. My father worked in a nursery shop on North Hollywood Boulevard. My brother Tak did gardening. My father had to sell potted plants. We heard about Pearl Harbor on the radio. It was about noon. I was sixteen in 1941, a senior in high school. What amazes me was that, within that afternoon when the news came out, there were four agents and they came to the door. I was sitting at the dinner table, and they had my father pack a few things and took my father away.

Oh, really, on the same day?

Oh, yeah, it was a matter of less than two hours.

Was your mother there?

Oh, yeah, we were all there. It was a Sunday, a non-working day.

What were your reactions?

(long pause) In the case of my father, when the news came out, it was "This isn't happening; it's not real." Then he went to bed and took a nap. He could see the whole thing from a bigger perspective, from all the people in Japan and in America. The idea of war. I really couldn't say what was exactly happening.

On Monday, we went to North Hollywood High School, and one of the female teachers came up to me and stood near me and said, "You don't think your people are going to come to California and bomb us, do you?" I didn't quite know how to answer that question! She felt she had to say something patriotic. There was also a male teacher who was worried or concerned about us. Just the way he talked to me, it was like, it's gonna be hard times. There were just a lot of things said to us. On my brother's gardening route, there was a friendly lady on his route. But after she came out to pay Tak and give him his paycheck, she said, "The only patriotic thing I can do is that I have to let you go."

What was the hardest part about leaving home and relocating to Manzanar? Any vivid memories?

I would say it was thinking, "Gee, this isn't going to make me cry." This is what you say to yourself. I was just speaking to a friend a couple of weeks ago, and we thought that, on the bus, some of us turned out to become lifelong friends. So, it was the beginning of lifelong friendships. They lived on the same block as us, and I just kept up with them.

So you and your family took a bus from Los Angeles to Manzanar. Where did the bus pick you up?

I would guess it was North Hollywood, but I really can't say.

And you and your family were able to stay together on the bus?

Yeah.

So you and your family did not have to go to an assembly center?

No, we went straight to Manzanar. People complained because at the time, Manzanar's barracks were really rickety, but the thing I remember is the friendships I formed.

So tell me about Manzanar. What were your first impressions? What were the first days like?

What was extraordinary is I don't know how soon it was, but the only thing organized and encouraged by the camp authorities was the church. They had a church in one of the barracks and it was jam-packed. People were also standing outside, and there was a piano inside and people were singing. It was the only thing being done during the first week for people to connect in any way; so even though people may not be normal churchgoers, they were assembled and doing something together. People were crowded outside the barrack trying to participate in the service going on inside!

So this church service happened in April of 1942?

Yes. The other thing that I remember was making friends and finding out how different they were from you, their slang and the way they talked.

Were you near the Terminal Island group who came to Manzanar?

Yes, in Block 10. The people from North Hollywood joined the Terminal Island group.

What was your reaction to the barracks?

The feeling of making do. The thing I couldn't control was the dust. I hated it. I can still remember getting preparations to leave Manzanar in 1944 and thinking, "Gee, it will be so great to leave all these dust storms!"

Now, you became a storyteller for the boys at the Children's Village after your family was sent to Manzanar?

Yes.

How did that come about?

There were no comic books there. They say there were no radios, but I talked to one of my good friends at the orphanage and he remembers someone who had a radio, but the radio station didn't come on until after 5 p.m. There were no stories, and a child's mind—I remember something quite extraordinary. I remember when I first started telling stories and the children would come around with their eyes wide open and their mouths open. They were listening with all ears. And the next time they would see me, they would say, "Tell us a story! Tell us a story!" The mind needs story; it's kind of food for the mind to grow. It became an easy thing. I think what was extraordinary was that the story that remained was the story of Jean Valjean [of *Les Miserables*], and the second was from Homer. I recited some of the ancient tales of Odysseus.

You recited this from memory?

This is the other thing—I talked to a friend and he said, "Oh, no, you read from a book!" And I told him, "I trust your memory more than mine!" I don't remember having a book because *Les Miserables* is about a thousand pages, a biggish book. But if he said so, then I may have bought one growing up and carried it with me to Manzanar. But if someone asked me, I would have said I told stories from memory because I had read these books so many times. But no question about it, *Les Miserables* was the main story.

So you just started telling stories to kids. How did you end up at Children's Village? Did you go to Children's Village at night to tell the stories?

No, since I was a graduate of the Shonien in Los Angeles, when there was an opening in the boy's section, I guess that I was interviewed by the Matsumotos [Harry and Lillian, the superintendents of Children's Village] and I was hired.

Okay, so you were hired by the Matsumotos to be a staff member?

Yes, I guess you could say that.

What were some of your jobs? Or was it mainly storytelling?

It was kind of minimal. I don't recall any kind of formal duty. I think it was just to be sure that everything was in order. I do remember one instance when someone had an appendicitis attack. He smelled very terrible. We were right near the hospital, and we had to be sure to get someone to take a look at him and operate on him. Other than that, I don't remember any kind of work type of thing. I don't recall any type of paperwork done. That was sixty-five years ago, so there wasn't so much—

The only thing that struck me was going to the dining room for the first time, and, before sitting down, the children stood in their places and sang a song (singing), "God is great and God is good, and we thank you for this food. Amen." And that was the same song that we sang at the Shonien way back in the 1930s, so it carried over from the Los Angeles Shonien. I do remember the food was better quality at the Children's Village. I think they had a pretty good chef up there.

The Shonien group came to the Children's Village in June of 1942. Did you start working there immediately?

No, no, there were at least two predecessors, both of whom I knew, and that may be the reason why I got recommended. The first one was Jack Nakahayali and the second one was John Nagayama. I believe that I followed John Nagayama. These people all left camp; John Nagayama went to Wheaton College [in Illinois, near Chicago]. So during that transition, when they were getting ready to leave, John Nagayama may have mentioned my name, since he was one of my very good friends in West Los Angeles when I was going to junior high and high school.

I see. So did you start working at the Children's Village in 1943?

Yes, I think I started working in autumn of 1943.

Did you get paid?

Yes, I think the pay scale was twelve, sixteen, and nineteen dollars. Twelve was for regular work, sixteen was professional, and nineteen was for people like doctors and teachers. I probably got sixteen. That's my guess. Earlier, I was working and I used to deliver heating oil to the barracks to the group in Block 10. Each block had an oil tank. Trucks would deliver oil to the tank. Each barrack was heated with an oil burner fed with oil with a stack that went up to the roof. We would get the oil from the main tank at the top of the block, and we would fill our individual big cans and knock on the barrack door and fill each apartment's stove. That was twelve dollars. Before that, I also worked making camouflage nets for twelve dollars. So I guess that working at the Children's Village was sixteen dollars.

Okay, so the books you read and recited were from Les Miserables *and* Homer. *What were your most vivid experiences of being at the Children's Village?*

I guess the storytelling.

What were the children like as you read the stories?

What struck me was their rapt attention. At the same time, I would say that *Les Miserable* was the story about orphans. In so many cases, the children's own childhood stories and early family life were very sad to quite miserable. In one case, the father was in prison for trying to murder the children; he was deported to Japan. The phrase we used to use back then was the mothers had nervous breakdowns and they would be institutionalized. There were also terrible stories about that. One of the mothers tried to escape. They were just kind of overwhelmed with family problems and couldn't handle them. She was a friend of my mother's. She wrote a letter to my mother about how she ran across the fields—like something out of a terrible movie—and the supervisors were running after her and ran her down into the bushes and dragged her back into her barred room. But I don't know if the children knew this specific story; the stories I heard most were about their fathers, how they were violent and abusive. And of course their simple emotions are either anger or guilt, like there was something wrong with them. It was a scar that they carried. So I think that . . . I was pretty amazed how, at the Manzanar Children's Village reunion in 1992, so many of them remembered the stories from *Les Miserables* so vividly and in such detail.

Yes, they do. Now did you read these stories only at bedtime? Did you read during the day?

I think the regular routine was that we would tell stories in the evening. Sometimes, some of the older boys would help out with stories also. The cut-off age was eighteen. There was a family of about five brothers—but two of the brothers in their teens were in the Children's Village.

The Matsunos?

Yes, and the Isozakis too. Tamo Isozaki [See COPH-OH 2332] had stories to recite also. You know, there was no television set to turn on or movies to go to. Once again, what was so astonishing was how rapt and open eyed these children were during storytelling. This is an aside: When I told some of the stories I remembered in Block 10, one of the results of that was one of the boys, after he grew up and married in California, named his first daughter Cosette, who is a character in *Les Miserable*, the girl who was saved by Jean Valjean. That kind of astonished me when I came back after the war and met his daughter. He told me he was so moved by the story that that was the name he picked for his daughter.

Wow! Now were you in school at the same time you were working at Children's Village?

No, I graduated in December of 1942 or the end of the year.

You mentioned religious services when you first got off the bus. Did you regularly attend religious services?

Yes, since my father was a minister, I ended up being a Sunday school teacher. What's so embarrassing is that after all these years, I don't read the Bible as consciously as I used to. I would say it's a worthwhile book to read, but I'm not a believer of the Bible. Back then, it kind of embarrassed me in later life because I would meet some of the boys and they would tell me how much they appreciated my Bible lessons. I wouldn't confess, but I guess I was at an earlier age when I felt strongly in those things.

Was there a Christian church?

Yes, there was a Protestant, a Catholic church, and then a Buddhist church.

And so you taught for the Protestant church?

Yes, there may have been two churches, one for Japanese speakers. My father was there for only a short while, because he was at mostly other camps for men detained in Missoula, Montana, and in New Mexico. But anyway, there was a barrack set aside for the church service.

When was your father released to Manzanar to be with his family?

I'm not quite sure of the sequence because I left Manzanar in March of 1944, and we all got together after the war on the south side of Chicago. And that was the next time I saw him, after 1945. I was a student at the University of Chicago. My mother was one of the last to leave camp and had left Manzanar in August of 1945. It took her about four days by train.

When you left in March of 1944, did your other siblings go with you?

No, my older sister Ieko left camp the first year in 1942 and went to New York to become a nurse. At the time, cadet nurses were being recruited by the army, and she worked in New York. It was very harsh because they got these young people to come in and work long hours, so in 1946 my sister contracted tuberculosis, a more virulent form than what she had when she was younger. She was never in good health after that. It was a hard life. I've heard numerous stories of girls whose health broke down because of overwork. She became well again and died in 1995.

What about Sam? When did he leave camp?

Sam contracted tuberculosis in 1935, and he was in a sanitarium at Manzanar. After the war, there was a sanitarium close to Los Angeles. He died in the spring of 1947 in Los Angeles.

And Saeko?

She married in camp and had a son in camp. I think she had one of the first babies in camp. She was married in 1942, and her son came in 1943. They left the camp in 1944. She joined her husband in Madison, Wisconsin.

And Takuo?

He left before I did in 1943 and left for college. John Nagayama, Takuo, and my brother-in-law all went to Wheaton College to study with Billy Graham. It was in Wheaton, Illinois, a Christian college.

Now, after leaving camp, you and your brother William went to the University of Chicago. What did you study?

They had no electives. We did a lot of readings in the great books. It was truly an extraordinary experience. We got there and the president of UC talked to us during an assembly and said, "This isn't a very good university, but it's the best one around. Don't worry about the professors. There's only two things good about the university, and that's myself and the students." (laughter) "Don't worry about anything else they tell you that you won't be held accountable for, and the only thing you will be held accountable for is the things that Plato said, Aristotle says, Shakespeare, Tolstoy. Don't worry about anything else they tell you. It's probably not worth much anyway." So it was like: feel free!

So did you and William get your degrees there?

Yes, our Bachelors of Philosophy in 1949.

Thank you so much, Mr. Hohri, for this interview.

You're welcome.

Chapter Four
The Children from Terminal Island:
The Matsuno Family

Before 1942, approximately 3,000 Japanese and Japanese Americans resided and worked in the fishing industry and canneries on Terminal Island, a small area off of San Pedro in Los Angeles County also known as "Fish Harbor."[1] On the island, residents developed their own culture and created their own dialect by combining Japanese and English.[2] Considered tough and "outsider" even in their own ethnic community, Terminal Islanders proudly referred to themselves as *yogores*: "dark and dirty on the outside, but pure and clean of heart within."[3]

Terminal Island was such a close-knit fishing community that people who were not born on the island but had moved there to live and work were considered "foreigners."[4] However, after the Pearl Harbor attack on December 7, 1941, the FBI treated all the Issei and Nisei fishermen on the island as foreigners by arresting and removing them from their homes because they were considered "suspicious" and a potential threat to national security.[5] Their arrest left Issei and Nisei women with the responsibility of caring for their families. The strain of prejudice and war was felt even further by these women when, after President Franklin D. Roosevelt signed Executive Order 9066 on February 19, 1942, the first action to be taken by the government was the removal of Terminal Island residents from their homes.[6] With the earlier arrests of their husbands, they were especially burdened with the

---

[1] The Terminal Islanders, Furusato: *The Lost Village of Terminal Island* Web site <http://www.terminalisland.org> (1 Jan 2008)

[2] Ibid.

[3] Ibid.

[4] Mary Matsuno Miya, Interviewed by Celeste Cardenas, 13 March 1993, CSUF-Center for Oral and Public History.

[5] Robert Okamura, "Incarceration of Japanese Americans During World War II: Sites-Terminal Island," Five Views: An Ethnic Sites Survey for California (Sacramento, CA: State of CA-Resource Agency, Department of Parks and Recreation, 1988), 182. Okamura writes that among the first members of the Japanese American community to be questioned and removed from their homes by the FBI after December 7, 1941, were Issei and Nisei fishermen living on Terminal Island, "even before civilian exclusion orders were issued by Lt. General John DeWitt, commanding officer of the Army's Western Defense Command"(183).

[6] Ibid, 175.

responsibility of finding alternative housing for their families after armed soldiers gave them forty-eight hours to leave Terminal Island on February 25-27.[7]

Consequently, the nine brothers and sisters in the Matsuno family were left without parents after the FBI arrest of their father, who had moved his family to Terminal Island in 1936 to become a fisherman.[8] Their mother had been placed in a state hospital in the summer of 1941, which left the eldest siblings with the struggle to keep the family together after exclusion. After removal, the older Matsunos—John, Susie, Isa, and Mary—lived temporarily in a hostel, while the younger Matsunos—Shioo, Shiro, Tatsue, and Takatow—were sent to the Shonien.[9] Fourteen-year-old Mary and the youngest child Setsuko Betsy (born on November 4, 1941) would later join their siblings at the Shonien in preparation for removal to Manzanar, and the Matsuno children would have no contact with their father for two years.[10]

Of the nine Matsuno siblings, two were interviewed for the Center for Oral and Public History's Children's Village Project.[11] Mary Matsuno Miya recalls her daily experiences of going to Manzanar High School and working in a pickle factory and the graveyard shift at the Manzanar hospital, and her brother, Takatow Matsuno, discusses his experience as a six-year-old boy being transferred to the Shonien after his father's arrest and then going to Children's Village.

---

[7]Ibid.

[8]Miya, Interviewed by Cardenas, 13 March 1993.

[9]Takatow Matsuno and Tamotsu Isozaki, Interviewed by Richard Potashin, Manzanar National Historic Site (National Park Service) Oral History Program, 24 January 2003.

[10] Miya, Interviewed by Cardenas, 13 March 1993.

[11]Takatow Matsuno (with Tamotsu Isozaki) has also been interviewed by Richard Potashin for the Manzanar National Historic Site Oral History Program.

Mary Matsuno Miya[1]

Interviewed by Celeste Cardenas

How old were you when you went to Manzanar?

I was fourteen.

You didn't go directly from Terminal Island to Children's Village. You went to an orphanage?

Yeah. We went to the Japanese Children's Home [Shonien in Los Angeles].

How long were you there?

We were there roughly from February to July, 1942, I think it was. June or July 1942. I remember when we came on the bus into Manzanar, there were all these people. They were all Japanese, and they were all brown from the sun. And here we are, we were all white because we were just arriving at Manzanar, and this is the desert, below sea level. And I remember when we were going on the bus to Children's Village that Children's Village was directly the last barrack in the back, and there was the hospital to this one side. And there was a road, and Children's Village was here in Block 29, in front of the hospital. The hospital was right across the street from us.

Did the staff allow you to take any personal belongings?

Well, they just packed everything. They packed everything for us. But I think the evacuees were just allowed whatever they could carry, that was it.

You had no choice on what to take?

We didn't have much anyway, so it didn't matter to us. When you're a child, you can get along with anything. You find that out. You don't have to have a lot of things. If you have clean clothing and a change, that's enough. As you get older, it's different. We just accumulate more worldly goods.

One thing about the Salvation Army and about the Japanese Children's Home [Shonien], they packed all the bedding—all the beds, everything—and took it to camp. When they were there, they needed every bit of it. They

---

[1]COPH-Oral History 2489 was conducted on March 13, 1993, in Monterey Park, California.

wanted the ones from San Francisco shipped to camp, but they had had a fire at the Salvation Army home, so somebody must have set it on fire. There was nothing to send. I remember Mrs. [Lillian] Matsumoto [See COPH-OH 2492] talking about it.

Did you make friends with the people outside the Village?

Yes, across the street. Wilbur Sato was in Block 29, but I knew Wilbur before the war. They lived across the street in Terminal Island.

But you did make friends with people outside the Village—

Oh, yes, because we went to school also. They had school. They called it a secondary school, but it was located way down there, in roughly Block 8. So the school was right down there. So Block 8 would start down here again, and each block is composed of fifteen barracks, and then two bathrooms for men and women, and a laundry room in the middle.

So you went to school with the rest of the kids. How was the education? How good was it? How much did they teach you?

Oh, we had speech, we had English, and we had bookkeeping. I don't think we had any sciences or anything like that. I don't remember that. I was there from the ninth to the twelfth grade.

You graduated there?

Yeah. We were the last graduating class, in 1945. Tamo and Takeshi Isozaki [See COPH-OH 2332 and 2337] were both classmates of mine, but they were older. The Salvation Army kids were all older, and they weren't really in the right classes. What they did in camp was make one class for each year of school. So to catch up to belong to this next grade, I think I had to go to summer school to catch up [in order] to be in this one class with the rest— ninth grade, or whatever it was. We didn't have A and B classes.

Was the education of high quality? How would you describe it?

It was called secondary school, so it wasn't the top. I don't know how they recruited their teachers, but we had a lot of older people, like the principal and the bookkeeping teacher. Dr. Potts, she taught English, and she was also, I think, principal of the school. The superintendent—I can see her face, but I can't remember her name. We had a wonderful teacher who taught drama and choir.

What was his name?

Lou Frizzell.[2] He was in the movies [in the postwar years]. He was from Pasadena [California]. Tamo Isozaki and his kid brother, Takeshi, were very close to him. From what I understand, they used to help him grade the papers.

In camp, did they ever emphasize Japanese? Did they speak Japanese?

They were teaching Japanese. There were a lot of Japanese schoolteachers, so they had Japanese school for whoever wanted to go. Probably at that time it was like free maybe. It was next to nothing, probably, if you wanted to go learn.

Did you go?

I remember I started to go, and then I didn't go. I remember it because I remember this one husband and wife, and their daughter was in my class. Their name was Ban, B-a-n, and they were from Boyle Heights. They taught Japanese, and there must have been others that taught Japanese in different parts of the camp where they lived.

Were the Bans in the orphanage, too?

No. They lived in barracks within the blocks.

How long were you in Children's Village before you got transferred with your brother and sister?

That same year.

So you were there less than a year.

Oh, yes, definitely. I don't really know when I left the Village. When my sister Susie and brother above me moved out of the Village—after we got there, they had to leave because that was the agreement that was made for them, that they were going to be transported there only. Then they were going to go—my oldest brother John was there already, and they were going to get an apartment and go live in the barracks. I begged them to take me, so they took me. When they got the apartment, they took me. That's why I wasn't in the

---

[2] Actor Lou Frizzell served as the music and drama instructor at Manzanar High School. He is best known for playing the character Dusty Rhodes in the 1970s television show, *Bonanza*. In 1976, he played himself in the television movie *Farewell to Manzanar*.

Village for long—but I would go and visit. And then I had a boyfriend in the Village that was from the Salvation Army.

Did you keep in touch with him?

Well, he's one of them that I should have talked to at the Children's Village reunion, but I didn't.

How about your social life at the Village? You said you were dating—

Well, I was out of the Village then. He would walk me down to where I lived and everything. Then all the girls were chasing him all over the camp. I remember that. He made a comment to my sister about that, that I had chased him. I never chased him, but I remember all the girls were chasing him.

Did you go to dances, movies, and stuff?

No, we just spent time together. I don't know. I don't remember. They would have movies probably once a week or something like that.

When you were in the Children's Village, did you have activities like sports?

Oh, yeah. We had a team called the Fighting Nines. This was after I left the Village, but we had a baseball team called the Fighting Nines, and my little sister was also on it. She was known as the home run queen because she always hit home runs. Then the boys had a terrific basketball team.

In the Village?

Yes. Most of the kids came from the Village. Tamo Isozaki was on it and his three brothers were on it. Maybe more than that, but there were three that I remember. They were great. They used to beat the Terminal Island team. And Terminal Island was—what would you say? Like a gang?

Terminal Island, were they like the tough kids?

Yeah. Terminal Island was actually like a ghetto of all Japanese. I remember there was a Russian girl that lived on Terminal Island. Her family lived among the Japanese. Oh my God, they used to tease her. She spoke Japanese fluently because she lived with them, but if you weren't born on Terminal Island, you were a foreigner. We were from Los Angeles, so we were foreigners.

Were you treated differently?

Yes, definitely. I mean, prejudice goes on wherever you go. Even within your own people, it's worse. It's worse. But then you have to learn to forgive because we were only children. We were children. And your parents are working, and they're not aware of what you're doing.

Was there a big difference between the rest of Manzanar and the Children's Village? Was the Children's Village better off? Or were the barracks better?

I don't think there was any difference. The only difference was that, at the Children's Village, instead of parents, you had matrons or men that took care of the boys. They looked over you. To me, I think every person is different. I think the boys got more love than the girls did. There were two sisters who were matrons that were formerly in the Japanese Children's Home [Shonien]. They grew up and they became matrons. And they were matrons at that time in the Village. Some of the older ones, they were very strict. [The staff on] the boys' side too was strict, but we didn't hear of it from my brothers, my younger brothers.

They were stricter with the girls and a little bit more lenient with the guys?

Yeah, because you've got strict teachers, and the other teachers might be very lenient. People don't all come the same.

Two of the girls that grew up at the Village worked inside the Village?

Yes. They became matrons.

Did you work there too?

No, I wasn't an adult. You were an adult if you worked there.

Did you work anywhere inside Manzanar?

Yes. I worked in a Caucasian mess hall. I used to baby-sit for the people that worked within the camp because I worked in the mess hall where they would come and eat. I got to know them, and then they would ask me to baby-sit. I also worked at a pickle factory. We used to pickle, so we could eat them at the mess hall. I remember they used to come and pick us up when I worked there. I remember they used to come in a flatbed truck and go all over and pick you up. You'd just sit there on the back of the thing with your legs dangling. (chuckles)

Did they treat you okay at work? Were they nice to you?

Oh, yeah, because you're just with the people that's in the camp. In other words, the people that are directing you are actually the ones teaching you how to do the things. They were incarcerated too.

I worked in the hospital, too. We were kids. In the hospital, there were a lot of Caucasian nurses. I remember one of the other girls younger than I, we'd sit there—we worked graveyard. And we'd get this great big book out and look at the pictures and look at weird things. (chuckles) We were young and didn't know any better.

There was one guy that was in there from day one. His name was Pete Kondo, and he was a famous baseball player in Japanese Town in the Los Angeles area. He was in an automobile accident, and then he was paralyzed. So we all used to go see him. He was the number one customer in the hospital. (laughter)

Was he sort of cute?

He was okay, I mean, we were friends. I remember my older brother knew him, and they came out to visit once. This nurse took him under her wing, after she left the hospital. Her name was Thelma McBride. She still writes to me. Every Christmas, I get a letter from her about what's going on. She took care of him. And I remember she brought him one time to Los Angeles, and we all went up to the hotel at that time. We all went up to see him and everything, the people that were in the hospital. I guess he must have passed away. She's not too healthy. That's what she said in her last Christmas letter.

My older sister Susie worked in the hospital. I don't know if it was the boiler room in the laundry or something. I never went there for a doctor's visit or something, so I don't remember the doctors' offices. All I remember is, I went there to get my teeth fixed. So they must have had places where you went. That one ward had babies and women. We didn't have a separate ward for just babies. I remember I got to see a two-pound baby. That was the smallest. And a ten-pound baby. And I wasn't even eighteen.

What did you think about the facilities in the Children's Village? How were they? The staff, did they have enough staff members to take care of you?

Well, I suppose so. We always had to say our prayers. God is good and God is great, and we thank him for this food. Whatever they served us, we had to eat every bit of it. I blamed them for giving me ulcers. I'm fat now, but I was small when I was young. But anyway, what happened was, because I was petite, I couldn't wait to be excused from the table because I would run to the toilet and puke.

On purpose?

No. Because it was too much. It was too much food. See, you couldn't be excused until everybody ate what was served. So, therefore, you had to eat everything there that was on your plate. I don't think that's right, when I think back about it. But I mean, maybe I'm the type, but I know when I worked, I had ulcers and stuff like that.

So they didn't treat you all that well. I mean, they treated you well, but they forced you to eat the food?

Well, if nobody could get excused from the table, you had to eat your food. They were very strict with us, but I guess, in a way, that was right. It was right at that time.

Was the food good? Did they serve good, healthy food?

I can't remember that it was good food. I didn't know about diet or anything like that. We always got rice, though. We always got rice. I can't remember milk. When I was growing up, I could not take milk. I don't have the enzyme.

Did the staff mistreat anybody? You or anybody else you know?

I never saw anybody get whacked. They would be strict. I mean, I was aggressive, so therefore, maybe that's the reason why.

What religion did your father teach you?

Buddhism. My father used to always make me pray when he was out fishing. He would ask me to pray.

And was it practiced in the Children's Village?

No.

Did they make you—?

We had Christian services.

Did they make you go to them?

Yeah. They'd take us to church. I remember when we were at the children's home [Shonien], we used to go to Union Church, the one that closed on San Pedro Street. We used to go there before we went in the camp. And then a lot of the people that were there, the matron and the—what would you call them? Not the matron, but the man. I don't know what you call them. But their wives and them would be Christians, and they would practice. I remember one of them said to me, "When you get kissed, you become pregnant." (laughter) I remember that. I believed it for a long, long time.

Who told you that, if you kissed a guy, you'd be pregnant?

One of the wives of the—I don't know if he was a reverend or if he was— [that] takes care of the boys, or what. I remember his name, but I won't say his name.

Who took care of talking to you about woman necessities? Did anyone talk to you about birth control and all that kind of stuff?

They didn't believe in birth control or having intercourse or anything like that. I mean, you just didn't talk about those things.

Is there any way your life has been affected in a major way by being at Manzanar camp? Has it changed your way of thinking?

Of course, because those were the years that you were growing up and your foundation is laid. We had some kind of guidance while we were in the camp, I would say. If we were in a different environment with no coaching or anything like that, we wouldn't have been exposed to Christianity or any religion or no upbringing.

What religion are you, if I may ask?

None. I believe in all religions because they all come together by a superior being. I don't believe that we just came to be. Maybe that's true, and a lot of people believe that.

Do you remember the hapa *[person of mixed-race heritage] kids in the Children's Village?*

You know, the kids that were different, that were half Japanese and half—

Were they treated any differently than the other kids?

Yeah, the *hapa* kids. They didn't stay long.

In the Village?

Yeah, they were adopted. Most of them looked more white than Japanese. Why, I don't know.

Were they different—the hapas?

Yeah, because they were—I remember this one kid's name—I don't know if his name was Tojo [See interview with Dennis Tojo Bambauer, COPH-OH 2335], or not. Like I say, when you're different, you're treated that way. Like on Terminal Island, I told you we were different. My mother was sick. My mother lived with us, and she used to take walks and go all over the island. And she used to make this smock that she sewed and wore. But she just liked to walk. But the kids used to always tease us about her, so that in itself was hard on us.

My sister Susie don't even like to talk about Terminal Island. She can't stand it. But she's older than me, four years older than me. I learned to accept and forgive in a way because we were kids. Kids say the meanest things, and if you don't have no supervision—and the kids on Terminal Island didn't have no supervision; the mother and father were both working—they're not aware of what goes on. Or just so small-minded.

Who were the hapas *mistreated by? The other children?*

Yeah, the rest of the kids.

Did the staff treat them differently or just the kids?

I don't know. I don't remember the staff mistreating them.

Why did they treat them differently? Because they were different?

Yeah.

Out of anger, jealousy, or—

I think, what it is, it's like anything else. If you're not normal by what is normal—if everyone's all the same color, and if you're black—yeah, they were treated differently. But what happened was, they disappeared, so they were adopted. They weren't there any longer. But we kept getting more new babies,

I guess from out of wedlock or whatever it is, from other camps, or whoever they came from. We had babies in that 1944 Easter Sunday picture.

How about around the Village and outside in the community? Did the orphans or the people in the Children's Village experience any kind of prejudice?

No, because the kids all played sports and things like that. They participated in that and you had the competition wherever they played, on the school basketball courts, or wherever. They were very good. They were outward going.

   I think in our time when all this was happening, a lot of the kids I knew had their mother in an institution. And they were able to communicate, and they gave up their secrets to you. I didn't realize until the other day what it means to some kids to cover their past, just because I'm not that way. I guess that's why I expect them to be that way. But I could see where they want their past not brought up, because there's too much hurt for them. They can't face up to it. Well, I can't talk for them because I had both parents. One was sick and one was—but still I had both parents, where they had one or none. It must make a lot of difference.

Do you know why the orphanage at Manzanar was called Children's Village?

My brother called it the orphanage, and I always tell him that I hate that name because it wasn't an orphanage. Whoever picked that name, I would never have thought of it. It's a good name. It was a village full of kids. What an appropriate name. I never thought to ask why they named it that. But they did talk them into making that. The way they set it up and everything; it was all planned. Mrs. [Lillian] Matsumoto said they went down there to check on the progress of the building and stuff like that. And she said that's why we left late for Manzanar.

So you were fourteen when you went in there. You were a teenager. How did you feel? You were not an infant, so you knew what was going on. You had feelings that the younger kids didn't. How did you deal with that? Were you scared?

No. I could say that because I've never—in all my life, I don't get scared. It's a funny thing to say. I guess maybe it's because I had trust. Growing pains.

It is how you're brought up. I believe so, too. When you think about the Village, what is your most vivid memory of it?

Well, we had a typhoid shot. We had to get typhoid shots, and that made us sick. I mean, we were down.

How often did you get them?

Once.

But you were down.

Yeah. I never heard of people getting typhoid shots. It's to prevent the disease, but we got it in camp. That's all I remember. We all got the typhoid shot. That stands out because I guess it affected us, all of us. We were down for at least two days, and the pain and the swelling and everything like that. But I remember that. I don't know why.

Did you have privacy in the camps?

Privacy? There were no doors in front of the toilets. There was just like a wall like this. In the showers, it was just one big room with showers on two walls.

What if you wanted to be alone? Did you have a place to go?

No. There wasn't anything, unless you went for a walk or something out in the field, out in the firebreak, or something like that. The sand was so bad. Wind storms. You couldn't see in front of you, and you would get sand all over everything. It was horrible. But the stars at night in the desert! You could see every star in the whole continent. Then when it thundered, you'd think the whole sky was going to come down on you.

What did you sleep on?

We had straw mattresses.

Comfortable?

Oh, no. They're like—they're not like regular.

What about emotional support in the Village? Who provided that when the kids needed it? Did anybody provide it?

I would say—see, I know about the boys more than I know the girls, because my brothers would tell me. Those guys would support them. John Nagayama and John Hohri [See COPH-OH3786]. The older guys would look after the younger guys. And my brother was a very unusual person. He was very—not softhearted. Tender. I mean, I don't think—I say this, not because he's my brother, but as a person—he would never turn a person away. I could turn a person away, but I don't think he was the type that could. He was always gentle, and he was always trying to find out if he could help the younger sisters, or whatever.

Why did you not tell these stories until now?

Nobody's asked me before. (laughter) Well, I think what I tell you is what I believe in and what happened to me, and things I could tell you. There was so much tragedy in some of those kids' lives before they were in the Village. I used to feel for them. I used to really feel for them. And I always felt lucky because I *was* lucky, because I had parents, and I could understand how they would feel.

Thanks for the interview.

You're welcome.

Takatow Matsuno[1]

Interviewed by Noemi Romero

Do you know your birthday?

May 14, 1935. I was born in Los Angeles, right in downtown, on Jackson and Alameda Street.

Before camp, what is your most vivid memory?

We used to live on Terminal Island. This was just before the war. We used to play on the railroad tracks. We'd go to school. Well, I guess we used to walk a mile or two down to the school, maybe about a mile down.

My father was a fisherman then. He would go out fishing and come back. When the war broke out, as a kid, I must have been terrified because there were three FBI people that came to the house, and they came searching all through the house. My other brothers were saying, "Don't be afraid! Don't be afraid!" When the FBI came in, they searched the house without any kind of warrant or anything. They just came in. They said that our father was an enemy spy or whatever, and we didn't have any rights. We had to leave Terminal Island in forty-eight hours.

From there, we came to the Shonien, which is in Silverlake, California, and we stayed over there. My oldest brother John was eighteen or nineteen, so they didn't take him then. My oldest sister, Susie, is the one that kept us together, and she went with us to Children's Village so we would all be together, more or less. She would be like my mother because my real mother was in the hospital.

When your mom was first taken, and then your dad, do you remember the feelings that you had?

Yeah, I remember my mother making me cereal with sugar and stuff like that. She used to make rice. We used to get rice, and then it was stirred up with a little sugar and it used to taste good. You remember some of them things; but as time goes on, you forget. It's like saying, "I should have learned my Japanese language then." If you're not around it, you don't know it.

---

[1] COPH-Oral History 2339 was conducted on March 19, 1993, in Monterey Park, California.

But the day you were separated from your mother, and then your father, what do you remember? Were you detached? Were you crying?

I probably cried.

But it's not like something that stands out that you remember?

You know—I block it out of my memory.

Because it's something so significant, you have to remember something.

I really don't. I think I don't even want to remember those things because, like I said, I just block that all out of my mind. It's just like when I went into camp, guys from Terminal Island were saying hi and everything to me. I didn't even know them. When all of these things are happening, you just live one day at a time. You forget all your friends and everything else.

Can you tell me about your relationship with your brothers and sisters before camp? What do you remember?

Well, yeah, there was an incident with my brother, Shioo. We were down on Terminal Island. Shioo is about six years older than I am, so I was maybe about five years old and he must have been about twelve or thirteen. We were on Terminal Island, and, being the youngest kid, I had to go out and do what the older ones told me. So we were down where they had the roundhouse on Terminal Island. They took the roundhouse out, and there was a big rock quarry where all the rock was, and we would have to go down to the rocks to set cans up, so we could throw rocks and knock the cans down. They hit me with a rock and I started bleeding and bawling like mad. Shioo got me on his back and said, "Oh, I'm a fire engine." (chuckling) He carried me all the way home, and that must have been about a mile away. He just kind of rocked me, and I went home. That's one thing I remember. Our family is pretty close, our whole family. Very close.

Do you remember anything about the Shonien [orphanage in Los Angeles, California]?

All I remember is that they used to have a lot of shrubs and stuff, and we used to run around inside. The Shonien was in Silverlake. In fact, I've been up there a couple of times before, but not recently. I don't know what's there now. But my memory of Mr. [Harry] Matsumoto, the old man, is that he took me down from the hill to get a pair of shoes. We used to run barefooted when we lived on Terminal Island. We weren't the richest people. We were poor, and I remember getting some shoes when I was at the Shonien.

Were these shoes new or hand-me-downs?

Brand-new shoes. Mr. Matsumoto took me to the store, and I got a brand-new pair of shoes. (chuckling) I think they hurt me, too. (laughter)

Were all your clothes and shoes new or hand-me-downs?

I can't remember any of that. We had clothes.

Overall, did you have enough clothes?

Yeah. Well, over at Manzanar camp, there were four seasons. When you're up near the mountains, it gets cold. I remember the wind storms. They had wind storms you couldn't believe! You'd get out there in the old tar-papered barracks we were in, and a lot of stuff is coming through them.

I remember my father used to have a victory garden at Manzanar. In between the barracks, he would grow grapes and stuff, and he'd try to make his wine out of them. We used to eat the grapes off the top, and when they'd turn to raisins, we'd eat the raisins. (chuckling) He used to make tobacco leaves and make his cigarettes. We used to go in the firebreaks and my father, who used to love golf, used to drive the golf balls. Good golf balls then, you know, were rubber, and they didn't have rubber in them days. But when they'd get a golf ball, he used to drive them. My brother and I used to go out on the firebreak, and we either had to catch the golf balls or find them. (chuckling)

Do you remember the ride to Manzanar?

I remember going to Manzanar. There were three buses, and we had a motorcycle escort going out of Los Angeles up to the county line. I think when we hit Kern County, they stopped and we kept going. There must have been a flood or something near Red Rock Canyon because you could see that the highway was eaten away.

What happened when you reached camp?

When we reached camp, all these people came looking at us because the three buses were for the Children's Village. We had been moved from the Shonien; I don't remember if there were some Maryknoll people with us either. We went to the Children's Village, and there were three barracks. One was for the kitchen and for the Matsumotos. I think there was also a reading room or something. The next barrack was for the older girls and a nursery. I was in there for a little bit. Then the third barrack was for the boys, and the other side was the big boys' side.

Where was your father?

We didn't know where our father was. The FBI had taken him away. He was transported to all different places. He was in Santa Fe, New Mexico, and then I think Louisiana and Alabama. All different places.

What was it like to be at the Children's Village?

When we were in the orphanage, we were pretty well-disciplined. We were kind of converted to the Christian way. Then there were some Catholics from Maryknoll there too. I remember we went to Sunday school. (chuckling) Every Sunday, we would go. The Children's Village had a mess hall in the first building where we would go and eat, and we would say grace and everything.

In the back of the Village, we used to have a pear orchard, and they had a garden with a gazebo. I remember that.

What about school when you were at Manzanar?

I remember going to school, but when you're that young, it's hard to remember a lot of the people! Even now I kind of remember their first names, but not their last names. From the orphanage, we would go to school, and then we'd come straight back to the orphanage. We didn't have any time to dilly-dally around.

How long were you in Children's Village?

From 1942, after the war broke out, I guess, until about 1943, right before 1944, right before the Easter Sunday picture was taken, because my father came back to camp.

During this time, did you know why you were in the camp? Did you know why you were in the Children's Village?

Well, my parents weren't around, so we had to go into the Village. Who was going to take care of us, you know? There wasn't anybody around that could take care of us.

But going back, did you know what was going on? What did you know? You were so young! You were what, about six years old?

Yeah.

Who would bathe you? Did you take your own bath? Did you have help?

Well, when I was on the little side, they'd get a brush and scrub us down. When you got older, if you didn't wash yourself, they'd scrub you down. (chuckling)

So it wasn't anything gentle?

No. You go in there and you go in the shower, and, if they see you not washing yourself, they'd scrub you down.

Did you like taking showers? A lot of kids just don't like taking them.

I like showers.

I read that the older children would wash their own laundry, but the younger ones had their laundry done for them.

No, we never did our own laundry, but the older ones did.

How would you describe your room conditions?

I remember if you peed in your bed, you'd go through the swat line, or whatever it was.

Did you ever?

I think I have, yeah.

There were some kids in the Village that had a problem with that.

There were some that had problems, yeah.

Did you ever ask yourself, "What am I doing here?" Because you were younger, did you have a full understanding of what was going on? What did you think?

Well, when you're small like that, it's kind of frightening when you see all this going on. That part there wasn't too bad. Well, the only thing that I can remember that was bad was when the FBI came to our house on Terminal Island. That was bad. Then, when we got out of camp, going to school, you know, we were "Jap, Jap, Jap." (chuckling) It was kind of really bad for a young person, but we overcame that.

Can you give me any specific time where you felt that racism here in America after the camp, in school?

Gee, I don't know, I just let it pass. Well, I went to junior high school, and it was almost like 70 or 80 percent black. That was at Lafayette Junior High School. There were a few Hispanics. I've got a picture of my junior high school class picture. But I don't know, there were a few times when I was a lot younger that all that stuff came up. In general, I guess I used to have to fight a little bit. A lot of the stuff I forget.

Did you fight verbally or did you get into fistfights?

Yeah, I'd get in fistfights. You know, "You Jap this and that," and then— (chuckling) then you fight a little bit. But that's when you're like in elementary school and stuff. In junior high school, they still had gangs and things then too, you know. I mostly stayed with my own people, the Japanese people. I've gone out with different other people too. I've mixed, but when they had socials and all that, I would go to the Japanese socials. They would be anywhere from Puente to Long Beach or Gardena. We used to do this in one night, drive around (chuckling) just to see how these dances were. This was like on Saturday night during my high school days, around 1950.

Returning to the Children's Village, do you remember if the children who were hapa *[a person of mixed-race heritage] had it worse off than you guys had it? What treatment did they get that was different than yours? You mentioned to me a child who was half-German, half-Japanese.*

Because they were half, they weren't pure Japanese.

What specific things were done to them?

Well, they were picked on more because they were different people. I mean, you look at them and it's obvious. If you're Japanese, you're Japanese. If you're half-German and half-Japanese or half-Mexican and half-Japanese, you have Japanese blood in you, but you were mixed. So when the *hapas* were in the orphanage or even when they were going to school, it's obvious and they'd get picked on and they would have it worse than I did.

By other students or the staff? By the instructors?

I think from everybody, more or less. They used to have problems. They used to urinate in their pants and stuff. I mean, hey, this isn't a regular thing.

Because they were frightened?

Yeah, they were frightened and things like that.

Do you remember any specific event that happened that a hapa *child went through? Was somebody looking down at them and you could tell? Any specific story you can tell me?*

Not really because I was too young. I mean, there were things that happened, but to me, it was like everything in general. I remember some incidents, but there are some things that you just forget. (chuckling)

You went from your house on Terminal Island to the Shonien and then to Children's Village at Manzanar. How did you adjust?

It was the same because you were like in a room where you have beds and stuff. You had different cots or beds and there was a whole bunch of you, so you were just confined to one room. You slept there, you got up, you ate in the mess hall, you came back to your room, or you went out and played in the yard, went to school, came back, ate. They had programs. They'd give you an allowance. I forgot; they'd give you fifty cents or something.

Like a dollar fifty, depending upon your age?

Yeah, something. It was something, but it wasn't too much.

What did you do with that money?

Oh, you could do whatever you wanted to do with it. You'd buy candy.

Is that what you did?

I really can't remember. I remember that each barrack in the Children's Village had their sections, like one end was for the small boys, and the other end was for the big boys. And right in the middle, they had a storage room and the bathrooms and the showers. I remember going into the storage room and stealing some candy. (chuckling)

From the storage room?

In the storage room, yeah.

How was the food at camp? Was there enough food? Did you ever want more food or was there always a lot?

That's another thing: You had to eat all the food that was on your plate. You eat it or you don't leave the table. You eat everything up. They forced you to eat it.

Did you ever have a chance to get seconds?

I don't remember that part, but I know whatever food they gave you, even if you don't like it, you eat it. You eat the food. If you're going to throw up, you hold it until you go out.

Did you ever throw up because of bad food?

I don't remember that either, but I know we had to eat the food that was served in front of us.

Was it tasty? What do you remember?

Mutton. Or old lamb. Stinky lamb! I like lamb, but I don't like mutton. It was mutton and it stunk. They used to have stew, you know, and they'd make it and it would stink and taste bad. (chuckling) It seemed like they gave you leftover stuff that's not fit for people to eat. I remember that.

I learned how to barbeque lamb or shish kebab and it's very good. We take it camping. My wife makes it all the time. You marinate it for about three days and put it on the barbeque and, oh, it's good. But if you talk to any of the older Japanese people, and you say lamb . . .

Did the Children's Village ever have a pet? Did you ever have a dog, a cat, or anything like a pet?

No, they didn't allow that.

When you were in the Children's Village, did you blame anybody for not having your parents with you?

You know, when you're young like that, you can remember one thing one minute, but the next day it'll be gone. As long as I got to eat and play and do what I do, it was really nothing. But some of the emotional stuff gets to you.

Can you tell me the difference between the Shonien and the Children's Village? Was there any difference in staff or the way they cared for you?

Well, when you're little, you just do what they tell you to do. Some of the older kids, like Tamo Isozaki [See COPH-OH 2332], were in the Village and he took care of us. When we did anything bad or did something, they would have a swat line and we'd have to go through the swat line. All these kids would be lined up with their legs open like this and you'd go through. When you'd come through the swat line, you'd get hit. (chuckling)

And who would hit you?

All the kids in the orphanage, all the way up the swat line.

So you'd hit each other? Is that how you disciplined each other?

Yeah, they used to do that.

What other ways did they discipline you?

I don't remember any of the staff taking a strap to me or giving me a whipping.

You mean any staff members?

Yeah, as a staff. I don't remember any of that. All I remember is, when we did something, the discipline was to go through that swat line and we would get hit. Later, you'd get revenge on the ones that really hit you. (laughter)

Did any of the staff ever put you down or hurt you emotionally? Anything that you recall?

Well, the staff is not like your mother and father, but then the Asian custom isn't like the Nisei. The staff was not like how I treat my granddaughter now. You know, I give her a lot of love and attention. Well, you don't have that with the older Japanese people. Even in the orphanage, you don't have any of that.

I can remember one thing. When they had Christmas, the older staff would give us gifts. I remember Mary Honda, and she didn't want to come to our Children's Village reunion. She's the one I cherish because she gave me a little Archie funny book. I mean it was something that you'd get from someone older. When you get a gift like that, you remember that as a little kid. I remember getting that. That's one thing I remember, and I never forgot that.

Did you have any other specific toys, toys that were just yours? Or were the toys that you had for everyone to share?

The toys were for everyone to share, as I remember. More or less, they had toys in the little children's side. We used to play marbles. Naturally, when you play marbles, you keep the marbles that you win. We used to play in a ring and play marbles. And we used to play tops. We used to look in the Sears and Roebuck and Montgomery Ward catalogs because that's all you'd get to look at when you were in camp.

What other games did you play?

We used to play "Capture the Flag." Do you know what "Capture the Flag" is? There was a big open field like this, and you had one side here and one side here. They'd have a middle point, and you come out and cross to the other side to capture the flag. Well, if you come out and this guy comes out after you and you tag him, then you take him as a prisoner. If you could get over to the other side and get their flag and run all the way back to your side, you won the game.

Children's Village also had a baseball diamond, [and a] basketball and volleyball court. Did you ever participate in any of these games?

I remember the older children always playing in these games and we'd go see them. Tamo Isozaki and the others had a team. I think they called themselves the Zeros, and it consisted of a lot of the orphanage's older boys. We used to go watch them.

They had a baseball diamond that was way down near Highway 395. After we got out of Children's Village, we lived right near the baseball diamond. The camp also had an outdoor movie theater that you'd go out to once a week. I forget what day it was. They also had a judo place and an auditorium.

When you were down at the Children's Village, to whom did you go to for emotional support?

I don't know. I guess I would go to my sister, probably my older sister or my brother. They were all protective of us younger ones.

Do you mean your older brother and sister, John and Susie?

No, John and Susie weren't in the orphanage. Well, Susie was there for a little while, but she went out because she was too old. But she kept us together.

So you're talking about Mary?

Well, I think more or less my brothers. They were more protective of the younger ones like my brother above me. My brother Isa was still in there and Shioo was in there. Mary was there. But they got out. Susie, my oldest sister, was in there just for a little bit, and then Isa was in there for a little bit, and so was Mary. Then it was like Shioo, Shiro, me, Tatsue, and Betsy. There were five of us that were more or less left behind, and my brother Shioo kind of looked over us.

So when you cried when you were sad, you went to him for that support?

No, you kind of more or less kept it to yourself because you have all these other kids around. You know, if you cry (chuckling), you really didn't have a mother or father to go to and cry on their shoulder. So, being a young kid, when I stop and think about it, it's nice to have a mother and father you could always go to.

Did you feel that the staff was there with emotional support for you?

No. (chuckling) The matrons were kind of mean, you know.

In what way? Would they yell at you?

Well, there were different ways to discipline you. We had to be disciplined. It's not like it's your own parents. I mean, the matrons are not my mother or whatever; they're just strict and they tell you to do this and that. I mean, you don't question them because it has to be done. They just tell you, "You do that, or else." It's not like you're going to get love and attention. Even if you do something good, it wasn't really there. Now you could talk to the staff. I wanted this one matron to come to the Children's Village reunion, but she was a real, real strict person. I wanted her to come because, hey, those days were them days, you know what I mean? You forget all your ill feelings or whatever. We're adults, so that kind of thing doesn't bother me now. I'm not going to keep a grudge. We're adults now.

Was there any staff member that you were attached to?

Tamo Isozaki. As I remember, when we were in camp, he used to always carry a Bible. I mean, you're brought up a Christian when you're in the orphanage and you look up to your elders. There was Tamo and another person, a *hapa* named Kenny. I don't know where he is anymore. But, yeah, I looked up to Tamo. He was real good.

John [Sohei] Hohri [See COPH-OH 3786] used to help out at the Children's Village. He was in Shonien back in 1934 and 1935, from what I understand. You read about his brother William Hohri a lot in the papers and stuff. Well, John Hohri—this is the good part—used to tell stories to us little guys. He had a knack for telling you a story at nighttime and keeping you in suspense until the next day. He would talk to us about Jean Valjean in *Les Miserables* or Jack London, a lot of different stories, and the older guys from the other side would come over and listen, too. (chuckling) That's how good he was. He'd go in a slow way, and then this happens and that happens. I mean, we were all attentive and we'd just listen. He'd tell all these stories. I remember that. That was real clear in my mind. He used to do that. I think he lived across the street in Block 29.

You were little when you were sent away to an orphanage. Even as an adult, it would hurt to be pulled away from your family, and you cried. What memories trigger that?

Well, I guess you have that experience, and then you get over it. I mean, I don't think you ever get over it, but the situation is you learn how to survive. And this is the thing: If you don't survive, people are going to step on you. And that's what you have to do. You have to do whatever you have to do.

So your main adjustment was going from Terminal Island to the Shonien?

No, I think my main adjustment was when we left camp.

That was more of an adjustment?

More of an adjustment than the Village. Actually, for us younger ones, I think we had more fun in the camp because we had no responsibility. Everything was furnished, but we went out for adventure. We would sneak out of camp and go. This was after we left the Village and lived in the barracks. When we were in the Village, we were regimented where we had to do different things and that was it. I mean, you'd sleep in this one room, you'd go to the mess hall, and you'd come back. Then you'd go to school, and then come back home. We didn't dilly-dally anyplace going anywhere like we would when we got out of there. Then it was different when we moved to the barracks. We weren't as restricted as we were when we were in the Village, so during that part of camp experience, we adjusted real quick.

Thank you for the interview.

You're welcome.

Resident number 5 is Robert Yamashita, number 10 is Tamo Isozaki, number 14 is Tak Isozaki, and number 17 is John Nagayama. This is a picture taken in front of one of the Children's Village barracks.

Staff gardeners developed and maintained the grounds of
Children's Village.

Staff with babies, (l-r) Ruth Takamune, Fuji Kajiwara, Taeko Kajiwara,
Maseo Deguchi. Second baby from left is Lillian Ogata.

Mr. & Mrs. Marvin Crites with Harry and Lillian Matsumoto and orphans. Mr. Crites was an employee of the school at Manzanar.

December 1942: Harry and Lillian Matsumoto, Mrs. Crites (nutritionist), Mrs. May Ichida and Captain Ainozuke Ichida both from the Salvation Army staff who accompanied the children from San Francisco. Mrs. Ichida was a nursery school teacher at Children's Village.

Choir director Louie Frizzell practices with the singers.

Taeko Nagayama and Lillian Matsumoto

Lisa Nobe Wong, Lillian Matsumoto,
and Taeko Nagayama.

Takatow Matsuno

Matsuno family, clockwise from left (starting with man in white shirt): Isao, Shiro, Mary, Takatow, Susie, Tatsuye, Kozan (holding Betsy), and John.

Chapter Five
Family Life:
Reuniting with Parents

Many of the orphans sent to Children's Village were "temporary" or half-orphans, who were reunited with one or both parents during or after the war. In some cases, these temporary orphans had been placed in an orphanage prior to the war by their parents because of financial hardships, the illness and/or death of one parent, or neglect and abandonment. Being sent to an orphanage had a deep impact on parent-child relationships, especially when the relationship was already tenuous or distant. However, for many children, the parent-child reunions were just as, or even more, stressful and traumatizing. According to Donna Nagata and Wendy Cheng, intergenerational communication studies on Holocaust survivors, Armenian genocide survivors, and Japanese American detention camp survivors show that "trauma combined with ethnic and racial discrimination had a particularly strong silencing effect in the family."[1] Amy Iwasaki Mass adds that the consequences of trauma include not only this "silencing effect," but also "psychological defense mechanisms such as repression, denial, rationalization, and identification with the aggressor to defend ourselves against the devastating reality of what was done to us."[2]

As a result, for many Nisei orphans who had not seen (or never seen) their parents in years, reunions with their parents were usually strained, as fathers and mothers had also been traumatized by prejudice, removal, and incarceration. Even more damaging was when parents were forced by wartime circumstances to take on the parental duties that they had abandoned years earlier. In the following interviews, the memories and stories of parent-child reunions that former Children's Village orphans Ira Iwata, Herbert Suyematsu, and Sam Tanaka share reveal the anger, devastation, and rejection that these former orphans experienced during and after camp.

---

[1]Donna Nagata and Wendy Cheng, "Intergenerational Communication of Race-Related Trauma by Japanese American Former Internees," *American Journal of Orthopsychiatry* 73 (2003): 276.

[2]Amy Iwasaki Mass, "Psychological Effects of the Camps on Japanese Americans," in *Japanese Americans: From Relocation to Redress,* ed. Roger Daniels, Sandra C. Taylor, and Harry Kitano (Seattle: University of Washington Press, 1991), 160.

The three interviews in this chapter provide a glimpse of what these parent-child reunions were like after months or years of separation. Sent to the Shonien at the age of four and then detained at Children's Village from June 1942 to November 1943, Ira Iwata was reunited with his father during the war, after the War Relocation Authority (WRA) located his father in Colorado. In the following excerpt, Iwata discusses not only his memories of the Shonien and the Children's Village, but his struggle to survive in Colorado during the war after he and his brothers were reunited with his negligent father.

Herbert Suyematsu and his two siblings were also placed in the Shonien, but the circumstances were directly the result of wartime military restrictions on the Nikkei community. The FBI arrested Suyematsu's father in 1942 because he had moved more than five miles away from his stated place of residence for a job. After his father's arrest, Suyematsu's mother became mentally ill and was sent to Patton State Mental Hospital, located in the city of Highland in San Bernardino County, California. In the following excerpt, Suyematsu recalls his reunion with his father and mother at Manzanar during the war, after his two-year experience as an orphan at the Shonien and the Children's Village.

Reuniting with parents was potentially even more difficult, if you were a sixteen-year-old teenager. Sam Masami Tanaka was three years old when his mother was sent to a sanitarium for a variety of illnesses. Unable to care for his children and afraid of being deported, Tanaka's father gave them up for foster care. Tanaka and his three siblings lived with a Japanese foster family for six years until they were sent to the Salvation Army Children's Home in San Francisco in 1939. Ironically, he and his siblings did not know until after the war that their father was also relocated to Manzanar after he was released from a Justice Department internment camp in Santa Fe, New Mexico. Only after the war did Tanaka and his siblings live with his father—until his father once again left them. In the following excerpt, Tanaka discusses his life as a young teenage boy at Children's Village, as well as the effects that foster care and relocation had on not only his relationship with his biological father, but also his identity as a father to three sons.

Ira Iwata[1]

Interviewed by Cathy Irwin

And so when your family moved to California, you and your brother Robert were sent to the Shonien. Do you remember your feelings or your first impression of the Shonien?

Oh, I remember the first day.

What was that like? What were your feelings?

It was traumatic for both my brother and me. All we did was cry, sit there and cry! Eventually, we got used to it. There was more companionship there at the orphanage than there was at home.

Did any of your family visit you while you were at the Shonien? Did your father or any of your uncles ever visit you?

I don't ever recall my father visiting, but my uncles used to come out every once in a while.

Were there any otonas *[adults] or other children who you remember helping you?*

Oh, yes. One of the *otonas* was Ruth Takamune. Alice Kaneko. Of course, Lillian Matsumoto, naturally, and Harry Matsumoto. Mr. [Rokuichi "Joy"] Kusumoto was the one who ran the orphanage.

Do you have any specific memories of them being really nice to you or helping you? Because you were just a child, four or five years old, do you have any memories of them taking you outside and playing or—?

You probably have never seen what the orphanage was like. It was at 1841 Redcliffe Street, and it was expansive. They kept adding on additional grounds right next to it. As far as my memory goes, it was a lot of fun because there were a lot of kids our age, and all we did was play games and things like that. Kickball and hide and seek and so forth. For us, there were a lot of

[1]COPH-Oral History 3775 was conducted on August 9, 2007, by phone (the interviewer in Claremont, California, spoke to the interviewee who was in Lakewood, Colorado).

pleasant memories, but it was very structured. You got up in the mornings, you lined up, you brushed your teeth and washed your face, stood in line, went to breakfast, and you sat at a table assigned with one *otona* at each table. You said prayers because the home was run by a Christian church. From there, we would line up as we got ready to go to public school. We went to public schools.

Do you remember where?

Micheltorena.

Oh, Micheltorena School.

It was an elementary school right off Sunset Boulevard. We would line up to go to school, and we all walked. Of course, they handed you a brown bag, a lunch bag, as you left and went to school. And then you traded your peanut butter or bologna [sandwich] at school with the other kids. (laughter) It was a lot of fun. As a rule, the kids from the orphanage did well in the public schools.

Did you enjoy being at school? Did you ever experience any prejudice when you were a child at the Micheltorena School? Or did everyone pretty much get along?

I would say we pretty much got along. It wasn't until after Pearl Harbor that it was a lot different.

Did you enjoy any activities or sports as a child?

Oh, yes. Naturally, when you have a group of kids like that, we played a lot of baseball, basketball. But then, in elementary school, I wasn't that keen on it. But just being around the kids, we enjoyed it.

Do you still keep in touch with people who were at the Shonien?

I do with a couple of them. Mits Yamasaki is married to my aunt, and one of my uncle's sisters is his wife's sister. They're sisters to each other. And so he is the brother-in-law to my uncle. Mits Yamasaki. He was one of the older boys there. He looked after us.

So you were at the Shonien from 1935 to 1942, until you were relocated to Children's Village. How old were you in 1942?

In June 1942, that's when they loaded us on a couple of buses and took us to Manzanar. But they let us finish fifth grade, which I was in.

So you were about eleven or twelve?

I would have been eleven. In July, I turned twelve.

Do you remember when you heard about Pearl Harbor?

Oh, yes. Yes, like I said, there was Mr. Kusumoto. I forget his first name, but he brandished his samurai sword. He lived up on the hill and he came down the steps. They had us all congregated down there. And he was hollering, "*Bansai! Bansai!*" (laughter)

With a samurai sword?

Yes. I don't know if he had that much allegiance to Japan, but he was a very good man.

Is that how you heard about the Pearl Harbor attacks?

Oh, after that happened, then we had to put up dark nightshades at the Shonien. We had to keep quiet during the day because they had a lot of people working up on the hillside there in governmental wartime jobs. We had to be silent. And we got some scares about air raids that proved to be nothing. We had to walk to school. And if we had a dime or two to go to the store or if we wanted to walk in the streets, we used to tell them [Caucasians] that we were Chinese.

Oh, really?

Yeah, because the Chinese could walk along the streets, and the Caucasians didn't know if they were Japanese. That was the only thing that I could remember doing during the time shortly after the war broke out. Things changed quite a bit in the schools. The teachers were okay. There was a big resentment against the Japanese kids from the orphanage for still being there in the school.

From the students?

Well, yeah, I'm sure they got that from their parents too. It wasn't blatant. You got snubbed.

Did they ever name-call?

Oh, yeah. Oh, yes. I'm hard skinned about that.

Did the teachers ever intervene?

Well, there were never any fights. I don't recall that much name-calling or anything like that.

Did you have a curfew? I know you were only eleven or twelve.

Oh, yes, I remember curfews. We had our own curfew in the orphanage, and we had to be in by eight or nine o'clock.

So you mentioned that you remembered leaving. Do you remember being sent to Children's Village? What was that day like?

Yes, very dusty. (laughter) Very, very dusty! You got off the bus, and then you got sand in your eyes from the wind blowing all that dust around. There was no vegetation or anything around there. It was all just dust and sand.

Did you take a bus?

To Manzanar, yes. There were two buses. They had a guard on each bus.

How did you feel about that? Did you get nervous?

Not at that age. You're so busy talking to the person next to you. They were singing songs and things like that. So my first impression when I got to the camp was, they had these guard towers with a soldier standing in there, and that was kind of intimidating.

Oh, my goodness. Do you remember the songs you sang on the bus?

No, I don't.

You were really young, but were you told where you were going?

I'm sure we all realized it. I don't recall specifically. All they had to tell us was that we had to move on to these camps. I'm sure they told us the truth.

What did you take with you?

I don't recall. As far as clothes, I think the Shonien and Lillian Matsumoto and the rest of the staff probably packed luggage with our clothes in it. You never knew which clothes you were going to wear from one day to the next because, for all you knew, you could have someone else's trousers. They didn't identify; they didn't put numbers or names on the clothes or anything. If it fit you, then it's it.

Were you and Robert able to stay together?

Well, there was a two-year difference. I was in a group of older kids, and he was in a group of younger kids. As far as being in the orphanage itself, in Children's Village, we were able to see each other quite often. It was a lot different than Shonien.

So how old was he?

His birthday is also in July, so there was exactly a two-year difference. If I turned twelve, he was ten.

What was the difference between the Shonien and the Children's Village?

Oh, big difference. At Shonien, everything was very structured, like I told you. We got up, stood in line, and did things like stay in line to get your lunches to go to school. And when we went to dinner, breakfast, or whatever, you all stood around and said prayers and then sat down. At the Children's Village, there were not that many disciplinarians to look after you. So we got away with a lot, and it was more lenient over there. But it was still somewhat structured.

Do you remember, on the first day, meeting children from other homes? Or were you the first?

We more or less stuck with the other kids from Shonien. And then the others came in from Maryknoll [in Los Angeles, California]. Within the Children's Village itself, we kind of had little—not fights, but tension. It took a while, but we got over it.

What was a typical day—or I don't know if there was any "typical" day at Children's Village—but what was it like?

As little boys do, we would go around looking for little gophers and snakes (laughter) and things like that. We'd form a circle and pit one against the other. We were mean kids. (laughter) Anyhow, we also chose teams, chose sides, and played baseball, football, whatever. We played in the sand; that's all there was, just sand. Then they had orchards. It was in the Owens Valley. And they had pear orchards; we used to pick green pears. In our Children's Village, there was a special barrack, and we had a place where we could store tools, and so forth. It was a lot cooler. And we would bury the pears in the sand in there for a week or two and then dig them up and eat ripe pears. There were several things I remember. And we'd look for scorpions and look for snakes.

What was the weather like for you? How did it affect you?

It was hot. I remember we got there in June [1942], and it was hot and windy and dusty. In the winter, it did get cold. We were snowed upon a few times. As kids, you adapt to things and situations. It wasn't all that bad. The biggest thing or the biggest problem I had was the school. At Micheltorena [elementary school in Los Angeles], we kids from the Shonien were all getting good grades for the most part. But when they put us all there in the Children's Village, they had all Caucasian teachers. And it was very disruptive. We used to call the kids from San Pedro and Terminal Island *yogores*—they were very aggressive and loud.[2] The teachers could not handle them. They used to throw sand at them and all that.

They used to throw sand at the teachers?

Oh, they did anything. I mean, sixth grade at the camp was a total failure. I did not learn a thing. In fact, half the class failed. We had to go to summer school. That didn't do much either, I guess. Eventually, we got people, college graduates or ex-college students who had a couple years of college to teach us. They did the best they could without certification. But I had problems starting in seventh grade. Of course, I went to school for about a half-year or six months or so, before they sent me to Littleton, Colorado. And when I got there, I was so far behind. There was no such thing as remedial courses, and I just barely hung on.

So how long were you in Children's Village?

I was there from June of 1942 until November 15, 1943.

Okay, so you were there long enough. Sounds like the schools were not adequate at all.

Apparently, they got better. But I wasn't there to see any of it.

---

[2]Local residents of Terminal Island called themselves "*yogores,*" which means "dark and dirty on the outside, but pure and clean of heart within." See The Terminal Islanders, *Furusato: The Lost Village of Terminal Island Website* http://www.terminalisland.org (accessed January 1, 2008).

In his interview, Dennis Tojo Bambauer [See COPH-OH 2335], who is hapa *[a person of mixed-race heritage], said that he was teased a lot. Were you teased a lot for being mixed-race?*

No, I wasn't teased as much as he was. He was a few years younger than me, maybe four years younger than I am. But yeah, because his last name was Tojo—Bambauer came later—he was ridiculed more for having the name Tojo.[3] My brother and I and he, as far as I knew, were the only *hapas* there. Yeah, we were teased too.

Oh, you were—for being hapa?

Yeah, the last time I talked to you, about a week ago, I said that they called me *keto* [a white person; also carries the derogatory connotation of "hairy beast"]. I thought that was derogatory. We just assumed that they were talking bad about us. I don't recall being called nasty names like that. Just *keto* got in my craw. Then when we moved to Littleton, Colorado, they called us Japs, so . . .

Oh, my goodness! Before you move to Littleton, can I ask you a couple more questions about Children's Village?

Sure.

What were your impressions of the food there [at Children's Village]? Was it okay?

I was told that we got the same kind of food as the food at the hospital. Our barracks were just like the hospital barracks. Lillian and Harry Matsumoto had to go to the army and request barracks just like the hospital barracks for the kids. And apparently, they built barracks just like they did at the hospital.

So the food was good, then, because it was similar?

Well, the food was a lot better than they were getting in the mess halls in the camp, I think.

Did everyone eat together or was it disorganized?

Oh, we ate in groups, just like at the Shonien. You had a bunch of boys, and we sat with the boys or pretty much our age group.

[3]Dennis Tojo was unfortunate in having the same last name as General Hideko Tojo, the Prime Minister of Japan from 1941-1944 who ordered the Japanese attack on Pearl Harbor on December 7, 1941.

Was there anyone at the camp, a particular person or event, which really stands out in your mind? Was there anyone who made life bearable?

Oh, yes, there were two. There was one, John Sohei Hohri [See COPH-OH 3786].

Can you tell me a little more about what he did for you and the other kids at Children's Village?

Yes. Again, he wasn't a certified [staff] or an *otona*. My understanding is he was finishing up high school or [had] finished high school. And there was one of the jobs that paid seventeen dollars a month, or I don't know what they paid. But he was definitely an influence on most of us kids out there because he read us books, the classics. *Les Miserables* [by Victor Hugo, published in 1862].

Wow. He read you Les Miserables?

Jean Valjean. About how his life was, and so forth. He had us intently listen to a chapter at a time. The next night we would be in for another chapter. So he made it very interesting, and he was also there for help. Then there was another man; he had polio. His name was John Nagayama [See Taeko Nagayama, COPH-OH 2492], I think. I should remember his name, but I'm not sure. But he was one of the *otonas* there, and he had polio. He had a definite limp. He read stories to us. He was into religion. I do recall he eventually left the camp and became a reverend. And he was also influential.

Were there any other activities or clubs that you enjoyed that made camp bearable?

As far as any organized club of any kind, no. At eleven or twelve years old, we just wanted to go out and play marbles.

Did you ever have to do chores or work at camp as a child?

I can't think of that many at the camp because there were so many other people that did the chores around there. There would be a lot of older people who would make little ponds and bridges and things like that. As kids, we didn't do anything but sit around and watch them, play our own games, and so forth. It was really no chores. Well, the older ones probably had dish washing and clothes washing and ironing. But they didn't entrust that to us kids.

Did you have to attend church when you were at Children's Village?

No, but we did attend church on special occasions in Los Angeles. We had *otonas* who were semi-qualified to teach the Bible, and every once in a while a reverend would come to the Shonien. We had Bible classes; I know I read the Bible twice. I never knew what I was reading, but I read it twice. (laughter) We had Bible classes, church services every Sunday. We put on Christmas programs for the board.

How about at Children's Village? Did that happen?

Oh, we had our own informal church services within the Children's Village barracks.

Was it Christian?

Yes. I don't know if the kids in the Catholic schools took to it, but it was still Christian.

Yes. So you were at Children's Village until November 1943 and got to leave early. How did that happen?

I don't know if it was the War Relocation Authority who located my father or if it was Lillian Matsumoto who located my father in Littleton, Colorado. But when they located him, apparently, they made the arrangement to send us back to Denver, Colorado. I do have—they gave me an identification card that said "Citizen, Indefinite Leave." I still have it. It's got my picture with my name on it, and then I was fingerprinted.

You're kidding!

It says: "Citizen" and "Indefinite Leave." United States War Relocation Authority. I'm leaving Manzanar and going to Littleton. I had this with me on the train. They sent an adult with us. He was going to Chicago [Illinois], so he took care of us until we got to Denver. In the meantime, we had to keep the window shades down. I remember that.

And so, they found your father or he found you?

They found him. If it were up to him, he would have left us and okayed us being adopted by somebody else.

Wow. What was he doing in Colorado? Was he still working?

Well, he was doing sharecropping. He would work on somebody's farm, and that's where he was. He was in Littleton, Colorado, and they had a little chicken coop place for us to stay.

You stayed in a chicken coop?

Oh, yes. It was converted into livable quarters. No electricity. No running water. No telephone. That was one of the most miserable times of my life because he was doing the same thing that he did with my mother. He would leave my brother and me for two to three weeks at a time, and we had to rummage on our own.

How did you survive?

I don't know, either. I don't know how we survived. There was a grocery story in Littleton where we were able to charge [groceries]. He used to charge over there, and the owner was kind enough to let us charge. So in that way, we were able to do a little bit. But when it came time to pay up—I remember the last year we were there—he did not pay it. He just took off and moved on to somewhere else.

So you and your brother were basically on your own from the time you were about twelve or thirteen. It must have been hard. Did your father live in the camp for a while?

No, he was in Colorado at the time the war broke out.

So he didn't have to go to camp. Was it more difficult outside of camp than inside?

Very much so. The problem was the parental neglect, in this case. But then, shortly after the war ended, my uncle, Lee Iwata, came home and the first thing he did was visit us. And naturally, his brother, our father, wasn't there. He [Uncle Lee Iwata] got concerned with us being by ourselves so long; he eventually brought us into the city and found us jobs as houseboys. So that's how we survived.

Were you going to school at this time?

No, I was on the farm living with my brother Robert. I missed a year and a half of school. But my other brother [Arthur] was staying with my other uncle, and he was able to go to school. But it was too far for me because I started high school; I was high-school eligible. And so my uncle Lee came out and brought us back to the city. And the first thing he did was find us jobs as houseboys. So we lived there, ate there, went to public schools, and that was it.

Were you really behind in high school for a while?

Very, very much so.

Were you able to catch up and graduate in time?

I eventually did. I missed a year and a half of school, so I graduated in the same class as my brother and eventually my wife!

Oh, was that how you met your wife?

I met her at school, yes. When I graduated in January, I was a nineteen-year-old. And they graduated in June. And when I graduated, I didn't have anywhere to go. That's when I went into the army.

Oh, you went into the army? At nineteen?

Yes.

How long were you in the army, and did you serve in any of the—?

I was in the Korean conflict. I spent some time in Korea and Japan, but I became ill. I was totally paralyzed. I had Guillain-Barre Syndrome (GBS). You become paralyzed, but eventually things start working back and you get use of your extremities. I spent some eight or nine months in the Simmons army hospital here in the Denver area, and I was there until about November 1953.

Oh, my goodness! That was a long time. So you went into the army, and then when you came back, you were in the hospital for eight to nine months. And after that, did you get out of the service?

Yes, I had a medical discharge.

Did you ever experience discrimination in Colorado after the war?

Oh, yes. More so than anywhere.

Did they call you names?

Yes, when I first started school. Of course, I was a dumbbell because I didn't get an education at camp. So I was so far behind. It was pitiful.

So you were a houseboy for four years, when you were in Colorado?

No, not that long. It was about two-and-half years.

Two-and-half years. So you had to just go to school and then go straight back home to work?

Oh, I did play football.

Oh, you played football. Did that help you make friends?

Oh, I made friends in school, sure. But I suffered two concussions and that was the end of my football days.

Oh, wow.

I was able to spend more time with the people who took us in as houseboys. They were very nice.

Was it a Caucasian family?

Yes, it was. She was from Louisiana.

Oh, really. Do you remember the names of your . . .

Yes, her name was Mrs. Tempest. She was very refined. She came from a very cultured family.

After the army, what did you do? Did you choose a career? Did you go to college?

I tried to go to college. One year, I went to the University of Colorado at Denver. I wanted to take an engineering course, which was a mistake. I was failing two courses. I was going on the GI Bill, and they called me in and said, "You are failing these two courses; let's give you an aptitude test." So they gave me an aptitude test, and they found out my highest score was in social work. And they told me, "There's no money in that." (laughter) So, the next highest score was art or visualizing things. So they said, "Why don't you go to drafting school? And that way you'll stay in the engineering area." So I went to drafting school and then got a job as a draftsman.

So you became a draftsman?

Yes.

So after that, you went to work as a draftsman. Because of all your experiences in the camp and in the army, what became really important to you after all these experiences?

The first thing that I would say: I would never turn out to be a father like my father was. But I did not know how a husband should act or how a father should act. So it was a little difficult, but I never tried to be mean to my kids. It was the most important part, I guess.

You said that you met your wife in high school. What is her full name?

Sumiye Shiramizu Iwata.

When did you marry your wife?

Well, shortly after I got out of the hospital! (laughter)

Oh, really! So in 1954? Wow, you've been married for a long time! (laughter)

Yeah, I think the last time I counted, I think it was forty-three—or fifty-three years! I lost ten years there! (laughter)

And how many children did you have?

Two girls. Rebecca and Deborah.

And do your children and grandchildren know about your camp experience?

In fact, when they were living in Virginia, my older daughter has a son and a daughter and he was a senior in high school and the daughter was in middle school. And we were visiting them. We got off at Dulles Airport [Washington Dulles International Airport in Chantilly, Virginia], and my granddaughter said, "Hey, you're going to be our show and tell!" Of course, we came to find out that our grandson was studying the World War II era and the camps and he said, "Would you guys come out and talk to our class?" So we did. We went to his class, and the next day we talked to her class. There were questions about our experiences. We didn't have any advice to give them: just, don't get involved in another war!

Thank you for the interview, Mr. Iwata.

Oh, you're welcome.

Herbert Suyematsu[1]

Interviewed by Reiko Katabami

Where and when were you born?

I was born January 26, 1936, in Brawley [Imperial County], California, near the Mexican border.

Any memories of Children's Village life?

Well, during Christmas time, I think, there were a lot of gifts, toys at that time. That's what I remember thinking.

Oh, so the toys were given to the children?

Well, there were toys, or whatever, but then I don't remember what happened after that because I don't remember having any particular possessions.

So the toys were everybody's possession?

I don't know about others. I don't remember having any particular possessions of my own.

Do you remember bedtime? What time did you go to bed? Nine o'clock or something?

Everybody had to go to bed at the same time. Whatever the normal time was, we went to bed.

Were you ever involved in mischief?

No. I wasn't that sort. I'd just do the ordinary things.

What about your brother and sister?

During that time, they never came to mind.

But you did see each other in the Children's Village?

---

[1]COPH-Oral History 2336 was conducted on July 18, 1993, in Los Angeles, California.

I never remember making any effort to see them. If they were there, maybe then I knew that they were my brother or sister, but I don't remember any experience with them being around.

Do you remember interactions between boys and girls at the Children's Village? Were they separated?

Well, when I was in the children's ward, the children were together. We didn't have much contact with other groups, like older boys or other boys. Then when we were in the boys' room, we didn't have much contact with the other children or anybody else. So we were always in our own group. I thought that was the normal situation.

Did you know any children from the barracks who visited the Children's Village?

I don't think any of that happened.

Did you experience fear and loneliness while you were in the Children's Village?

No.

Were you a carefree child?

I guess so.

Did you always have someone to talk to if something happened?

No. There was no occasion where I needed to talk to anybody.

During the winter season, was it warm enough for you inside the Children's Village?

I don't remember feeling cold or anything, so I must have been okay.

What about summertime? Was it hot?

I don't remember being uncomfortable. That wasn't what remains.

What was the climate like at Manzanar?

We knew that it was snowing in winter, but we didn't suffer from the cold. If it were hot during summer, I don't remember suffering from the heat.

But you experienced the wind and dust?

Oh, dust storms? Yeah. After Children's Village, when I lived in the barracks, I would walk out in the open where dust storms occurred. I remember the stinging effects of the small stones in your face.

So after Children's Village, you lived together with your father after he was released by the FBI and came to Manzanar?

Yes.

Where did he live?

In the bachelor's quarters. There was one corner of Manzanar where single male adults were assigned; so then he was in one of those barracks.

Do you have any idea how many bachelors were living there?

No.

How long did your father live there, before you joined him?

I don't know. He lived there, and then we got together. Then later, my mother was released, so the family was whole again. In that period, we moved to three different places.

Do you remember your mother or father and Executive Order 9066?[2]

We never . . . the parents never talked about those things—about that—to us or to each other, apparently because the only information I got about that was from history.

So your mother was in the hospital when you were sent to the Shonien and she stayed in the hospital after you departed for Manzanar?

Yeah. See, she was in the [Patton State Mental] Hospital [in the city of Highland in San Bernardino County, California] until she was released, but I don't remember exactly when. We moved three times [at Manzanar], and the last barrack was in Block 18. That's when my mother came back.

---

[2]On February 19, 1942, President Franklin D. Roosevelt issued Executive Order 9066, which gave the secretary of war and the US armed forces the authority to define military areas along the West Coast and to exclude from these areas anyone who was considered a threat to the United States. This order eventually gave the military the power to send 120,000 people of Japanese ancestry to concentration camps.

When you say your mother was released, was she recovered from her disease?

Well, probably — although whatever she suffered came back again. Throughout her life she wasn't normal, and then sometimes it got worse. Other times, it was not so bad.

So, she was maybe in much better condition when she was sent to Manzanar?

Uh, probably.

Was the hospital a private hospital?

Oh, no. It was a state mental hospital.

What was your mother's disease?

Well, I don't know what she had actually during the wartime, but then I did witness a manic-depressive situation. So that's what she had at that time. There was an incidence of a manic-depressive condition, but the usual case was persecution. She was always hearing the neighbors plotting against her, or something like that. So it seemed like a mixture of various diseases.

So your mother was released from the hospital and came to Manzanar to join your father?

No, no. We were with our father first, and then mother came.

And then your whole family stayed at Manzanar?

Yes.

Until the end of the war?

Yes.

Was the Children's Village a better facility than the barracks? Were the gardens around the Children's Village beautiful?

Well, when we first got there, there was nothing, but I think some people got together and made some sort of park near the Village. But we weren't comparing our facilities with other barracks or anything. That wasn't the thing that remained in my mind.

After the Children's Village, you and your two siblings joined your father. What was your reaction to your father?

I don't remember any emotions. Something happens in your lifetime, and another thing happens in your lifetime. Whatever happened wasn't painful, so there was no complaint.

Do you think your older brother had more of a reaction?

Probably, yes.

How was living in the barracks after the Children's Village? Was it different?

Well, it was just our group in one room, but other than that, I don't know what to say. It was different, but it wasn't something so different that one complained about it.

I'm just wondering, after your mother was hospitalized and your father was arrested, you went to the Shonien. Who took care of the family property?

Well, see, that's a complete blank for me. I don't know what happened after they both disappeared. I don't know who took us to the Shonien or what happened or how long a period that was. It's a complete blank for me.

After the war, did you contact the state and regain any of your family property?

Well, let's see. Before the war, we had a large console radio. The government confiscated radios and things, so I remember, sometime after the war, we were allowed to pick up the remnants and get it back. What was left of the property was a little piece from the big radio. That's the only thing—I don't know what other items we owned that disappeared.

So did you eat with your father in the mess hall at Manzanar?

Well, yeah. Outside of the Children's Village, the situation was somewhat similar. There was a double-sized barrack for dining for the rest of the population. I don't remember having to stand in line. Well, in a normal situation, there was a short line. We did not have to wait a long time. I don't remember that happening.

Other informants mentioned that the Children's Village served much better food than the barracks. Did you think so?

I didn't have any basis for comparison. Well, maybe—it wasn't too important to me. We had food in the Children's Village, and then we had food in the regular blocks outside. But food wasn't a big part of my life, so it didn't seem to matter. I don't remember anything very tasteful, but then it was of little interest to me. I don't remember anything about that.

Generally, after the Children's Village, you went to a much [more] open space, but you lived with your father. Did you have any contact with the other kids on your block in camp?

Some, but not that much, actually.

What was life in the barracks with your father like?

Well, it's another phase. Normal kids go to school, play, but I don't remember anything special.

Did your family eat meals together in the dining hall?

Yes.

After meals, did you mingle with other families or other kids?

I don't think so.

So after the meal, you came back to your barracks?

I think so.

Do you remember your father having friends in camp?

Well, during the earlier periods, I don't remember; but in the last block, Block 18, in the next building, Block 17, there was a family that was close to my parents. And they remained such after the war, so there was a long period of friendship. That's what I remember. Then several buildings over was the Matsuno family, and my family had contact with them.

After you left Children's Village and lived in the barracks, did you continue at the same school in Manzanar? Did you continue the same grade?

Well, I remember when we were in, maybe, second grade, the Village manager had to sign the report card. So in the middle of the school period, when we left the Village, my father had to sign the rest of the reports. So there was a period where part of the school year I was living in the Children's Village, and then the other part I began to live with my father.

But school itself is the same school?

Well, at that time, because each grade—the second grade was located in a different location from the other—it seems to be scattered about. It didn't seem to be where all the grades were located in one block or anything.

Although you left the Children's Village, did you keep going to the same school in the Village?

Same school. That had nothing to do with the Village. It was outside.

Did you have any inconvenience or frustration at the time outside of Children's Village life?

I don't remember anything special, uncomfortable, pleasant, or unpleasant. I just existed.

When you were with your father, did you receive pocket money or something?

No. I don't remember spending money on anything. Allowance for spending money? I don't remember that being in our family at all.

When you were with your father, did you feel like a family?

[no response]

You don't remember?

No. You know, you're born and then you exist and you don't question whether that's the situation or whether you have a better situation. There was no particular complaint, so I wasn't hoping for any other kind of life.

In the barracks after the Children's Village life, did you have any special memories with your father or with your siblings? Any vivid memories?

Uh—no. (chuckles) Nothing special. Let's see, the faucet in the early morning, I guess, iced, so there was an icicle—There's nothing that I can remember special. It was just a normal life. Normal for that situation, I guess.

So you played mainly with your siblings?

Played?

You didn't play with anybody else?

No.

And you stayed inside the barracks?

Well, we must have gone outside. I don't remember playing or doing anything special. We must have been doing something outside. What did I like to do? I don't remember any particular thing.

Did your father work in Manzanar?

There were a little bit of jobs available for people, and there was construction of a large auditorium there. I think he was part of that. But, see, when you're behind barbed wire, you don't have to work. You're fed, and that's it. The jobs available were, I guess, for extra money.

So your father was working a little bit?

Yes.

What was he doing?

Carpentry.

So he was mainly building—

Well, he was part of the crew that built the auditorium is what I remember; but after that, I don't think there was anything.

He was mainly working inside the camp?

Oh, yeah, never outside.

I guess you were freer outside of Children's Village. How was that?

I didn't feel any restrictions. I didn't feel restricted in the Children's Village. I don't know if there was a rule to keep us inside, but there was no urge to go outside either.

So your mother joined you in Manzanar?

Yes.

How long were you with your father until your mother joined you?

I don't know. Maybe a year. I don't know. I have no idea.

Can you describe what happened when your mother joined you?

I sort of remember thinking that I don't know this woman. I didn't remember —I guess I didn't remember exactly what she looked like. Like, if she were walking in the city, then I probably wouldn't have recognized her. But, I don't know, I was six years old, I should have remembered. My relationship with my mother wasn't that close to begin with, so probably there wasn't that normal child-mother relationship.

When you were reunited with your mother, how old were you?

Probably nine.

And you didn't remember her?

When I last saw my mother I was six, so then— but a six-year-old child should be able to remember their parents, right? I guess I didn't—yeah.

I guess children need parental care, parental love. When your mother joined you, did you feel like a family?

No, I don't think I was close to my mother emotionally. I don't know how my brother and sister felt, but I didn't feel that I was very close to her, so she was almost like a stranger when she came back.

Were you closer to your father compared to your mother?

Well, if it's just a comparison, probably. But I don't think I was that close to either one.

Did your mother join you at mealtime?

Probably.

As a child, did you feel insecure about the future?

The future never occurred in my mind. You lived day to day.

Okay, so never specific. So you never had any difficulties at Manzanar?

Apparently not. There was no special pain or painful memories.

That's good. Did you enjoy school?

That wouldn't be the word for me. But then, I didn't find it unpleasant either. We all went to school, and it was a normal condition. I didn't feel any complaints.

After camp, after the end of World War II, where did you go?

My father got a job as a farm laborer somewhere in Culver City. Then, my father came down with rheumatism, so he wasn't able to work anymore. So then we moved to Los Angeles, and we were living on welfare. It says on the document, "Culver City." Actually, we lived in the Gardena region. It was all farm area then. Our family and another family lived in that area as farm laborers. The other family lived in the barn; we were in the house. The house was for farm laborers, but we weren't there for very long.

So after a short period in Gardena, you moved to another place?

We lived in a hotel on East First Street in downtown Los Angeles.

Did you live in that hotel for a long time?

Yes, that was a hotel that housed all Japanese. It's not a fancy hotel. All the rooms were single rooms, so the families were in single rooms.

At the time, did your mother work?

She was working in a fish cannery. She traveled to San Pedro [Los Angeles County]. Later on, she worked as a cleaning woman in various houses.

As a child, do you remember feeling motherly love from your mother?

No, I don't think there was much of that there.

Was it because of her mental breakdowns?

I don't know if that—I don't think that's the reason. Some families are not that close. I don't think we were very close in that way.

How about your father? Did you feel fatherly love as a child?

Well, maybe, but then the concept of love was not within the realm of my childhood experience.

When you left Children's Village, did you have any sentimental feelings about it?

I don't think so.

Did you have any reactions when you left Manzanar camp?

No special emotions. As each change occurred in my life, it was something that occurred without any value attached to it. It was just the next phase of my life.

So you don't feel any impact of camp life on your life?

As a child, there wasn't much suffering, I think.

I see. So after camp, as you gradually became an adult, did you feel the impact of camp life?

I don't think so. For me, it wasn't a bad experience, so it's a different situation for adults. But for kids, it wasn't too bad.

The Japanese people lost their property during relocation. In your case, your family also lost property. What was your reaction?

It's not emotional because I wasn't attached to the property emotionally. As a kid, I don't remember having any things of my own that I was attached to. They disappeared. I didn't feel a loss. I mean, I never thought about losing my own property, if I had any. I'm pretty sure that if I lost the property I have now, it would be a much stronger effect. So being a child, if I had toys, I wasn't even thinking about those kinds of things.

Did you think evacuation was wrong?

The purpose of internment was racial. A two-year-old kid or a six-year-old kid is not going to be a military threat. So it was nonsense.

You received $20,000. Of course, it's not enough, but how did you feel about redress?

Well, it's more than nothing. Many people didn't have anything before they died. I never thought we would get anything, so something is better than nothing.

So do you think the apology to the Japanese American people by the American government was a good sign?

Well, apology is not meaningful, when it's not really meant. There's a law that says the president has to apologize; that's following the rules. But what's the personal emotion of everybody who has to apologize? It's not there, so it's just form.

Do you feel it's important to tell your story to others?

I don't think telling your story is going to change people much. If one is going to correct injustice, knowing about the history isn't going to have that much effect. It's how people who stereotype think—that mental process has to change. With those types of people, knowing the history of another group doesn't make any difference to them, it seems. People who think in simple terms or stereotypically—plus if they have power—become dangerous. In order to correct the situation, first you have to teach people to think clearly or fairly. You can't treat people in terms of groups because that's not meaningful. A dangerous thing to do is to try to keep those people out of power!

Thank you for your interview.

You're welcome.

Sam Tanaka[1]

Interviewed by Reiko Katabami

You went to Children's Village at the age of?

Twelve.

Until the end of the war.

Well, no. I left camp in June of '45.

June '45, so before the end of the war?

Yeah. The war ended in August.

Yes, August 15th. I'll ask later about that. So, in Children's Village, did you attend Sunday service?

No.

You didn't have to go, so you didn't go?

I went when I wanted to go. See, we didn't have a Sunday service at the Village like we did at the Salvation Army [in San Francisco, California]. Like I said, Maryknoll [in Los Angeles, California] was Catholic. I didn't know if the Shonien [in Los Angeles, California] was Christian or Buddhist. The Salvation Army was Christian. So we went to whatever church we wanted to.

You visited, though, with Catholics?

I went to a Catholic church once, but I didn't go to a Buddhist church, because I couldn't understand what they were talking about.

That's what I thought. Do you know some kids who went to the Buddhist church?

Not that I know. I went to the Christian church now and then, but if I didn't feel like going, I didn't go. Nobody said you had to go.

---

[1]COPH-Oral History 2333 was conducted on June 28, 1993, in Cerritos, California.

How did you view Mr. [Harry] and Mrs. [Lillian] Matsumoto [the superintendents of the Children's Village] and other hakujin *[Caucasian] staff? Did they take care of you?*

Well, like I say, when you're young, you don't really worry about how well you're being taken care of as long as you're being taken care of. Really, your needs are really not that much. As far as I would look at it, I would say they probably did what they had to do. Through the years, I look at it as, it's not so much what *they* did, it's what people they hired to do for us that counted. It's just like saying it's their job to hire you as a nurse to take care of the infants, but if you did something wrong, then it was up to them to reprimand you or dismiss the staff and get somebody else. I really don't have a lot to say in that area.

Okay. What about the hospital, the medical care?

They had a hospital.

In Children's Village?

No, in the camp. Manzanar had a hospital that was like a community hospital. If you got hurt, you went there. You didn't pay. But they took care of you and whatever was wrong. From my own experience, I broke my arm when I was, I guess, thirteen.

How?

You know what the horizontal or parallel bars are?

Oh, yes, I know.

Well, I was playing on one of them and missed my grip, so I broke my arm. I went to the hospital, and they reset it and put a cast on. It was like 9:30 at night, so I had to stay over in the hospital that night because, by the time they put the cast on and by the time it dried, it was too late. So I had to stay over and I said, oh, well.

Did you break your bone?

I broke my wrist right here. Then another time I had to go to the hospital, when I got bit by a squirrel. (laughter)

I can't imagine.

Well, they're wild, right?

Hungry.

So he bit me on my finger, so I had to go and get it taken care of, take shots, whatever. Another time I had my appendix taken out. Back then it was like a two-week ordeal.

Would you describe it?

Well, when I went to the hospital, it was like 4:00 in the afternoon, and at 6:30 they did the operation. I stayed in the hospital for ten days at that time. I couldn't do anything for almost a month. I couldn't play, or whatever. The technology back then wasn't as knowledgeable as now. Other than that, I had no other hospital. I guess they took care of whatever they had to, and they did whatever they needed to.

How did doctors find out that your appendix needed to be taken out?

Well, I had a stomachache.

And then you went to the hospital?

Well, actually, I went to school and I got a stomachache, and I stayed at school until lunchtime. I told them I couldn't walk anymore, so they sent an ambulance to me, and they took me home to the Village. Then I went to bed, and my stomach still hurt at 3:00, 3:30, so they had to—see, we didn't have a telephone either, so they had to walk to the hospital, which was like maybe half a mile, quarter of a mile away, and go get an ambulance again.

So an ambulance took you to the hospital?

Yeah.

It must be difficult to describe, but comparing the hospital to today's hospital, was it different?

I don't think so. You figure you have private, semi-private rooms, and they have curtains, whatever. The nurse and the doctor would come visit you just like they would if you were in a hospital here today. But how good the doctors were, or how good the nurses were, you would never know. As long as you got well, you figured that's all.

Okay. Did you feel safe in the hospital at Manzanar?

Well, yeah, I guess I would say so.

Did you feel safe at the Children's Village?

In the Village? Oh, yeah. Because, like I say, you had older people, brothers and sisters, whatever. If you really had any problem, you can talk to somebody.

By the way, where did you get your nickname, "Sausage"?

I have to go back to San Francisco. My Japanese name is Masami, and the kids started calling me "Salami." From there, it ended up with "Sausage." I guess whoever wants to call you what they want to call you, they call you, and I got stuck with that.

So the Japanese kids called you "Salami" at first?

Yeah.

Not the hakujin *kids?*

No, the *hakujins* called me Masami.

Do you remember some of the staff from Salvation Army going to Manzanar?

There was only this one Japanese couple that went to Manzanar, but they did not go to work in the Village.

Where did they go?

They went to another block. I remember the lady, or wife, used to come and help now and then, but she was not working as a staff member.

Did the staff ever counsel you at the Children's Village?

When you say "counseling," it wasn't really counseling. Only except, like I say, what the big brother or your supervisor would do for you or tell you. But he wouldn't really counsel you in the same sense—I look at counseling, as someone trying to teach you something.

Give advice.

Yeah. It was more like you did what the other kids did, or from what you see you did, or you should know better. (laughter)

So the supervisor just listened to your story, but didn't teach you anything.

Yeah, well, there really wasn't that much teaching in that respect.

Did you experience any physical or mental abuse?

No.

I read that, in the schools at Manzanar, there were not enough textbooks, enough books, and not enough facilities.

Well, let's put it this way. In that instance, I would have to say, in certain classes, not all, you wouldn't be able to take the book home and do your homework. You had to do it there, or you had to borrow. If they gave you half an hour to do your homework and you didn't finish, you either didn't do it or you had to ask permission to take a book home. I remember that they would make copies and give it to you, so that you wouldn't have to worry about taking a book home.

What about your experience? You also couldn't get a copy?

Well, I'd have to say, I wasn't a very good student (laughter) because I didn't really care if I passed or if I didn't pass. That's the kind of person I was then. If the teacher wanted to fail me, fine, fail me. It wasn't a matter of not learning or trying to learn. I guess I went to school because I had to be there, not because I wanted to be there or anything else in that sense. The teachers that were teaching, to me, they wanted to be there to teach. They weren't forced to teach.

So the teachers were willing to teach you? They were not forced to teach?

I don't think they were forced to teach, but I think all of the teachers were *hakujin*. Whether they liked you or not, I had feelings. Half the teachers I didn't like and half of them didn't like me, so it didn't bother me. So if I did homework, I did it. If I didn't, I didn't. Whether they, shall we say, flunked me or passed me was up to them.

Do you know some kids who failed?

Oh, yeah.

In that case, where did they go?

They didn't go nowhere; they'd do the class over.

Okay. Did you ever cut class?

Yes.

Why? It was not fascinating?

Number one, I didn't like school. I didn't care for school, really.

Most children don't.

When I used to cut class, I used to fight.

Fight for what?

You say, "for what," but it's—

The fighting is meaningful?

No. Towards the end of camp, it got bad because we used to have a club that we used to play. It didn't matter if we beat them or if they beat us; it would always end up as a fight.

Was it serious fighting? Beating?

Oh, yeah.

Wow! Were you injured?

Not injured, not in the sense that you got injured in that way. I mean, you were kids, and you fought. Then it got to a point where they start ganging up on you in school. But if you didn't go to school, they couldn't gang up on you. So I cut class. If the teacher asked where I was, I said I went home, didn't come to school. We didn't have to bring absent notices.

Oh, I see. So it's easier to cut classes.

Yeah.

As a boy, you were separated from your sisters in Children's Village. Did you keep in contact with them?

Yeah.

In your case, what did you talk about with your brothers and sisters?

Nothing in particular. If I had a problem or wanted to know something, I would ask them. Just a normal conversation, or whatever came up.

Okay. How about dating? Did you have a girlfriend?

No, not really a girlfriend.

Did you like someone?

Yeah, I guess. Well, let's see. I'd have to be what, fourteen? We had a boy's club with kids basically in the same age group, but they lived in different blocks. Basically, we would play basketball, baseball with them. Then socially, every once in a while, we would get another girl's club in the same age group and have a dance. It was maybe once in six months, once a year, but sometimes more often. I never really had what you'd call a girlfriend. Never really dated anybody in that sense. At that time, I think my interest wasn't that much, as far as a girl was concerned.

That's interesting. How about other boys? Did they date?

Oh, yeah. People had girlfriends and boyfriends; but to me, where did they go? If they had a movie, okay, they go to the movie together. At night, maybe they just sat around and talked to each other because they couldn't go anywhere. I know we had a canteen, but there wasn't really an area where you can go and sit and talk, or whatever. Well, they had a couple of parks that they built. People just went for walks, or whatever.

Okay. Do you have any vivid memories of Children's Village?

Oh, I have memories, yeah.

What are they?

Well, living in a group of sixteen to twenty, everybody's not going to go to sleep at the same time when they go to bed. We used to go to bed at nine, but every now and then somebody would try and talk to somebody next to them, and the supervisor would hear who is talking but couldn't tell exactly who the person was, so they had to ask. Nobody wants to say anything because they figure, well, if I say something, I'm going to get punished. When I say "punished," I mean that they'd have to stand in the corner or something like that for half an hour, or whatever. But nobody would say nothing, so they would make all of us stand up until somebody would say, yeah, it was me. Sometimes we would be standing there half an hour before our bed or an hour. They wouldn't let us go to sleep. Then we'd get mad because we'd know who did it, but the guy wouldn't say nothing. So the next day, we'd beat him up.

No wonder it's a vivid memory.

Well, but then there are fun memories, too. I guess in every life, regardless what kind of discipline you get, you learn by discipline and you learn that you have to be disciplined in order to become stronger. Being that I was in an orphanage, I guess I learned a lot quicker than a lot of other kids.

Do you think so?

I believe so, yeah.

You learned a lot.

Well, it's just like they say, the sooner you're on your own, the faster you learn, regardless what you learn. You learn the values of living, life, and responsibility a lot sooner and, to me, you appreciate certain things more. As you grow older, you look back and you think some of the things weren't as bad as they really seemed. But you don't want your kids to go through what you did, or some other kid that you know. It gets to be, shall we say, a spoiling fact when you have kids. Regardless how good times are, how bad times are, you don't want your kids to be in the same situation as you, so you try and give them more, but yet you're not really doing them right when you do that. At least, I don't think so. That's why—well, I still have two boys that live at home.

At the end of the war, did the staff try to get families or foster care for the children in Children's Village?

Yeah. They tried all they could to reposition kids that were orphaned or deserted. I think this is what Mr. and Mrs. Matsumoto worked a great deal on.

To transfer the kids.

These are the things that, as a youngster, I'd never realized or seen until I started growing up. And I thought, whatever happened to so-and-so? How come he was only there six months?

So children didn't know what was going on, when they left.

Yes, or even after—this is hard to say.   But it's my feeling that after the Matsumotos left, there was a *hakujin* lady [Eva Robbins] that came and took over as supervisor, or coordinator. This is where I think a lot of the young adults—now when I say "young adults," high school age kids—felt that they were mistreated by her because, what she would do is, she would try and place people by just placing them, not trying to find a respectable couple or family for John, Jim, Jane, whoever. I know for a fact that there were kids that had a hard time after they left, and they were still in the minor-age brackets.

How about you?

You know, I guess no matter who you are or what you are, everybody has a different concept of what happened and why it happened. It's just like even myself, I could tell you things that wouldn't interest you, but, on the other hand, I think it is part of my growing up. After I got out of camp, my father came back, but then left us again more or less because he didn't want to be responsible. But, by then, I was seventeen years old.

You parted from your father at seventeen?

Well, he parted from us. (laughter)

Did you feel deserted, or a sense of desertion?

Yeah. Well, see, like I say, in the past, I never really knew my father because I hadn't lived with him long enough. When I did live with him after the war, it wasn't like a father-son relationship. When I did live with him, it was just like, well, he's just another man in the house. If he said something nasty to me to the effect that I didn't feel which was right, I would tell him so. If he didn't like it, like I say, I can walk out that door. Because that's the type of relationship we had already. I mean, here I am seventeen years old, or sixteen years old, and not really knowing him, and he's going to tell me what to do and what not to do? It's kind of hard.

Oh, I see. Yeah, I understand.

It's hard for *me* to stomach.

As a father's words, you can't accept.

Yeah.

Maybe it was because your father came illegally to the United States?

Yeah. I believe that had a lot to do with it. But still, there had to be thousands of others in the same position. But then, see, they became citizens later on because they knew what they had to do. Whereas my father—this is a feeling that I had towards my father—was the type of person [who] was always running away from something. To me, there was a little difference.

When you became a father, did you learn a lot from your father?

Oh, yeah. That's why I still have two boys that still live at home, and yet they're almost thirty and over. I don't tell them, no, you have to move.

Well, they don't feel like leaving.

Well, no. They don't feel like they *have* to leave either. I tell them—and I tell my wife the same thing—because I never had a home of my own when I was young, my boys have a home that they can come home to, and they can bring their friends home. That's what I want them to have. It's different when you have things when you are young. Like I say, it's kind of like spoiling them, but it depends on how you spoil them.

I guess you are a good father.

Well, yes and no.

Because, as you told me, you learned well in your world. I think you learned earlier.

Yeah, I learned a lot earlier than a lot of kids. I can't say I learned any better, but I learned to be independent since I was like, shoot, five or six years old. When you go back into your childhood, okay, it's just like, say, in your case where you lived with your mother and father, they probably tried to give you or do things for you as much as possible, but being that I was living with a foster parent, they're not going to give me everything. They're going to give me whatever I need.

Did you feel parental love from the first foster family that you lived with, when you were small?

Not really. I guess I was, shall we say, young and free, so I didn't really—well, since I had my brothers with me all the time, I had no problem in that sense. My brother and sister probably replaced my father and mother because, when I needed something, I went to them.

How did your older brothers and elder sisters manage those problems? They needed parental love, too.

Well, I guess you really do.

Do you think they helped each other?

Well, see, we were close in age.

Do you think you had an advantage because your age difference is so close?

Not so much an advantage, but the companionship is a lot easier.

To overcome difficulties?

Yeah. It's not like a twelve-year difference between two people.

Do you think a sibling can replace a father figure or a mother figure?

No.

No?

Not after I raised *my* family. Until you raise a family, you don't really know the true meaning of who you need and what you need.

Thank you for the interview.

Oh, you're welcome.

Chapter Six
Life after Children's Village:
Finding A Home

For many of the orphans, leaving Children's Village was just as traumatic as losing a family. Because the three orphanages for children of Japanese ancestry had closed during incarceration, many children were separated from caregivers and friends whom they knew and loved. According to Lisa Nobe and the War Relocation Authority's Final Report on Children's Village, approximately 50 percent of the 101 orphans who spent time at Children's Village were reunited with one or both parents, while "nearly 25 percent were divided among institutions and wage homes. Only a few were adopted or placed in foster homes."[1] Nine-year-old Celeste Loi Teodor and six-year-old Annie Shiraishi Sakamoto, two girls who were the last to leave the Village, were among the few placed in foster homes in 1945, at the very end of the war.

Both Teodor and Sakamoto had spent their lives in orphanages or homes for children of Japanese ancestry. Born to an unwed mother, Sakamoto was a baby when she was sent to one of the Japanese children's homes in Los Angeles (which one is unknown). She was three years old when she entered the Children's Village, and six years old when she left Manzanar and returned to Los Angeles to meet her new foster mother, Wilma Stuart. The meeting was an auspicious one, as the close bond between them continued even after Sakamoto became an adult. After Sakamoto married Doug Sakamoto in 1965, for example, Stuart continued to play a role in her life by helping to take care of the Sakamoto children, Robert and Michelle. In the following excerpt, Sakamoto recalls life not only at the Children's Village, but her life after camp as well, specifically with her foster mother, Wilma Stuart.

Although she stayed with Wilma Stuart and Annie Sakamoto for only a short term, Celeste Loi Teodor remained close to Annie Sakamoto and Wilma Stuart throughout her life. Like Sakamoto, Teodor was also raised in a children's home in Los Angeles, the Shonien. She met her mother after the war, when she was ten years old, but decided she would rather be in foster

[1]Lisa Nobe, "The Children's Village of Manzanar: The World War II Eviction and Detention of Japanese American Orphans," *Journal of the West* 38 (April 1999): 70.

care. Teodor was initially placed with Wilma Stuart, but subsequently was sent to two other foster care homes before she turned eighteen. The following excerpt from Teodor's interview gives her account of life at the Children's Village and the traumatic move to Wilma Stuart's foster home and the homes thereafter.

Sakamoto and Teodor were not the first children to be sent to Wilma Stuart for foster care. Born on December 4, 1900, in Corning, New York, Stuart was the daughter of a minister. While she was still a child, her family moved to California and lived in a Free Methodist community in Los Angeles. Both she and her two sisters became elementary school teachers for the Los Angeles School District. Along with being a schoolteacher, Stuart was also a foster care mother to many girls; at the end of World War II, the government placed in her care the last two girls from Manzanar's Children's Village. Interviewed at the age of ninety-three, Wilma Stuart discusses her early life, as well as her role as a foster care mother to Annie Sakamoto and Celeste Teodor.[2]

---

[2] Wilma Stuart passed away at the age of ninety-six on February 5, 1996.

Annie Shiraishi Sakamoto[1]

Interviewed by Noemi Romero

Do you know what happened to your parents?

I was born to a twenty-four-year-old farm laborer mother, and my father was a lot older. He was probably about fifty-six. He had a family of his own, and my mother was unmarried, so she didn't want to take care of me from then on. But I understand that she had me by cesarean [section] and I weighed only two pounds, so I was in the incubator for several months. The social workers tried to contact my mother and see if she wanted to take care of me after camp, but I think it was just before camp, and she said no. By that time, she was in camp and she had married. I understand I have half-brothers and sisters but have had absolutely no contact with them.

I met my father only once at age eleven, and it was on a street in downtown Los Angeles [California]. I understand that he passed away when he was probably in his sixties. He had diabetes and was insulin-dependent. My father tried to support me through the years, but he had his own family who knew nothing about my existence. He tried to send some support money to Miss [Wilma] Stuart [See COPH-OH 2488], and eventually he had to say he couldn't support me anymore, so Miss Stuart took care of me without charge. The government tried to help her because we were on welfare at the time.

But that's all I know about my family. A lot of times, I wish that I could find my mother. She moved to Chicago [Illinois] after the war. Maybe she passed away because she'd be in her seventies by now. She's probably about seventy-nine.

Do you remember your mother's name?

Her name was Jane Shiraishi. That was my maiden name. When she married, her name was changed to Mrs. Yata .

You told me that you met your dad in L.A. How did that happen?

I think Miss Stuart had something to do with it. She asked my father if he would like to meet me, and we did meet in downtown L.A. He was short,

[1] COPH-Oral History 2486 was conducted on July 11, 1993, in Los Angeles, California.

skinny, kind of dark skin, and maybe we looked alike. But he was very quiet. I don't recall exactly what we talked about. It was just for a short while. I don't even remember if we went out to lunch, or whatever. But after that, I think he died shortly. That was when he told Miss Stuart that he could no longer support me. He was just sending a little bit of money each month.

Tell me a little bit about Wilma Stuart.

Wilma C. Stuart is a Caucasian lady who was teaching school. She asked the government to release the last two children from the camp in Manzanar, and she wanted to take care of them. She had been acquainted with quite a few Japanese people, had visited them in the hospital, and wrote to them. When they left for camp, some of them stored their furniture in her garage. She kept correspondence with some of them in the camp. When they came out of camp, of course they came to see her, and, through the years, a lot of them have either passed away or moved away, but she does still keep in contact with several of them who live in the San Gabriel area [Los Angeles County]. Miss Stuart taught school for many years and retired in 1955. She took care of a number of foster children; among them were Celeste Teodor [See COPH-OH 3776] and myself.

How old were you when you were turned over to Wilma Stuart?

I was six years old when she first took care of us.

So you were tiny when you went to Children's Village.

I was only maybe about three years old.

Do you have any significant memories of your arrival at Manzanar?

My memories of Manzanar are of the high barbed wires, the tall searchlights, which would sweep the lights over our camp at night. The sweep lights would come in through the windows and I would hide underneath the covers, being afraid.

And why were you scared?

When it's dark and the searchlights are coming in through the window every so often, I was trying to think what was happening there, why these searchlights. Maybe they were doing that because they were watching us or afraid that we would do something wrong, like maybe run away. I must have been insecure because I would wet the bed at night, so of course, naturally, the people who were taking care of us would have to clean it up. But I don't remember—they must have scolded me, but I don't recall them ever spanking me.

You wet the bed many times throughout the whole time you were there?

Yes, I believe that; but once I got out of camp, I didn't do that.

And the lights would go on every so often during the night. Would that wake you up, or once you were asleep, didn't it matter anymore?

Well, only when I was awake would I notice it, but once asleep, I assumed that—

You got used to it.

Yeah. There was a social worker named Eva Robbins who took a special interest in myself, and I used to like to go to her house, sit on her lap, play the piano, or the typewriter.

I have been quite insecure in school because I remember one time that I must have done something especially naughty, which I don't remember, but I was locked up in a dark closet, was crying my head off, then spied some ink— it was in a bottle on top of some books—and spilled the ink over the books. What happened afterwards, I have no idea. It's blotted from my memory, so I must have received a good spanking.

I remember the bitter cold, the snow of the winters, and the humidity of the summers. The camp was right at the base of tall mountains on which could be seen the snow most of the time.

I liked the babies and used to climb up on stools to peer into their cribs and play like I was taking care of them. I don't really remember the older people who worked at the Children's Village, although one of them was Alice Kaneko, who I still keep in contact [with] occasionally.

You mentioned a social worker, Eva Robbins. Can you tell me more about her?

We kept in contact after camp. After the war, she came out from Indiana and visited Celeste and myself and took us in a car to some park, or maybe to the zoo. I kept in touch with her, writing her every year around Christmas, until she was in a nursing home. Probably she was in her nineties. Eventually, she passed away, and of course, after that, I lost contact.

For emotional support, is Eva Robbins who you went to during camp?

I believe so. I don't really recall that much about her talking to me, but I'm sure she thought a lot of Celeste and myself because she took the time to come out from Indiana to visit us and take us someplace. I'm sure we had a lot to talk over. Of course, that was so many years ago. I think it was maybe in 1948, somewhere around there. So I know she must have thought a lot about us and remembered us very much in camp.

Any other social workers you remember?

No, I do not remember any of the others.

How about the Matsumotos [Harry and Lillian], the directors?

I don't remember them at all.

Can you tell me more about what your school was like in camp?

I recall having a Caucasian teacher. On my report card, I got an *F* in behavior. Being locked up in the closet probably was proof of that. I think I was very insecure at that time, with kind of maybe a displaced feeling. Not being in a family unit, I had no parents to role model.

Can you tell me a little bit about the toys that you had in camp?

I don't remember having any toys in camp, no teddy bear or ball. Maybe that's the reason I didn't like to play with dolls. Really, I don't remember playing that much with other children. I just liked to look at the babies in their cribs.

Do you remember visiting anyone in camp?

The only ones I remember would be Miss Robbins, visiting her house a lot, and the baby room. But those are the only ones I remember.

Was there any particular baby you took a special interest in?

I took no special interest in any baby. To me they were all cute and cuddly. Of course, I couldn't carry any of them, being so young myself. I just liked to look in their crib and touch them and talk to them.

Why?

Maybe I had sort of a maternal instinct, because I myself was, kind of like, orphaned without a mother or father. Maybe that's where that feeling came from.

Did anyone visit you from outside of camp?

That I don't remember.

When you left camp, did you want to leave? You told me you didn't know where you were going.

I had no choice. I didn't know where I was going.

But you maybe wanted to stay there?

I don't recall wanting to stay there. I was just very apprehensive of the future.

Do you remember anything about the hapas, *the mixed-race children?*

No, I don't remember any of them.

The conditions of the food, do you remember—

No, I don't remember the condition of the food. I think we had rice and maybe oatmeal or hot cereal, but the food, I really don't remember.

You don't remember anything about not wanting to eat food or being starved?

No, I don't recall that.

How about the clothes that were given to you? Did everybody get the same uniform clothes?

I think they were allowed to bring in some of their clothes. But as far as the way we were clothed, I really don't remember. I assume that the State [of California] clothed us because we came from orphanages.

Do you remember getting new clothes or used clothes or anything like that, or shoes?

I don't remember.

Can you describe your bed or your pillow, in camp?

The only memory I have was hiding under the sheets when the searchlights would come in through the windows, being afraid. I think we were on cots, and there were rows of cots in our particular room. I think there were all girls. I don't recall any boys being in there.

How about when you were sick in camp. Do you remember someone taking care of you?

I don't recall being sick in camp. Although I understand that I did have bronchial pneumonia, apparently I was not hospitalized. I was treated with antibiotics, whatever they had in the 1940s, which they didn't have too much of.

Can you tell me a little bit about your feelings when you left Manzanar?

I was a little bit apprehensive because, on the bus coming from Manzanar, I could see the other cars, or the other buses, winding down the road. It was a steep mountain road, and I had my face pressed against the window and was wondering, where are they taking us, and what's going to happen to us? I still remember the scene of that and seeing those buses or cars going down the winding road. But as far as other reactions, I just don't remember.

And can you tell me your first encounter with Miss Stuart?

We were put into this front room, and we sat on the couch. She had some other children with her, and her elderly mother, and I think her sister Mary was there. Celeste and I sat together, and we were frightened. That's when we were fingering our rosaries and crying. Celeste was kind of the ringleader, and she said, "We don't belong here. We're Catholics." And we were crying. That's the first encounter that I remember.

What was your first impression of Miss Stuart?

We saw this—well, she wasn't really fat, but she was—I think she was middle-age, and we were just—she seemed like a nice lady, but we didn't really know what was going on, just that we were sent there for her to take care of us.

What did she tell you?

That I don't remember. Whatever conversation we had is a total blank.

Did you and Wilma Stuart talk about your first encounter later?

She told me about the first encounter, about Celeste saying that we didn't want to stay there because we were Catholics. Then she said, shortly after, Celeste threw her rosary into the fireplace, that this was when she broke her ties with the Catholic Church. She said that Celeste left after a few years, and I was the only one left, and she decided to keep me.

How about Celeste? Were you guys close in camp? Were you always together?

Apparently, we were close in camp, especially toward the end. But I don't remember my playing with her too much.

What do you remember of Celeste after camp, when you went to live with—?

She was a smooth talker. If Miss Stuart wanted to scold her or spank her, she somehow managed to talk her way out of it. She had a way of making people laugh, even the sour ones. She did have an impish grin. I remember her being very skinny and kind of laughing. It was not a throaty laugh, but it was a laughless laugh.

How did you feel when she was taken away, when you were separated from her?

I don't really recall that incident, but I was pretty upset when she left because then there was only myself. But I don't remember what I did at that time. Incidentally, maybe I'm getting ahead of myself, but when we just came out of camp, apparently we must have had some kind of Catholic training because we had rosaries, and I recall sitting on the couch in Miss Stuart's house and we were crying because we wanted to go back to the Catholic orphanage, and we felt that we wouldn't be able to continue our Catholic beliefs. But I understand that Celeste shortly after burned her rosary in the fire because Miss Stuart was very much a Protestant.

So, you're a Protestant now?

Yes. Miss Stuart was a Free Methodist, and I was a Free Methodist for many years until I married my husband. We're now Church of the Nazarene, which is Protestant, but similar to the Free Methodist Church.

What was your biggest adjustment when you came out of camp and into society? Did you notice anything different? Was it hard or easy on you?

The biggest adjustment was coming from a camp full of Japanese to an entirely white world and having to associate with white children because I had never really associated with them before, and I now had to deal with some of the reactions of the white children toward myself.

Can you give me any specific examples?

In the primary grades at the Bushnell Way School [in Los Angeles], which Miss Stuart also attended as a child, some of the children would taunt me and call me "Jap." One time when I was in junior high school, in the classroom, I had come up behind a white boy. I was just looking at his paper, just to be sociable, and he turned around and said, "What do you want, you Jap?" I remember that was like a slap in the face. That was when I fully realized that being Japanese was not such a good idea. For many years, I resented being Japanese and wished that I had never been born to parents. But that was also during the adolescent years, when a person's emotions and perspective of the world are so changeable and unsteady.

How about the discipline by Miss Stuart?

She was very strict because she had to be. She had her elderly mother to take care of, plus she had about maybe five to seven foster girls—all girls—so she would have each one of us do a chore.

What did you do?

I stood on a stool and did the dishes.

You were tiny.

Yeah.

In what other ways was Miss Stuart strict?

We could not really associate with other children in the neighborhood, and they did not come to our house. She, of course, had to keep tabs of us at all times. She didn't allow me to go to other kids' houses, or very seldom could they come to our house to play. This was especially true during junior high school and high school. Some of the teachers in the high school thought she was too strict because, when I got to college, she did not want me to go on choir tour. The teachers had to talk to her a lot, and eventually I was allowed to go on choir tour, which meant going out of state or going up north. So they thought, in that respect, she was being too restrictive.

Was she mean?

No, she was never mean. I just remember her swatting us a couple times. That was because we were really naughty.

How about in camp? How were you disciplined there? Did you ever get swatted?

I think I must have gotten swatted after I poured that ink over the books because that memory, what happened afterwards, is completely wiped out of my mind.

You said you were put in a dark closet?

I must have been naughty. I don't recall what I did. Maybe I hit one of the other kids or talked back to the teacher.

But you don't remember anybody being real strict or excessively hard on you in camp?

No. In fact, they were all nice to me, as far as I can remember. I don't remember anybody spanking me or saying cross words to me.

At Miss Stuart's home, did you have privacy?

No. We had to be like in bunk beds because there were five or seven of us. I don't really remember how many. So we had to have bunk beds. I think there were maybe three bedrooms. Her mother had one bedroom to herself, and Miss Stuart had one bedroom, and then we had a porch where some of us bunked, and then we had another bedroom where the rest of us were in.

When you were growing up and got interested in boys, what was Miss Stuart's reaction?

She didn't like boys. She had never married, never been on a date. Her mother, towards the end, was very restrictive. Miss Stuart never missed boys. I mean, she never missed the dating or wished she had. So she figured that she would do the same for me. In high school especially, she would ask another girl to spy on me and tell her what I was doing. I did have some boyfriends in high school, but if we went out, it was more in a group. It was never alone. So when I attended nursing school and after I had finished that, I moved out and lived in an apartment with two other girls for about two years. And then I dated boys.

Was it because Miss Stuart's mother never allowed her to have boyfriends? Was that why she didn't like you dating boys?

Her mother never allowed boys in. Her mother needed a lot of care, mentally. I think she developed Alzheimer's, so she required a lot of care. Miss Stuart didn't dare let her out of her sight because she would run out the door and run the streets and wander off down the street hollering, "Help me! Help me!" So Miss Stuart didn't have the opportunity to date anybody, except take care of her mother.

In pictures of you as a child, you were always smiling. Growing up, were you always happy?

I guess I could smile for the camera. Socially, I was kind of a loner. I used to like to sit under the walnut tree and draw for hours and hours, and read. The time that I had gotten a splinter in my knee, I recall when it got infected. I was out there sitting at the table under the walnut tree, drawing, but not feeling well because I developed a fever, and it happened that I had to be taken to the county hospital because septicemia resulted from just that splinter infection in my right knee. They had to lance it and give me antibiotics, and I stayed in the hospital for about a week.

Socially, I wasn't able to play with the other children or have them come over to my house. I sort of got along with most of them because I was a loner. I really don't think I developed normally socially. Being an adolescent in the junior high years, I was kind of rebellious and shaped under the restriction of Miss Stuart. I just recall having to live with a lot of very elderly women and being around elderly people. Some of them were sick. Then in high school, I was very happy. That's when I interacted socially with my classmates and remember the good times with them and making them laugh. I was kind of a cutup in class. Not a bad one to be expelled. Sometimes I was the teacher's pet.

So, you weren't shy.

I was shy in a way, but at certain times I could really make the class laugh.

Did you have any nicknames?

They called me "Annie Oakley" or "Annie Orphan."

How did you feel about that?

Oh, I thought it was kind of a compliment. They would say, "Annie Oakley, get your gun," or "Annie Orphan" because, obviously, I didn't have any parents. But I don't recall taking offense at that term.

What are your feelings towards your father and towards your mother?

It was kind of resentment for a long time, but I understood their situation because their own families didn't know of my existence. For quite a few years, I did have a lot of resentment because what they did wasn't really right in having me the way they did. But that's past. Meeting my father one time has helped. At least I knew what he looked like. I'll never know my mother.

You said you resented your parents for many years. How many years, or to when?

Oh, it was probably mainly in high school. My adolescent years were very unstable. Adolescents, especially when they are in the transitional period between the ages of twelve, thirteen, fourteen, need family stability, and when they don't have it, a lot of times they resent that fragmented family.

Did you ever blame your parents for anything?

Yes, I blamed my parents for not being able to take care of me and for being Japanese and being put in the camp for so many years. I did resent them, but the resentment was more during the junior high school years.

How about the government? What did you feel about them doing that? Did you even think of it?

Oh, I didn't think so much about the government as I thought about the parents.

Your focus was on them.

Yes.

Did you ever think one of them—well, maybe your mom—would come back looking for you?

From what I understand from the social worker, when they came to her home—I think this is after the war, in Chicago—the social worker asked my mother if she would like to have me back, and she told them absolutely no. To her, it must have been a very traumatic experience having me, and she wanted to forget that completely.

How do you feel that affected your life?

I think not coming from a stable family unit and having a father figure or a male role model has affected me. Only in recent years have I really appreciated the intact family that has the stability and the values to it. I think when I had the children—that's been over twenty years—I realized how important the family is, with a father and mother and the kids at home. Of course, no family is perfect, but . . . a family that's together is becoming extremely rare these days.

Thank you for the interview.

You're welcome.

Celeste Loi Teodor[1]

Interviewed by Cathy Irwin

Where and when were you born?

According to my birth certificate, I was born in Los Angeles, California, on June 24, 1936.

Nineteen thirty-six. Were your parents from Los Angeles, as well?

I think so; I never knew them.

You never knew them?

No, I meant I never knew my father and I met my mother when I was ten years old.

When you were ten. So, who brought you up in Los Angeles?

Probably the orphanage. See, you must remember, I was only five when I went to Manzanar. So I don't remember much before that, except I was told that I was in an orphanage in Los Angeles. And we were all transferred to Manzanar from there. I remember that I was in an orphanage, but I don't know the name of it. I think it was S-h-o-e-i-n or something like that—

Oh, the Shonien.

Yeah. That's where I was.

Did you have any other siblings with you when you were there?

No, just me.

Okay. And you don't remember your parents, either—

Not at all. I met my mother when I was ten years old and just for a few minutes. I didn't like her, so I told her to get out of my life.

Wow, where did you meet your mother?

---

[1]COPH-Oral History 3776 was conducted on August 9, 2007, by phone (the interviewer in Claremont, California, spoke to the interviewee in Las Vegas, Nevada).

I met her at one of the foster homes that I was placed in after World War II. And at first, she told me her name was Mrs. Young. I guess I did see her more than once. At first, she told me that she was Mrs. Young when I was at Wilma Stuart's [See COPH-OH 2488] home with my friend, Annie Sakamoto [See COPH-OH 2486]. And at that time, she had taken Annie and me out to an ostrich farm and we knew her as Mrs. Young. I didn't know that she was my mother until I was moved to another foster home called Aunt Jessie Bloom's. That was a very good foster home, but I wasn't any good, to say the least! So I was kicked out of there. But anyways, my mother met me there and then revealed to me that she was my real mother. By this time, I had noticed that she had been drinking alcohol and I didn't like her behavior. So, the first time I knew that she was my mother, I told her to get out of my life and to never return again because she wasn't good for me. And I was age ten or eleven.

Wow! So you were pretty spunky at that age.

Oh, yeah! You have to, to survive. You have to think on your own. You have no one else to think for you.

Were you living at Aunt Jessie Bloom's at that time?

Yes, when I told my real mother to get out of my life. Now before this, we had had several visits, but I didn't know her as my mother. I knew her as Mrs. Young.

And how did you know Wilma Stuart and Annie Sakamoto?

Annie Sakamoto and I left Manzanar together. We were very close to each other. Wilma felt I was a bad influence on her because of my—well, spunkiness, as you said. (laughter) So I was put in Aunt Jessie's house, which was much better. Wilma's home was very dysfunctional, as far as I was concerned. Annie might not feel that way, you know. Annie was there all her life, for the rest of her life.

Were there other kids at Wilma Stuart's?

Yeah, there were other kids there. But Annie was the only Japanese American there, and my ancestry is Japanese, Chinese, and American, of course.

I see. And were you able to keep in touch with Annie, even though you were separated?

Off and on, yes, as teenagers. But I couldn't do that much with her because Wilma would not permit it. She would forbid me.

What were your feelings as you moved from foster home to foster home, from Wilma Stuart to Aunt Jessie Bloom's home? What was it like? What were your experiences?

Well, by that time, I was depressed. I did not bond to anybody. And after Aunt Jessie, I went to a Japanese home. Now Aunt Jessie was not Japanese. She was Caucasian and had a very nice home. She was very good to us, and there were about seven kids there: Caucasians, one Hispanic, and me. And then, I just didn't behave myself; I was too wild, running in the streets and everything like that, you know. But to me, that was a very, very good home. So then the State of California and its welfare system decided to put me out in the country with this Japanese family. Well, the foster mother was sixty years old, and I was only thirteen. And she didn't speak my language, and I didn't speak her language. So that was the kind of home that I went to, although it was okay. When you are a teenager, nothing satisfies you; but in the end, I was very happy because I was able to make friends with her children who were ten years older than me. And to this very day, I've been always invited to all the reunions and births and deaths and everything.

What was the family name?

Nitake. So after I left and became a nurse, I became very good friends with the Nitake family.

And where were you in the country?

Baldwin Park [Los Angeles County].

Oh, Baldwin Park. That was the country then?

That was out in the country then! (laughter)

And where was Wilma Stuart's home?

Near Highland Park [Los Angeles County]. It's on Monterey Road in the Highland Park area. As a matter of fact, my friend Annie still lives in the same house.

Oh, you're kidding!

Wilma had a lot of property, and Annie is now the owner of both of those homes. She rents one out, and she lives in one.

I see. Did you know Mr. [Harry] and Mrs. [Lillian] Matsumoto when you were at the Shonien, or did you meet them when you were at Children's Village?

Well, you don't know who you've met when you are five years old. I didn't even know I knew them until after the fact, when I was told that they were the superintendents or the assistant superintendents at Children's Village. So I really didn't know them, no. But I knew their staff. And one that is very vivid in my mind is Ruth Takamune.

Can you tell me any memorable experiences or memories of Ruth that you can share?

Oh, she was a very loving mother figure. Whenever we got hurt outside, she was there. She taught me a lot; she taught me religion. Believe it or not, they allowed religion to be taught. I'm not sure if the other children were, but I was able to go freely in and out of Children's Village. And I attended the Catholic Church, I attended the Protestant Church—I attended every function there that had movies. I would walk to the movies. I had complete freedom. I have no idea if this was allowed or not, but I had complete freedom in the camp.

Did Ruth Takamune go with you to church or to the movies? Or did you get to just wander around?

Well, I could just wander around. Ruth Takamune was very busy with the other children, so she never left the grounds with me, anyway. She might have left the grounds with her co-workers or other children or for any group activity.

And so you were five years old when you went to Children's Village?

Yeah, five. I probably just turned six.

So you basically started school when you were living at the Children's Village.

Oh, yeah.

Do you remember school or going to school?

I do at the other orphanage, before camp.

What was that like?

Well, we were in kindergarten at the time. I remember that the school gave me a farewell. They said I was going to camp, and I said, "Okay." (laughter) They gave me a farewell party and gave me a rubber doll. I was so happy with that rubber doll because I could feed it and get it wet and not have to worry about it because in those days, they had metal plaster dolls or wooden dolls. And you couldn't bathe them or anything because you would peel the paint off. This I'm remembering, okay? (laughter)

So you remember, when it was time to leave to go to Children's Village. Do you have any memories of bringing anything with you? Did you get to take your doll?

I think so. Yeah, I believe I got to take my doll. All I remember is taking the doll and the clothes on my back. They probably packed everything to take up there; when you're five years old, you don't do anything. But I do remember the ride to Manzanar.

What was that like? What were your feelings?

Oh, I was happy because what do I know? I was not political or anything. (laughter)

So you just thought you were taking a bus ride somewhere?

Well, they said we were going to our new home. So, I'm not sure if it was a bus drive or truck drive. I remember that Lillian [Matsumoto] said it was a bus drive. But I don't remember a bus; I remember a truck because I looked at the bottom of the car and there was a hole in the floor and I saw the truck. Of course, it might have been the bus too. But it was nice. I enjoyed it. I enjoyed every minute of my stay at Manzanar.

Do you remember singing songs on the way to Manzanar?

Oh, yeah. We probably sang a lot of songs. Childhood songs.

What do you remember when you got there to Manzanar? Do you remember your first impression?

No. The most important thing to a kid of five years old is other children. It's not the place or anything like that. That's not what's important; it's if you have friends to play with. That's the most important thing; it's not what kind of castle we're about to enter. So the important thing was: oh, good, we can get out and run! We can be with our friends! We can go to the bathroom!

(laughter) We can do this and that. I have never had the experience—I have read a lot about camp life and what the private families had experienced like in *Farewell to Manzanar* and some other books I've read. They were taken away from their homes that they had all their lives. These are adults I'm talking about. And then they were thrown into this place called Manzanar where they had to stuff their own mattresses with straw. I never experienced any of that because I was only five and everything was done for us. But I don't remember straw mattresses at all. I don't remember things like that. I remember we had little cots, and we had our own little space that they fixed with a box to put our personal things in that box. It might have been a crate for all I know, standing up like a dresser. We all had our private little space with our private things. And everybody respected each other's things; they didn't touch it.

So there were a lot of other children with you. Who did you hang out with? Was Annie Sakamoto there with you?

Yes, Annie was there, but she was much younger. Annie and I are about three or four years apart in age difference. So when you're five—well, when I was six-years old, she might have been three. So you don't hang out with a two-year-old; you hung out with someone your age or older.

Who did you hang out with? Do you remember?

I don't know.

What did you play? What was your daily life like?

Well, we ate breakfast at the orphanage mess hall. We never had to stand in line or nothing like the other people did, and then we would eat. We had breakfast; they served us three meals. But if we didn't like something, we had to eat it anyways. Sometimes I'd stay there until midnight, but I still wouldn't eat it. I would not eat some of the food because I didn't like it. But I guess from the Depression era, you just didn't waste any food. I just remember only a few times when I sat there until midnight because I wouldn't eat something I didn't like. But I think that was the mentality in those days, even in private families. It was not only in the institution; it was private families, too, because a lot of my girlfriends later on told me that they could not leave the table without finishing their plate because their parents were raised in the Depression era.

What games did you play after eating?

We usually went outside and ran around and played. Now, they did have something like a playhouse, I remember this. And it was made of logs and stuff. So it was like a playhouse for the children on the grounds and I remember lots of grass and a little hill of grass. We would roll down the hill. Our bottoms were usually grassy. And we had a couple of pear trees there, and as a matter of fact, a lot of the private families wanted to come in to play with us because we were the only ones that had facilities. We had swings or what have you. And we had a playhouse, and we had lots of room to run on the grass. I remember lots of grass, but I have no idea how big that grass area was. For a five-year-old, it could be just an acre. But we had lots of things to do and lots of children to play with. As far as my case was concerned, the private families never made fun of orphans because they wanted to be friends with us in order to come in, be invited into the area.

So were they able to play with you?

Yeah, they came in. I let them in. (laughter) Maybe they weren't supposed to, but I let them in and we all got to play together. See, there weren't that many caregivers. I thought there were sixty to eighty kids there, so we always had lots of friends to play with. And then we were taken out on a little field trip, believe it or not, out of the camp. I remember it so vividly, and maybe that's why I remember we were in trucks. At the base of the mountain, there's a beautiful brook. We got to play around the brook, and I remember that. But I don't know how they let us out or what legal means that they had to let us out. But I do remember we were able to go out of the camp just to visit the base of the mountain.

What was the weather like? Do you remember being cold? Or hot?

During the winter, it was cold. In the summertime, it was nice, I thought. Of course, when I went up for the pilgrimage [Manzanar Pilgrimage] in April, my God, I thought I was going to die from the heat! (laughter)

So how many years were you in camp at the Children's Village?

From June 1942 to August of 1945.

So you were there basically the whole time?

Oh, yeah. The only time they let the older folks go was if they had a job or they went East or something like that, according to my history of it.

So you started kindergarten/first grade and were there until third or fourth grade.

I was in third grade because, when I got out of camp, then I was in fourth grade.

What was the school like at camp?

Well, I thought the teachers were discriminating against the orphans because they would never call on us and we always had our hands up to answer questions because we wanted to get to a superior class. But they would never call on us, so we were just left in the average class. All the classrooms they had for the superior class—so they had three individual classes. They had the low one, the average, and the more intelligent. And everyone one of those questions that they asked, I could answer. But they never called on us. So I thought it was not because I was dumber; I thought it was because I was from the orphanage. They never called on any of the orphans; they called on everybody else who lived in private families, but they never called on any of us. That's what I remember in my class.

Was it adequate? Were you bored because it seems like you could have gone to the superior class?

Well, I suppose so. I wasn't interested in school anyway; I was interested in recess, more than anything. (laughter) I've been like that all my life.

Did you have any impressions of a particular person or event that stands out in your mind, when you think of Children's Village?

Ruth Takamune. She's the only one.

Ruth Takamune. Did you stay in touch with her after you left?

Yes, I did. After the 1991 reunion, I think Tak [Matsuno. See COPH-OH 2339] was the one who organized it. But see, I was in Turkey, so I couldn't make the reunion of the orphanage, of Children's Village, and I regret that very much. But after he and Annie—Annie had gotten all the information and that's when I saw Ruth's name there. So I wrote to Ruth, and we started corresponding.

So she taught you religion when you were young?

Well, she taught all of us kids how important Jesus Christ, Mary, and Joseph was.

As a child in the camp, as you got older, like seven or eight, did you ever have chores to do?

Not that I remember. I don't remember any of that. I remember just playing, mostly. Well, the only thing we had to do was make our bed and keep our little cubicle clean. That's all. Those were our only responsibilities.

And so did you ever get sick as a young girl? Did you ever have to go into the camp hospital?

No. Apparently, I had had a touch of polio. That's what I'm told now, and I did have physiotherapy with my ankles because they were very weak, so I would go to the hospital to have physical therapy, I would say, once or twice a week.

But you don't remember that?

Well, I remember going to the hospital and having that, but I didn't know why.

I see. And were the doctors Nisei?

No, I don't know. I have no idea.

So you were in the camp until you were in the third grade, so you were about seven or eight years old?

Yeah. I have a picture of all the orphans.

The Easter one?

Yeah, 1944. It's in front of a beautiful mountain. Do you know who took that photo? That famous photographer, Toyo Miyatake. You know, he wasn't permitted to have a camera in camp, but I think he made this with a home-made camera. It's a beautiful photograph.

Do you remember taking that picture?

No.

So what was your best memory of when you were there? Do you have any vivid, good memories or really vivid, bad memories?

I have no bad memories of Children's Village that I can think of. I absolutely loved it there. The only bad memory I had was when we had to leave. We all cried our eyes out.

What was it like leaving camp and having to go to a foster home?

Horrible, scary, very scary. I was very close to a teenage girl called Nadine Kodama, very close to her. You know, after we left camp, we were not put right into Wilma Stuart's home. We were put into this Catholic high school. It was a boarding school.

In California?

Yeah. And I have no idea where it was, but we were put there temporarily. And I didn't like it at all. I remember I got in trouble from the head mistress, [who] gave me a good spanking in front of everybody! In front of the whole dormitory! And I felt so humiliated. That was worse than the spanking itself.

Did you remember doing anything wrong?

Oh, you know, when you're a kid, you do everything wrong. (laughter) I've always been rebellious. I remember Nadine comforted me. She was a teenager, and I was only eight. She comforted me. I tried to find her, but to no avail. Couldn't find her. I tried to find her because I did have her address from the 1991 reunion, but I never could find her. Ever. I remember Nadine. I remember Annie only because we went to the home together. That's all. And Ruth Takamune. Those are the only three people that come very clearly in my mind of who I knew over there. And I remember—I was giving my tearful tribute to Ruth Takamune, when we all met with Lillian Matsumoto at the Japanese American National Museum. One of the guys—he's in the picture that was taken for the *Rafu Shimpo* newspaper [Los Angeles]—told me, "Celeste, I'm sure glad that you gave a nice tribute to Ruth because we all thought of her as our mother." That's how wonderful she was to all of us kids. He was older than me, so he would remember a lot more.

So you left camp, and your first foster home was Wilma Stuart's?

Yes, after we left the Catholic school for girls. Annie Sakamoto and I both ended up at Wilma's. But for the State of California to put us in a home like that is just beyond me. My God, here they put us in a home with a woman who's never been married, never had any kids, and a religious fanatic at that.

And there were seven of you?

I think there were. You would have to get this figure from Annie; she would know better than me.

Wow, so she was alone with seven children?

Well, she had her mother living with her. Her mother was more reasonable; she knew how to talk to kids and everything. I got along with her mother fine, but I just didn't get along with Wilma.

And from there, you went to a Caucasian family, Aunt Jessie Bloom's home.

Yeah, Jessie Bloom.

Was that fine?

Oh, yeah, that was wonderful. All of these kids had something physically wrong with them, and I was hard to handle, so they put me in that home, too. I was incorrigible. (laughter)

And how old were you then? (laughter)

Eleven.

Oh, my goodness. So you were almost in junior high then . . .

Yeah, well, I was in sixth grade.

And how long did you stay there?

I stayed there until eighth grade. Two years.

And then you went to the Nitake family.

Yeah, I went to the Nitake family.

Do you have any vivid memories of your experiences at any of these foster homes?

Well, I did not become emotionally attached to them because once you are torn from a loving environment such as the orphanage—and everybody is so surprised when I say it's a loving environment; well, to me, it was. Maybe to other people, it wasn't, but I'm just giving you my impression. After you are torn from a loving environment, you become emotionally detached. And so I didn't become close to anybody. But I did like Aunt Jessie Bloom's, in retrospect. Aunt Jessie Bloom, I thought, was extremely fair and she did everything she could to make our lives happy. She did do that.

How many other children were living at Aunt Jessie's?

Oh, gosh, I would say about six or seven.

Oh, my goodness, that's another large family! Then you stayed with the Nitakes through high school?

All through high school, yeah. When I got stable in high school, I didn't get in trouble. I didn't make the best grades in high school. I was just an average student because I didn't work for it. All I cared about were my peers at that time—that's what you care about—and my social life there. I was extremely popular at Baldwin Park High School. I was a cheerleader, vice-president of my class, and the Girls Athletic Association president.

Oh, did you play sports?

Yeah, I did.

Which sports?

Well, I liked basketball and soccer. Baseball. I played them all. I really enjoyed my high school years. You know, you don't care about whether you enjoy your home or not, as long as you have your high school and your peers. They are the things important to you.

Was it a diverse high school? Were there a lot of other Japanese Americans?

Actually, no, there was only one in my high school, and just a handful of Mexicans and only one black family. So the rest were all whites. It was a wonderful high school. In fact, I went to my fiftieth reunion not too long ago.

Oh, you're kidding! Did you ever experience any racism or—

No. Well, I did when I got out of camp. Annie doesn't remember this because she was too young. I remember when we were walking down the street and someone came over and said, "Are you a Jap?" And to protect Annie, I said, "Yes, I am." And he threw a brick at my head. But that's the only time. It was soon after that there was absolutely no prejudice about us being Japanese. However, in fourth grade—I was nine years old—I had a girl friend from the grammar school. She said to me, "You know, Celeste, I would love to invite you to my birthday party, but I can't because my parents don't want any Japanese people there." Oh, that hurt. But I got over that. Those two incidents are the only times that I ever had any prejudice thrown at me. And then I started getting popular in junior high and then in high school. I think that's what saved me. That saved my life because I felt like, at last, I belong somewhere. And the most important things were my teenage friends. Nobody else counted.

Do you still keep in touch with your friends?

My best friend, yes, we do. We had lost track of each other for years because, you know, you get married, you have your life, they have their life, and all of a sudden, you all get together after everybody's kids are grown up and out. And then everybody's retired, so we can devote time to each other now. It is one big circle. So basically, I had a very happy childhood. Those are your formative years. So those years, one to six, if they are happy, everything else can be crap, you know what I mean? I was never molested, never sexually molested, never beaten, nothing like that. They were all pretty good to me, now that I look back. Of course, at that age, you think that they all suck! (laughter) But in retrospect, you kind of appreciate what they all tried to do for you.

Thank you so much, Mrs. Teodor, for the interview.

Oh, you're welcome.

Wilma Stuart[1]

Interviewed by Noemi Romero
with Annie Sakamoto present

Where were your parents originally from?

Well, I was born in Corning, New York. My father was a minister, preacher. He was a preacher in Corning and Ithaca in New York. My mother's health broke, and we moved to Iowa. Anyway, we didn't stay there very long. We decided to come to California. And when we came to California, we moved to this Christian community here, a Free Methodist community. I was just a little girl then. We lived here a while and even built a house here.

Then later we moved to San Diego. My older sister had graduated from the Christian high school up here [in Los Angeles], and she wanted to go to normal school, a teacher's college, so we moved to San Diego to put her in the teacher's college. Then she graduated from there. After she graduated, she taught a year or two there. Then we moved back up here [Los Angeles]. The church asked us to come back up here and teach in the Herman [Public Elementary] School over here [in Los Angeles]. It's called the Bushnell Way [Public Elementary] School now. So we came back up here, and I was just a little girl then. We've lived here a long time.

I went to Bushnell Way School and then to Franklin [Middle School]. I went up to our church school on the hill, and somebody hit my hand with a ruler, so my sister took me out and she took me over to another school. Then I went to a teacher's college in Hollywood to become a teacher. Down at the church, I was superintendent of the beginner's department for many years, for about twenty years.

What's the beginner's department?

The beginner's department of the Sunday school. Then I taught school. I taught public school for about twenty or thirty years. I started in Watts [a district in south-central Los Angeles], and I taught in Watts. I started there and then I wanted to change, but they wouldn't let me until I'd been there three years. After I taught school in Watts for three years, then I got a chance

[1]COPH-Oral History 2488 was conducted on July 11, 1993, in Los Angeles, California.

to move to the Euclid Avenue [Public Elementary] School in Boyle Heights. My older sister Mary was teaching in the Euclid Avenue School, so I got a chance to teach there with her. I taught there for about twenty years. Then I stopped. I'd had enough. (chuckles) So I stopped and retired.

Okay. Going back to the 1940s, can you tell me what you know about Manzanar [War Relocation Center in eastern California]?

I don't know anything about Manzanar. Annie was there, but I wasn't there. She was a little girl there. They were passing out the children to homes when the war was over, so I asked them if they had any they could send me. So they sent me over the two, Annie [Sakamoto. See COPH-OH 2486] and Celeste [Teodor. See COPH-OH 3776]. Celeste stayed with me for a long time. Annie stayed the longest.

How long did Celeste stay with you?

How long? Two or three years, I guess. Welfare didn't want me to keep both of them, so I let Celeste go. They put her in another home, and I kept Annie.

This might be a tough question, but who made the decision of who you were keeping and who was going? Was it you or was it Welfare?

The other one was a little older. I guess I liked Annie best.

Did you ever keep in contact with Celeste?

Yes. I still sometimes stay in contact with her, and she writes to me sometimes. I have a picture out here of her and her husband. I'll show you. She was a nurse. Then she got married. I have a picture of her with her married husband. She never had any children. She was a smart girl. And Annie stayed with me.

Can you tell me a little bit about Annie?

Well, she's a smart girl. She had almost *A*s in pretty near everything. She's been a very good daughter to me. She couldn't be better.

So Annie lives right behind your house?

She lives in the big house.

How did that transition happen? She was living here with you, and she grew up with you.

Then she married and lived over in—was it Alhambra [Los Angeles County]? Over that way somewhere. And she had one child, Robert. Then I got her to move over here and live in the big house. Then Michelle was born here. Annie has been a nurse for many years. She is taking care of me, and she's been very good to me.

Do you have any other children?

Yeah, I took care of foster children. Different ones. I don't know just how many.

They would come in and out of foster care?

Yeah.

Let's go back to the 1940s, right after the war. After camp, when the Japanese came out of the camp, did you notice any discrimination against the Japanese Americans?

I didn't notice.

Any incidents where Annie or Celeste came home and told you they felt that they had been put down because they were Japanese, or anything like that?

I can't think of anything. They were always nice to Annie, and she was good too, a good worker. She's a smart girl, very smart. She used to get *A*s in about everything. I sent her up here to a Christian school for a while, and she got *A*s in everything.

So when you first got Annie and Celeste, it was just you three living here in this house?

We weren't living here. We were in another little house back there.

But was it just the three of you?

Yeah. Then when I had Celeste and Annie, I also had Terry, a little Spanish girl. And we lived in a little house back here. It was very fair. And we lived there for a while. Oh, I don't know, I've built so many places around here that I can't keep track of them all.

Can you tell me your feelings or the way you felt about what the US government did to the Japanese? By that, I mean, how did you feel about the camps?

The government shouldn't have done it. They shouldn't have sent them. No, there was no need of it. They couldn't do anything about it. When I got a chance to get a child or two from there, I did.

What made you decide to take care of Annie and Celeste, and bring them into your home?

I don't know. I didn't know who I was getting. The welfare lady brought me Annie and Celeste. Then I got the other little girl from—her mother couldn't take care of her, so she put her in the welfare system. So I had the three of them for a while. Then later on I decided to let them go. Terry had already gone. Her mother had taken her. And I let Celeste go to somebody over in Alhambra. But I didn't let Annie go. I kept her.

What year did they come live with you?

What year? Do you know, Annie?

Annie Sakamoto: Nineteen forty-five, August.

So, right after Children's Village you came here?

Annie Sakamoto: Yeah, because the government started dispensing people from Manzanar. I think it was June, July, and August, and we were the last ones to leave Children's Village, so that was in August of 1945.

Wilma, do you remember where you were when the government issued the order to put the Japanese Americans in camp?

I don't remember the date.

Do you remember how you felt when you found out about it?

Well, I didn't really think it was right. I had other Japanese friends on the street here, and a lot of them had to go. I wrote to a lot of them and took pictures before they went. And when they came back, they came to visit me. Anyway, we didn't think it was the right thing to do, but we couldn't do a thing about it.

Did most of your Japanese American friends that lived around here lose their property? Did they lose their belongings because they could only carry what they could take?

I don't know. I expect something like that.

Did they express to you how they felt about going into the camps?

I probably heard a lot. I can't remember right now. When you get to be ninety-three years old, you can't remember everything. My mother lived to be ninety-eight. A car hit my father over here, when we were living in that house. We built that house. My father didn't go to a doctor, and septicemia poisoning set in his leg and he was gone in a short time. He died over there. He was old, too.

How old was he when he passed away?

Oh, I expect he was eighty years old or something. I don't know.

Is there anything else you would like to tell us before we leave?

Where that building is, and the next one, we had all that property, and my mother had a big garden there. A little Japanese girl and I used to go up and down the streets of this town and sell vegetables that my mother raised. That girl is still living over in South Pasadena.

Do you still see her?

I haven't seen her for a long time. I'd like to see her. She's pretty near as old as I am. She lived over there on the hill then. There was nothing but a dirt road out here for many, many years, just a dirt road. I guess I've told you enough.

Thank you, Wilma. That concludes our interview with Wilma. Thank you.

You're welcome.

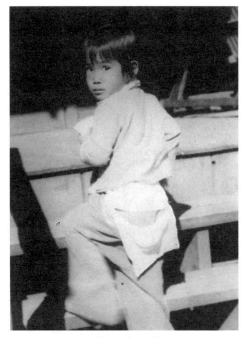

Annie Shiraishi Sakamoto

Wilma Stuart in 1950.

Celeste Loi Teodor and husband Peter

This photo by Toyo Miyatake taken on Easter Sunday in 1944 includes nearly all of the children and young adults who were residents of the Children's Village at Manzanar Relocation Center.

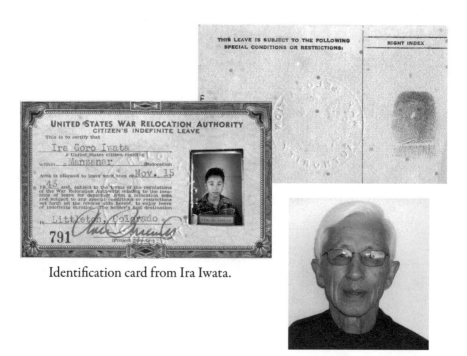

Identification card from Ira Iwata.

Fiftieth Reunion held at Rosemead, California, in 1992.

—(l-r: seated in front)
Susie Matsuno Watamura
Kenji "Gopher" Suyematsu
Takashi "Saber" Suyematsu
Takatow Sam Matsuno
—(ladies standing)
Fudge Kajiwara Okamoto
Taeko Kajiwara Nagayama
Matsuko Kodani Kaku
Haruko Isozaki Hirata
Clara Seno Hayashi
Alice Kaneko
Sachiko Sugimoto
Shizuko Sharon Okazaki Kodama
Harue Kodani Odaka
Jean Tatsuye Matsuno Takeuchi
Lillian Matsumoto
Annie Shiraishi Sakamoto

Sue Sumako Tanaka Asawa
"Betsy" Setsuko Matsuno
Nakako Nadine Kodani
Kazuye Suyematsu
Clara Niguma Yakushi
Mary Matsuno Miya
—(gentlemen standing)
Sohei Hohri
Tamotsu Isozaki
Aki Isozaki
Ira Iwata
Bobby Yamashita
Tak Isozaki
Shoji Tanaka
Mits Yamashita
Gene Murakami
Isao Matsuno
Masami "Sausage" Tanaka

Herbert Suyematsu

Mary and Mits Yamasaki

Gloria and Ronald Kawamoto

Chapter Seven
Being Mixed-Race at Children's Village

Prior to World War II, very few immigrant Issei in California married someone who was non-Japanese. As Paul Spickard writes, "The rate of outmarriage by Japanese immigrants in California was very low, because it was where the Japanese population was heaviest, because both Japanese and non-Japanese opposed the practice, and because the sex ratio in Japanese communities was not so lopsided as it was among other immigrant peoples."[1] On the other hand, while the Issei were strongly opposed to interracial marriages, some of their American-born Nisei children wanted to date people outside of their community, socialize at high school dances, and follow the American courtship rituals that potentially led to marriage.[2]

The social stigma and family opposition to interracial marriages in the Nikkei community, however, resulted in very few interracial marriages before World War II.[3] Consequently, many mixed-race children of unwed mothers were abandoned, sent to an orphanage, or given up for adoption and foster care.[4] At the Children's Village, out of a population of 101 children, an estimated 19 percent were of mixed-race ancestry.[5] The majority of these mixed-race children were recorded as third generation, American-born Sansei, and eight of the fourteen children were three years old or younger at the time they were placed at Children's Village.[6]

Many of these children suffered at Children's Village because of

---

[1]Paul Spickard, "Dimensions of Intermarriage: Old Barriers Fall," in *Mixed Blood: Intermarriage and Ethnic Identity in Twentieth-Century America* (Madison: University of Wisconsin Press, 1989), 47.

[2]Ibid, 50.

[3]Ibid, 51. According to Paul Spickard, "Just a tiny fraction of those older West Coast Nisei who married before World War II chose non-Japanese mates: 3.1 percent of the men and 2.3 of the women."

[4]Ibid, 113.

[5]Racial combinations of these mixed-race children included "Mexican and Japanese; Indian and Japanese; Filipino and Japanese; and Japanese and Italian, Irish, and French descent." See Helen Whitney, "Care of Homeless Children of Japanese Ancestry during Evacuation" (M.A. thesis, University of California, Berkeley, 1948), 32.

[6]Helen Whitney, 32, 34.

their mixed-race heritage. According to former orphan Takatow Matsuno, "*Hapas* [people of mixed-race heritage] . . . were picked on more [because they] looked different."[7] Dennis Tojo Bambauer remembers the teasing and name-calling in his oral history interview. Bambauer, who is part-Japanese and part-Caucasian, was six years old when he relocated to Children's Village, a move that was quite traumatic for Bambauer because he had spent most of his life outside of the Nikkei community. He had always thought of himself as white and had been accepted among whites at the Children's Home Society of California and in foster homes. In the following excerpt, Bambauer recalls the uneasy transition from the predominantly white Children's Home Society in Los Angeles to the all-Japanese American Children's Village at Manzanar.

Being placed in an all-Japanese American orphanage had a deep impact on Bambauer's racial identity and his desire later in life to learn about his ethnic heritage. For Ronald Kawamoto, who is part-Japanese and part-Mexican, his knowledge of being sent to Children's Village as an infant turned into a quest to find out why he was separated from family and relatives for the first two years of his life, and then reunited with his mother and sisters at the end of the war. In the following excerpt, Kawamoto discusses his struggle to find out what happened to him and his family during relocation and why he was orphaned.

---

[7]Takatow Matsuno, Interviewed by Noemi Romero, 13 March 1993, CSUF-Center for Oral and Public History. See COPH-OH 2339.

Dennis Tojo Bambauer[1]

Interviewed by Reiko Katabami

Can I ask you when and where you were born?

Birthday, October 7, 1934, Los Angeles, California.

Do you have any siblings?

I have two adopted sisters. I have six half brothers and sisters on my mother's [Anna Tojo] side and two half brothers on my father's side.

Tell me about your relationship with your parents. Right after you were born, you were sent to an orphanage?

Yes, the Children's Home Society [in Los Angeles, California].

Because?

Because my mother could not keep me.

And how about your father?

[My] father could not keep me.

In our conversation before our interview, you told me your parents actually didn't get married.

That's true.

Okay, that's why. How did you find your parents two years ago?

Well, I have some friends that are very active in the Japanese American Citizens League, and so I thought that maybe their friends might know somebody by the name of Tojo. It happens that my friends, who were helping me, live in Marysville, California, and my auntie Frances, who married my uncle, came to Marysville, and by luck my friends met her and we then discovered the rest of my family.

So you were very lucky.

---

[1]COPH-Oral History 2335 was conducted on August 16, 1993, in Sacramento, California.

Very lucky. I started looking for the Tojo family in 1957, and it took me this many years to find them.

And would you describe your parents?

My mother was Nisei and my father was Caucasian. They were not married, and I was born. After I was born, I was put in Children's Home Society.

So both are living right now.

My mother is still alive. My father passed away in February of 1993.

So your father died this year?

Yes. I saw him just before he died of heart complications and old age.

Did you have anything to talk about with your father? Did you feel fatherly love?

No, I did not know him that well. I only knew him for two months.

Before he died?

Before he died. And he was in the hospital.

So how about your mother? Did your mother remarry?

Yes. My mother Anna Tojo married a Japanese gentleman and had six children. So I have six half brothers and half sisters on my mother's side of the family.

How long have you known your mother?

Two years.

Okay, two years ago you met. Was it good?

Yes, it's wonderful.

Oh, that's good. How is the relationship with her going?

It's going good.

Do you talk about your past experience?

Mother doesn't like to talk about that, so we talk about the camp experience and things in very broad terms.

She was at Heart Mountain [Relocation Center in Wyoming]?

Heart Mountain, yes.

Does she talk about that?

Yes. My aunts and uncles were there, so they talk about it.

I'm going to ask about your own experience. You went to Children's Home Society right after you were born?

Yes.

And stayed there until—?

Until I was moved to the Children's Village, nineteen forty—when was the war?

Do you know who arranged that you go to Children's Home Society?

I believe my mother did.

And at that time, your mother was on her own?

No, she was living with her family and working part-time and going to school part-time.

Could you tell me about Children's Home Society? Where was it located? Is it still in operation today?

Yes, but they don't have any orphanages; they just put children into families for adoption. They don't have any orphanages, to my knowledge. The Children's Home Society was in Los Angeles on Adams Street.

You stayed there at Children's Home Society until six or something?

Yes.

Do you know who was in charge of Children's Home Society?

I don't know.

Do you know how many orphans were there?

Well, I was very young, but there were quite a few of us.

Do you have any idea what the age range was?

I remember just small children, five to six years being the oldest.

And the racial backgrounds?

Caucasian.

What about Japanese American?

I think I was the only Japanese American.

During those six years, did you just always stay there?

No. I was in some foster homes.

Oh. Tell me about that. When did you go?

I don't remember. But at one time I was in a Japanese foster home, and I think it was out in the Santa Ana [Orange County, California] area.

How long?

I think about a year.

Do you remember how they treated you?

Oh, nice.

They had children?

No.

What did your foster parents do?

I don't know what they did. I was too small.

Maybe something happened to them, and then you came back to Children's Home Society?

Yes.

Did you go to nursery school?

I don't remember.

How did you mingle with other orphans at the Children's Home Society?

Okay.

Did you play with them?

Yes.

Was there any racial conflict or physical or mental abuse there?

No. I didn't know that I was Japanese. I thought I was Caucasian like all the other kids.

Do you still have contact with the children that you met there?

No. I don't know anybody from there.

Okay. So for you it was a comfortable place at that time?

Yes.

So then, what was the reason for leaving Children's Home Society?

Well, the government said that, because I was Japanese, I had to go to a relocation center. They moved me from Children's Home Society to Shonien [where I took a bus] to Manzanar. What I remember is being with Japanese American kids on a big, grassy area. We boarded two buses and went to Manzanar.

How was it inside the bus? Did you sing or something?

Um, we might have, I don't remember. It was hot; I remember it was hot.

Outside? Inside?

Outside.

When you arrived?

Yeah.

What was the mood?

Well, we were told we were going on a little picnic. And then we got in that bus and we just kept going and going and going. And it was hot.

Do you remember when you arrived? What time did you arrive?

I think it was in the afternoon.

So you brought with you all you had from the Children's Home?

Which was nothing.

Okay. After you arrived in Manzanar, what was your reaction as a child?

My first reaction was the fences because when we got in there, the guards had to let us in, and there was a barbed wire fence and there were towers. I remember that. So I remember being scared when we first got there.

Do you remember any staff members who went to Manzanar with the children?

The only one I remember is John Nagayama [See COPH-OH 2494].

How about the Matsumotos [Lillian and Harry Matsumoto, superintendents of the Children's Village. See COPH-OH 2494]?

Oh, I remember the Matsumotos, yeah.

How about the other staff?

No, I don't remember them.

Do you have any idea what was your feeling then, at the time, when you went from the Children's Home Society to the Shonien [and then boarded a bus to Manzanar and Children's Village]?

Yeah. Because I had never been associated with any Japanese, I thought I was just—before, everybody was like me. Then when I got to the Shonien, everybody was different than me.

The Japanese [American] children?

Yes. They all had different faces than I had, and I found out that I wasn't the same as everybody.

So it was a shock.

Yes. I'd never been with Japanese [American] children.

Did you make friends there? How did you play with them?

Well, yeah, eventually we—

But at first?

I don't remember.

So it was a difficult period, when you went to the Shonien [and then the Children's Village]?

Yeah.

Tell me about how you were treated at the Children's Village.

By staff?

By staff or children.

By staff, I guess I was treated just like every other kid. Because I was half-Caucasian, I think the kids picked on me.

And they made your childhood difficult?

Yeah.

Can you tell me about it more extensively? Was it the same kids that attacked you? Who were those kids?

I don't remember. They gave me a nickname.

What was the nickname?

Gopher, because of my teeth.

I see. How did you like your nickname?

I didn't like it.

Can you tell me more in detail? How did they attack you?

Oh, they just ridiculed me because my name was Tojo.

Did they say what Tojo means or something?

Well, first of all, the name Tojo was not popular in the camp. Being mixed, half-Caucasian, I was kind of different, and they used to tease me.

Because of your name Tojo?

The name Tojo and not being full Japanese, being half-breed.

So you noticed what Tojo meant then, gradually.

Yeah, it was not good.

And you realized that Tojo was a—

War leader?

Yes.

Yeah. And he was bad.

He was their [Japan's] leader, actually. He was a lead student in a military staff college, or military academy in Japan. And then later he became the prime minister until the end of World War II. Then like the secretary of the army, he was appointed as minister. Japan wanted to go to war, so he played an active role in Japan's going to war.

So in America, he was the enemy.

Yes. And then Japan saw England and America like savage, brutal countries. Do you know anything else about Tojo?

Not a great deal.

So at this time you didn't know about Tojo, what Tojo meant.

No. I just knew that he was a general and that he was hated by Americans because he was leading the Japanese in the war, so that was not—he was not a nice person. So they used to tease me about my name.

Did you have counseling with the Matsumotos?

Not that I remember.

How about with other staff members, to discuss your case or anything like that?

No.

Did you make any friends at Children's Village?

Well, a few. Then after I left, a couple of people I got to know better.

Do you still have contact with some of them?

Occasionally. The Matsuno family. Tak Matsuno [See COPH-OH 2339].

How did you manage your emotions during the Children's Village period?

I got mad, had temper tantrums.

Did you fight back?

Yes.

Did you have anybody to talk to about this?

Not really.

Because you thought it was—?

No. Because they were different.

How about staff members?

One person that I talked to was John Nagayama, who was the dorm leader.

Was it helpful?

Yes.

So each time, if you had a problem, you went to him?

Yes.

How was dormitory life? How did you mingle with other children?

Well, we just had one big room with beds all around.

How many?

Fifteen maybe.

Do you remember staff members playing with children?

Yes.

Do you remember playing?

Yeah. I remember throwing sushi.

Was it a party or something?

Yeah.

Who threw the sushi?

We kids.

To you?

At me. We threw it at people.

This might be difficult, but compared to the Children's Home Society, was Children's Village a less comfortable place?

Yes.

Because of the—

Because of my difference in race.

Do you remember playing at the Children's Village?

I remember playing in a big grassy area. Kick the can and games like that.

With the staff members?

No, just with kids mostly. And I remember the older boys had a basketball team. I remember watching them play.

Do you have any memory of mealtime?

Yeah. At mealtime, I remember we got a lot of rice and brown gravy, a lot of it.

So you were not hungry.

No, we never—if we wanted more to eat, we always had more rice and brown gravy.

Do you remember the blackouts?

Well, the blackouts were when the military police made everybody turn off their lights at night, practicing, in case the Japanese attacked us, I guess; I don't know. It was kind of scary. They'd make you turn off the lights, and you had to stay in the building, and then they would patrol around the orphanage and make sure that everybody did what they were told to do. It's kind of a way of intimidating people, I guess.

From the staff members?

No, from the military.

Do you have any memories of your last days at Children's Village?

Yeah, I remember being told that I was going to leave, and then I think I was sent down to the military police, and I think they took my picture. And I remember them taking fingerprints so I could leave. I remember being very scared about leaving and kind of scared because of the police taking my picture and fingerprints.

Only you?

Only me.

Because—

Because I was leaving early.

Oh, you left early?

Yes. I left there in the summer months.

You went to Manzanar in summer?

I went to Manzanar with the whole group, but then I left Manzanar and went to Bishop, [Inyo County, California].

You stayed at Manzanar until when? Nineteen forty-three?

I think I left in June of 1943. I think I was there for two years.

No, just one year, because you went to Manzanar, I think, in June 1942.

I don't remember. Whenever I was there, I was there a short time.

Do you have any memories of visiting other barracks while you were living in Children's Village?

Yeah. I remember visiting Tak Matsuno's sister and some other members and friends of theirs.

How did you perceive the other barracks?

Oh, they were crowded and not—there was no privacy, I remember that. No walls. Just big rooms.

Do you remember how the adults at Manzanar treated you?

Oh, nice.

Because they didn't know you were living in Children's Village?

I don't know.

Did you talk to them, to Japanese adults?

No.

So you didn't feel any prejudice? They didn't look down on you?

I don't think so. Now, we're talking about the adults.

Yes.

No, I don't think so.

How did you feel in general during the Manzanar period?

Well, I guess I felt all right. You know, under the circumstances, you adjust, right? So we all adjusted pretty good.

You told me you were parted from your parents right after you were born?

Yes.

So you didn't miss your parents.

No. I never had any parents to miss.

Compared to the other barracks, there was no privacy, no partitions. How did you like the Children's Village barracks?

Well, there wasn't—I don't have anything to compare it to.

But other barracks looked bad or something?

Well, our barrack was just one big room with a heater in the middle.

Was it warm enough?

Yeah, I think so.

Really?

Well, I don't remember ever being cold, so—

I see. How were you taken care of in Children's Village by staff members? Do you remember?

Not really. I was too young.

Do you think the orphans were relatively well-behaved at the Children's Village?

Yes.

They were not punished?

I don't—yeah, we were punished. It wasn't cruelty, but we were disciplined.

So no physical, mental—

I don't remember that.

Did they explain why you were wrong or give you guidelines?

No, I don't think so. They just told you that you didn't do it right and do it better.

Okay. Do you know how the Matsumotos were perceived among orphans? What was their reputation?

I just remember them as being the directors.

And then they have subordinates.

Yes.

How about subordinate people?

The only person I had contact with was John Nagayama. That was the only one.

Can you describe John Nagayama?

Oh, he was a very nice person.

How old was he then?

I think he was probably eighteen.

He was like a social worker? Did other kids like him?

Yeah. He was in charge of our part of the dormitory.

Did you feel that you were protected during the Children's Village period?

Yeah.

How?

Well, because we were all together, and we had the older people looking after us.

Do you know [or remember] anything about getting a clothing grant?

No. In Children's Village?

Yes. A monthly grant: three dollars and seventy-five cents.

No. In Children's Village, all the clothes would be washed, and then you'd go get your clothes. And whoever got there first, or was the biggest, got the best, and the youngest and the littlest got what was left.

At the laundry?

Yeah.

You picked up anything you liked?

Yeah. That's what I remember because I always used to get the last leftover.

And how did you feel?

I didn't like it. I always got the bib overalls. I always got left with the bibs, maybe because I was taller.

You were taller?

Yeah, I was always taller, bigger, taller.

Because of being bigger, do you think you were also possibly teased? You were different also because you were tall?

Because of being Caucasian—my father was tall.

Okay, I understand. Do you think it's really important to tell your story?

Yes.

Not only to your family members, but also to others?

Yes . . . to my fellow workers.

Tell me about that. Are they also interested?

Yes. They're more interested in the family background because it's unique, but we also talk [about] the social issues [such as] the treatment of the Japanese during the war and Japan bashing today, things like that.

So in a way, your unique situation has also opened up the conversation?

Yes. It becomes the highway, the freeway. It starts out on one road and then we branch out.

The more you talked, the more you felt better?

Yes.

For you, which affected your life more, the orphanage life experience or the Manzanar internment camp experience?

Well, the camp experience, because if I hadn't had the camp experience, I probably would never have known parts of the Japanese culture, or I probably —yeah, I would have never been exposed to the Japanese because I would have been always exposed only to the Caucasians, I'm sure. I guess you'd have to say that was a positive effect of camp for me.

Positive?

Yeah. It was still the worst thing that America ever did to a group of people.

Any regrets in your life?

I regret not being able to be raised more in the Japanese culture, because I have decided to identify with the Japanese half of my family, and I missed that, the culture. It's very important. By me not having that culture or experience, my children can't have it either. So what's going to happen in our family is we're going to lose it.

Well, I appreciate your cooperation. I think I learned a lot. Thank you very much.

Thank you.

Ronald Kawamoto[1]
(with wife, Gloria Kawamoto)

Interviewed by Cathy Irwin

When and where were you born?

June 17, 1942, in Santa Anita [Assembly Center, in the city of Arcadia, Los Angeles County], California.

So growing up, were you taught anything about your Japanese or Mexican culture, or the language? Do you remember?

No, not really because my mother [Teresa Rose Kawamoto] never involved us kids in the Spanish culture, other than we knew our whole family was Spanish. And they spoke Spanish. But the kids, my cousins, we all talked English together. We didn't speak anything other than English. And hardly any of my cousins know how to speak the Spanish language because it wasn't taught to them at that time. I think that, a lot of the time, they wanted to be Americans.

Yes.

And they didn't want to speak other languages because of possible reprisals, so they spoke the English language. And as far as, like my dad [Yoshio Kawamoto], since he was gone fishing all the time, my only contact with my Japanese side is when he would come in from fishing and he would pick us up and go to his mom's house. And of course I couldn't understand a word that she ever said. (laughter) And Japanese was basically what she talked.

Did anyone else in your family speak Japanese?

My half-sister Hanako, my uncle Konie, and my father knew the language.

Oh, they did?

So that's the only connection we had.

So on the census forms, or when you had to check-mark the box identifying your ethnicity, what did you check? Japanese and Spanish descent?

---

[1]COPH-Oral History 3591 was conducted on February 4, 2007, in San Diego, California.

Yes.

That's great. Because some people had to figure out what to put—check-mark one? Why? What about the box that says "Other"?

Well, at one time, some of the applications would have white, black and Mongolian. So, of course, that's where I landed because I wasn't white, wasn't black. The Mongolian sector of the world. That's what we were. The Spanish, the Latinos, were put in that sector as well as some—some of the Latinos were also considered white! The Spanish were considered white.

Exactly. So where did you fit?

I could put one here and one there—

Exactly.

But I just checked the Mongolian sector. That's where I put my check-mark. Afterwards, the census began splitting categories up. Either you were Japanese —actually it was Asian Pacific.

Yes.

And then it became Latin, Mexican American. So it was kind of hard because there was Japanese American, Asian American, Spanish American, and Mexican American. So, whoa! I could fill all these columns! (laughter)

Yes, people have had a hard time filling out those boxes.

Very much so.

Getting back to your parents—did they ever talk about Pearl Harbor? Did they ever mention what they remembered? Do you remember them ever bringing it up?

Not a bit.

Do you know if your parents had to sell the Frisco Café [in San Diego, California] quickly?

I think that's what it was. They had to sell really fast like a lot of the families did. I mean, they had to sell things for pennies on the dollar because they were leaving. That's essentially what it was.

Wow. So you don't know what happened to their property?

No. I just know it was sold. As far as, like I said, their house on Island Street [in San Diego, California], they still lived on Island Street.

After the war?

After the war. But I don't know if it was a new house or the same one. I don't know. I have no knowledge of that.

Okay. Did they ever talk about the Executive Order? Or about how they were going to be assembled for relocation?

I just think they just started rounding them up! And—

You don't know how they heard about it?

I really don't, other than my father. I think my father would be the one because of the Frisco Café. The Kawamoto family had to go. As for my mother, my mother really didn't have to go to the [Santa Anita] Assembly Center because she was Mexican, so her decision to go in was on her own—to go, of course, with her husband. I mean, that's natural. And Sylvia, my older sister, is half-Japanese. Well, she *had* to go. So, my mother isn't going to leave my father *and* my sister. And then, I was born at the Santa Anita Assembly Center. So that was basically the reason.

So, did your mother ever talk to you about how it felt or her choice? Do you remember her ever mentioning it?

A: No, she really didn't say much other than the fact that I was born in a stable of one of the famous racehorses.

Really? So you were born at Santa Anita Assembly Center.

It was a racetrack, yes.

Oh, my goodness. So you were basically housed in horse stables?

That's where they were. And like you said, they used the straw for their beds and whatever they could cover the straw with. But she said it smelled of the horse. There were quite a few families housed in one stall. And the shower facilities and the bathrooms were not the best things in the world. And you take your time. That stuff I learned not from my mother, but from a lot of people who had been in camp. So my mother just never talked about it. I've tried to ask her questions about camp, about internment, about what happened, and she just never said anything. She just—that was it.

Yeah.

My father—after he got back from the war, or the service I should say, my father became a fisherman. I think he was a little bit—not ashamed about what happened; he was upset. And I think he figured the best thing for him would be to go out and go fishing. Plus, fishing at the time was a lucrative business, very lucrative. And he, we really didn't have anything to come back to. I mean, the Frisco Café was gone. I'm not really too sure if the house on Island Street was taken from him; I'm not really sure. So, he really didn't have anything that he could come back to, I guess.

No.

From what I understand from my sister Hanako, the little that she has talked about camp, they weren't in Poston [Relocation Center in Arizona] long. They weren't in Poston very long, and they got back. They came back.

To California?

To San Diego, yes. But Hanako doesn't know anything. I know more about the camps than she does! And I was born—she was three or four years old at the time. So I don't know if she's buried a lot of that herself. My other sister, Sylvia . . . she thinks she knows everything about it, but she doesn't. I mean that she was only one or two years old at the time. What is she going to know?

Yeah.

And as far as me knowing, I didn't know nothing.

Yeah, you were born at one of the assembly centers.

I mean the biggest thing I could have done to people was to wet on them! (laughter)

Oh, my goodness. (laughter) So your parents never talked about how they even got to the racetrack, Santa Anita.

No, just that they went . . . the whole family went. The thing that I've been trying to figure out is, since I had a grandparent, and I had a half-sister and an uncle, why didn't I go with them [to Poston Relocation Center]? Why did I go to Manzanar, to Children's Village, as an orphan?

Yes.

That's—see, this is what's so crazy about this whole thing. First my mom didn't have to be in there. Secondly, we go and then we get split up. Why a baby gets taken away from their mother for whatever reason—I have no knowledge of when—I have grandparents that could have taken me. Why that didn't happen—that's the biggest—I think the biggest stumbling block in my life has been trying to find out why this happened. Why did it happen to me? I'm probably not the only child that had this happen, but why? It's crazy to me.

Were your grandparents also sent to Santa Anita and then Poston?

Yes, but there is no number.

There's no record.

There's no record of them being in there because my uncle Konie and my grandmother and Hanako are not in there. Their names are not on the rosters, and that doesn't make sense. It shows the Kawamotos, just my father, my mother, my sister, and myself, and that's it. And there's too many holes, too many secrets that someone is not telling—and why? And if there was another Kawamoto family (and there were quite a few) why isn't my grandmother and uncle and half-sister on the roster? And they're not.

So were you and your siblings ever separated in the process of going to Poston? Or were you separated after? You were talking about how there were no records, or you're not sure if you were even sent to Poston.

Well, according to the papers, I have no records of my mother and myself *being* at Poston, according to the United States Department of the Interior. (narrator displays the documents) It shows…July 27, 1942…the Kawamoto name was originally misspelled in their Poston registry as Kawamoti. And the registry has a handwritten correction of the Kawamoto family: Yoshio, Teresa Rose, Sylvia, and Ronald were transferred to Poston. At Poston, according to the National Archives, the only matching searches of numbers show Yoshio at 4259A, Sylvia 4259C.

That's the family number?

That's the family number. And according to this, neither Teresa nor Ronald was listed with this family number. It's assumed that we would be 4259B and 4259 C, which would be wrong on the "C" part there. It should be 4259 B, since Sylvia was the "C."

Yes. So at some point, you probably were separated from some family members?

Oh, we were separated from my grandmother; Hanako, my half-sister; and Konie, my uncle, at Poston, because Hanako remembers being at Poston. But she remembers not being there long. The authorities let them go, from what she says. And that I don't understand because I thought they all had to stay in camp until 1944-45 or when they let them go. But she said that she wasn't in camp that long at Poston, so I don't really know anything about that.

And she doesn't remember living anywhere else besides California during that time?

No.

She recalls coming back to California.

Hanako just basically doesn't remember a lot.

And you were just a baby; you were just born, so you probably don't remember any part of being at Santa Anita or Poston.

No, I do not.

Do you remember Children's Village at all?

No.

You don't remember. Do you know how long you were in Children's Village?

From 1943 to 1945.

Wow, two years. So when you left, you were about two years old.

Two going on three.

Do you know what the process was to leave Manzanar since you were just a baby? Do you know if you were reunited immediately with—

No, I got a letter here from Manzanar. (looks for letter) Oh, right here. This one here is a copy dated January 25, 1945, from Manzanar Relocation Project, Manzanar, California. Got down "Mr." Rose Kawamoto. (laughter) "Dear Mr. Kawamoto, We wish to advise you that Ronald is ready to leave Manzanar. Will you please let us know immediately if you wish to come and get him? If so, it is necessary for us to have a time of your arrival in order to make arrangements at the gate for your admittance. If you cannot come, we would like to know at your earliest convenience, so that we can send him to San Diego. Please advise us of the actions you wish to take." And this is from Ralph Merritt, Project Director.

Oh, yes.

Gloria Kawamoto (RK's wife): Is he still alive?

I don't think he's alive anymore. This is dated January 25, 1945. So it was supposed to be addressed to Mrs. Rose Kawamoto. So your mother was already in San Diego, living on Eighth Street at the time?

As far as I know, when she got in trouble at Poston for taking me out—

So what happened? Do you know any of the circumstances?

Other than what the Manzanar Park [Manzanar National Historic Site] Ranger Kirk [Peterson] found out for me. She was taking me—she had a pass to leave and—I guess it was an overnight pass or weekend pass. And she was taking me with her. Well, I had no pass evidently. And from what I understand and from what transpired in some of the workings and letters, she got in trouble.

For leaving?

For leaving. But that is at Poston and some of this information suggests that I went strictly from Santa Anita straight to Manzanar, when that's not the truth because I was in Poston because I do have a Poston number. Except it's not registered. Again, if you go back to these papers, my mother and myself are not registered, but my sister and Yoshio are. They have a number 4259. I don't.

Wow.

At some point, like I said, either they took me away from my mother, my mother gave me up, or whatever. I don't know what happened, what transpired. That's all. My mother didn't talk about it, and my father was in the service at that point.

So at some point your family got dispersed.

Well, like I said, when my father signed up for the service—

This was in Poston.

Right. And he took his basic in Utah. Then they went to Fort Shelby, Mississippi, and my mother and my sister followed him.

But not you?

But not me. At that point or prior to that point, I think I was shipped down to Manzanar. This is where everything gets really hairy. What is really confusing is the fact of why. I'm a baby! Why didn't I stay with my mom and why didn't I go with my mother? And the only thing I can come up with, the only conclusion I can come up with is, and some of the papers kind of almost testify to it, that I was orphaned.

And you've talked to nuns as well?

Yes, the Maryknoll Sisters, a Catholic Order.

So the Sisters of Maryknoll. Why did you talk with them?

Right, they had dealings with the hospital and I almost certainly had some contact with them at the Children's Village. I learned this when I lived up in Portland [Oregon] because the Sisters of Maryknoll were up there and I tried to seek information from them. And they had no records or anything. And they said the best thing to do would be to contact National Archives or Manzanar or whatever.

Yes.

So I really don't know what happened at that point.

So you're not sure how you were sent to Children's Village?

No.

Or when?

When I was sent (reading document): "February 4, 1943, Ronald was transferred to Manzanar Children's Center."

Hmm. I wonder if you went with other orphans, or if you were the only orphan sent from Poston.

I was sent by myself because I'm the only one that is registered under the Kawamoto family or *this* Kawamoto family with the number 6010 or 60-1-10. There's a big hassle there.

Yes. So none of your siblings went with you?

No.

Wow. There's a famous photograph by Ansel Adams with you and other babies in the Children's Village nursery.[2]

Right.

So obviously the letter from Ralph Merritt to your mother suggests that at some point you were reunited with your mother. Do you remember being reunited at age three?

No, I don't because I don't remember anything. Not until I was probably four or five years old do I have any real recognition of my parents. And at that point, it was just basically my mother and my sister.

Yes.

So I don't remember anything prior to that.

As you got older, did you feel like studying Manzanar?

I did. My ex-wife's uncle was involved in the redress.

Were you involved?

No, I wasn't involved other than the fact that, since my name was in the National Archives, I received the gratuity [twenty thousand dollars] just like everybody else did because of it. My mother had to fight for it.

Oh, really?

Because she wasn't going to get it. They said that she didn't *have* to go in. And she went voluntarily. And therefore she wasn't eligible for it. But she contacted Senator [Daniel] Inouye from Hawaii and, of course, he wrote letters and stuff on her behalf and she did get her money at that point.

That's great.

But, no, I wasn't really involved in it; but because my ex-wife's uncle was involved, I asked him. I told him my story and he was completely awed and

---

[2]See Ansel Adams, "Nursery, Orphan infants, Manzanar Relocation Center, CA (1943)" Call # LOT 10479-5 no. 25, and "Orphanage, Manzanar Relocation Center, CA (1943)" Call# LOT 10479-7 no 15 *The Library of Congress: American Memory* <http://www.memory.loc.gov> (3 July 2008).

amazed that they would separate a child from their mother at such an early age and for no reason. So he searched, and he couldn't find anything. I've asked people through the Ninkai-Jinkai and also the Japanese Benevolent Society in Portland and they've said the same thing. Nobody's ever heard of it. They just said that they couldn't find any information. If it weren't for the Manzanar [National Historic Site] Park Ranger Kirk [Peterson], I'd still be looking.

Yes, this is fascinating. And do you feel the government's letter of apology and the little money that they did give people made up for everything that a lot of the Japanese had to go through?

I would say not. Because you figure a lot of your Japanese, they lost a lot of stuff. They lost valuables, their homes, and their businesses. Some were fortunate enough to have friends take it over for them and get back. But [for] the ones that didn't, it played a hard part on them. I think, like with my father, I think he felt that, since he went in with the service, and one of my uncles went in the service, that his family shouldn't have been placed in the centers. Like I said, my mother never really talked about it. My father never, *ever* said anything. And I never really questioned either of them about it, other than my mother later in life. I questioned her and I got a lot of, "What do you want to know for?" and "It is water under the bridge." Well, no, it is not. It is my life. Something happened. I want to know what happened. Was I given up for adoption? Because I ended up in Manzanar. Why all the circumstances?

And no one is saying anything?

No one is saying anything. Of course, my mom, she's dead now. She can't. And my father, he's passed on as well. He can't. My grandmother passed on, but she couldn't speak the English language. Hanako, my half-sister, really doesn't know anything. My other sister, Sylvia, thinks she knows, but she's not telling. And I'm—to me, I'm saying, it's my heritage, it's my life. It's something that happened to me. You're oblivious to what happened because you were with my mother. And I wasn't. I was left alone in the care of Japanese people. I'd like to find out who took care of me. I'd love to tell them, thank you!

It's interesting how the War Relocation [Authority], the National Archives, doesn't know either.

Gloria Kawamoto: (shows document) Yes, what happened—it says he came from a foster home. How did that happen?

See the thing is, you really don't—I want to know for my own self-gratification where I came from. With my parents both mixed-race—my mother of one, my father of another—I want to find out why this happened. I'm curious. I've been curious, since I was up in Portland [Oregon] living amongst the Japanese [American] community all that time. I really want to know. Everybody has roots. Everybody has a connection. I'm kind of out there on my own.

Thank you for the interview, Mr. Kawamoto.

You're welcome.

Chapter Eight
A Life in Pictures

On January 14, 2007, when the Japanese American National Museum in Los Angeles held a special event focusing on the Children's Village featuring former assistant superintendent Lillian Matsumoto, they included a special presentation by former orphan Lillian Ogata Bonner.[1] Bonner, who had flown from her home in Houston, Texas, to participate, provided a moving slide show about her life during and after Children's Village. In the audience enjoying her presentation were former orphans, friends, and Lillian Matsumoto herself.

"I'm honored to be here with Mrs. Matsumoto who more than likely held me in her arms in Children's Village," Bonner said to a news reporter, Gwen Muranaka, after the event.[2]

Born in Tacoma, Washington, on September 30, 1942, Lillian Ogata was immediately given up for adoption. She was one of eight babies sent to the Children's Village, where staff had prepared a baby's room with cribs for infant orphans.[3] In 1945, as Children's Village and Manzanar Relocation Center were in the final stages of closing, Mr. and Mrs. Frank Hattori of Yerington, Nevada, adopted three-year-old Lillian and provided her with a Japanese first name, Yoshiko (today, she refers to herself as "Lillian Yoshiko"). They also adopted another Children's Village resident, Kenneth Hattori.

The following pictorial autobiography includes pictures with commentary from Lillian Bonner's July 14, 2007, presentation at the Japanese American National Museum. Along with pictures of Bonner as a child at the Children's Village, this presentation includes family pictures of the Hattori family, who later moved to San Francisco, California, and became part of the city's Nikkei community. In addition, Bonner proudly presents her family: her husband Dr. David C. Bonner, and her two grown children Marisa Yoshiko, an architect and mother of five children, and David Frank,

---

[1] "'Because They Might be a Threat': Memories of the Children's Village at Manzanar," Japanese American National Museum, Los Angeles, California, January 14, 2007.

[2] Gwen Muranaka, "Emotional Return to Children's Village," *Rafu Shimpo* February 3, 2007, 1.

[3] Helen Whitney, "Care of Homeless Children of Japanese Ancestry during Evacuation" (M.A. thesis, University of California, Berkeley, 1948), 30.

an executive MBA at the University of Wyoming, who is also a former air force officer and 2000 United States national champion in judo.

This is a picture of me in a white Easter dress in front of the timber porch. I am standing very straight. I was two-and-a-half years old here. This was a staff picture and was given to my mother when I was adopted. From the appearance of this picture, Village staff took excellent care of the children.

In the photo of me sitting on the Village lawn area, notice the hastily made timber fences in the background. Volunteers took care of the surrounding lawn. On a recent Pilgrimage, I found that the lawn has long since disappeared into the desert environment.

Here I am with an attendant and three other Villagers in the rose garden. This photo was taken in 1945. I look much older; I was three years old. I was adopted at the age of three at the end of the internment period by Mr. and Mrs. Hattori of Yerington, Nevada. Friends told me that volunteers planted roses in the Village. Notice again, timber fences in the background.

My uncle, George Inai, was my adopted mother's younger brother who fought with the 442nd in Italy. I do not know where this picture was taken. My uncle was very lucky and survived the war. He served in the Service Unit of the 442nd and his name is engraved on the World War II monument in Los Angeles, California. My uncle died in 1972 in San Francisco, California.

My new mother, Josie, was so happy to have me in her home in Yerington, Nevada, where my parents owned and operated a dry cleaning business. My mother presented me with a brand new buggy and doll to celebrate the joyful occasion. This picture was taken in our new backyard by our home and business. My parents were among the lucky few Japanese who were not interned during the war because they lived outside the western zone.

This picture was taken in Yerington, Nevada, also in front of my adopted parents' home. My brother Kenneth was also a Villager and was adopted at the end of the internment, about the time Manzanar was disbanding. The picture was taken in 1947. My brother and I are about a year and a half apart.

This family portrait was taken in 1952 in San Francisco, California. Around 1947, my parents sold the Nevada business and moved to San Francisco where my father felt that there were more business and educational opportunities. My brother and I lived in San Francisco until we each married and moved away. Our lives were very full, rich and loving, indeed, growing up. My mother made certain of that!

My brother and I were both busy in scouting, church, school and music lessons. I started piano-organ lessons at the age of six and continued until my adult life. I have since been a volunteer organist for over twenty-five years. It was always a pleasure playing for my Japanese extended family at our little Episcopal mission church, Christ Episcopal Church, in San Francisco. I started to help with church services when I was nine. I was able to play very simple hymns at that time and rarely missed a Sunday in my entire career as organist. Perhaps my mother fed me properly! I simply loved music and my dear parents gave me the opportunity to do so.

These are my children, David (3) and Marisa (8). In 1973, I married David Bonner, at that time a Ph.D. student in Chemical Engineering at the University of California, Berkeley. We moved to Lubbock, Texas, for his first teaching assistantship at the university there. Our daughter Marisa was born in Lubbock.

DAVID BONNER
2000 NATIONAL JUDO CHAMPION

My son David started taking Judo lessons when he was only six years old. He simply loved the sport and never quit! In 2000, when he was 20 years old, he participated in the US Judo Championships and I never dreamed of him winning gold. David won two gold medals in one day, both in the junior and senior divisions! I have come to the conclusion that children always surprise you. I love my son very much and he is the apple of my eye.

Although David is no longer in the US Air Force, this is a picture taken in 2003 when he was commissioned as a 2nd Lieutenant. David enjoyed his military training very much and was very proud of the medals he earned along the way. He is now working on his MBA and would like to pursue a sports management career.

This photo of my daughter's family was taken in Lausanne, Switzerland, in 2004. Marisa married a European, Antonio Balta, and they now live in Lausanne where they both attended the engineering university. Pictured are my daughter's five children by the water of Lake Geneva. Marisa certainly has her hands full, raising children and working part-time as a licensed architect.

My adopted mother Josie had such a strong, loving, and devoted influence on me that, in retrospect, I can see that I raised my daughter the exact same way! The miles do not separate us, as we are in constant communication about every other day. I miss her very much.

My daughter's master professor designed the Beijing Olympic Stadium for the 2008 Olympics. It is called the "bird's nest." The Swiss architectural firm Herzog and de Meuron based in Basel, Switzerland, was responsible for the project. They have other famous buildings world-wide.

This photo was taken in 2006. I am very proud of my husband for all of the work he has done in chemical engineering and for society. A few years ago, David was named Distinguished Alumni in Engineering at the University of Texas at Austin. The family attended a formal dinner and presentation at that time. Five alumni were honored.

Index